COLD KITCHEN

Caroline Eden

COLD KITCHEN

A Year of Culinary Journeys

BLOOMSBURY PUBLISHING
LONDON · OXFORD · NEW YORK · NEW DELHI · SYDNEY

BLOOMSBURY PUBLISHING
Bloomsbury Publishing Plc
50 Bedford Square, London, WC1B 3DP, UK
29 Earlsfort Terrace, Dublin 2, Ireland

BLOOMSBURY, BLOOMSBURY PUBLISHING and the Diana logo are trademarks of
Bloomsbury Publishing Plc

First published in Great Britain 2024

ISBN: HB: 978-1-5266-5898-2; EBOOK: 978-1-5266-5897-5; EPDF: 978-1-5266-5896-8

2 4 6 8 10 9 7 5 3 1

Typeset by Newgen KnowledgeWorks Pvt. Ltd., Chennai, India
Printed and bound in Great Britain by CPI Group (UK) Ltd, Croydon CR0 4YY

To find out more about our authors and books visit www.bloomsbury.com
and sign up for our newsletters

For Noriko Kumagai, with love

CONTENTS

CONTENTS

A Subterranean Homecoming

Home again. Home again to this subterranean kitchen, cold as a larder, quiet as figs...

Carrying the malt reek of breweries, the wind pushes against my shoulders as I unlock the black door to my flat. Inside, shutting out the night, I take off my shoes, put down my holdall and, treading over a drift of junk mail, I move carefully over the hallway's cracked floorboards, feet sidestepping splintery crevices. Then, turning right, I descend a tight curve of flagstone stairs where, at the bottom, the kitchen opens up.

And it is there that I enter an underworld of silence, where everything is interior, ill-lit, zoomed-in and thoughtful. Without recent life energy, the kitchen exudes a particular and comforting mustiness, proving its bearings deep beneath Edinburgh's cobblestones.

Untied by travel miles — eyes red, throat parched, tongue sour — I sit down at the heavily carved dark oak kitchen table and slowly begin to feel myself soften in the peacefulness and diffused light. Shoulders, weak and achy, begin to drop, facial muscles relax, then lower back and arches of feet.

Sinking into the wooden chair, and its split leather seat, I am grateful to be here. Here, in this modest-sized room that requires fifteen paces to cross its entire length. Because over the years, it has become important to me, this kitchen, and I have let myself become entangled by it. Somewhere safe and promising

I

to return to, somewhere capable of soothing my pathological restlessness, at least for a while. A hitching post, not unlike a familiar dovecote for a messenger pigeon.

And it matters, because when I write, it is here that I write (in a little office off to the side). And because when I cook, it is here that I cook (on a little electric stove). As the Egyptian writer Naguib Mahfouz put it, 'Home is not where you were born; home is where all your attempts to escape cease.'[1]

So, now home. Home to the kitchen's wordless welcome.

~

With its union of practicality and magic, a kitchen is a portal, offering extended range and providing unlikely paths out of the ordinary. Offering opportunities to cook, imagine and create ways back into other times, other lives and other territories: Central Asia, Turkey, Ukraine, the South Caucasus, Russia, the Baltics and Poland. Places that have eased into my marrow over the years, shaping my life, writing and thinking. They are here, these lands I return to, in this kitchen. In my notebooks, photographs and handwritten recipes. In the fabrics and dried fruit, and plates and pottery and bread stamps and hollowed-out gourds for holding spices. In flea market finds, knives and forks, table runners and embroidered napkins. In the memories I keep of kitchens elsewhere, in short-term rented apartments in Bishkek, Istanbul, Yerevan, Rīga and Almaty. All of this is unpacked in the kitchen, ready and waiting to be indulged and transformed into new things – pieces of journalism, recordings, essays, books, recipes and meals. Wanderlust mellows here. Longed-for places are suddenly not so far away. Not unreachable, but present. Held again in the hand and heart.

The outside world comes home here, making it possible to be in two places, or times, at once, with just an iota of effort and imagination. No other room in a house is as capable of transforming the everyday into the otherworldly. The kitchen is a treasure room and a birthplace. A rich hunting ground.

In *The Ethics of the Dust*, published in 1866, John Ruskin, art critic and polymath of the Victorian era, asked: 'What does cookery mean? It means the knowledge of Medea and Circe, and of Calypso and Sheba ... It means the economy of your great-grandmothers and the science of modern chemists ... it means English thoroughness, and French art, and Arabian hospitality.'[2] Ruskin understood the far-reaching capabilities of cookery and food, how the kitchen is a place where history, nature and culture collide.

One ingredient or dish can conjure up a single moment, or an entire expedition; a whole city or just one unforgettable meal. The feel of nubbly peppercorns between fingers is to revisit a Cambodian pepper farm, the scent of fresh mint is a cup of Moroccan tea poured in the Atlas Mountains. Each encounter in the kitchen can be a form of wayfaring. It is a pleasingly deceiving domestic territory, interior yet outward facing, one that teaches you that sometimes it is sufficient that the mind, not the body, travels.

And it demands that you be physically present, at least for some periods of time. To care for it, this room of ripening and decay, chaos and discipline. To take pride in its cupboards and their contents. To keep an inventory. To manage and adjust. Look after it and it will give back, with its tools and alchemy, and its unique ability to nourish, inspire and host.

You can write a story, or a whole book, and send it from a laptop to an editor from any café, airport or hotel room in the world. You can delight, temporarily, in the buzz of being detached from family, friends, neighbours and responsibilities. But a kitchen is grounding.

Left too long, the kitchen will become sad and fly-haunted. Left too long, things will turn and rot. It is an exchange. This is how we became friends, this cold Edinburgh kitchen and me.

~

Subtle dramas play out day by day, hour by hour in this room, which so artfully reflects and collects the crumbs and details of daily life. Rows unfold over dinner. Accidents happen. Blood is spilled from a knife nick. Fingers are burned on oven racks. Sugar scatters across the floor. Bills are calculated. A birthday is toasted. A dog laps water from a bowl in the corner.

When I stand at the hob cooking, or at the counter chopping, I sometimes try to picture those who stood in the same spot before me, sautéing, boiling and swearing. Just as it is now a domestic atlas of my own private world, it was once theirs. If you stay anywhere long enough, associations, past and present, begin to form. Ghosts appear.

But finding a kitchen, which would become central to my sense of home, was, until I moved in, an idea and ambition as distant to me as my famous dead neighbours, born in other centuries, their names carved reverently into sandstone. At 52 Queen Street, in 1847, James Young Simpson inhaled drugs in his dining room with some physician friends, thus discovering the anaesthetic power of chloroform.[3] Across the road, at 17 Heriot Row, a young Robert Louis Stevenson was nursed by his beloved nanny, a strict Calvinist nicknamed Cummy, in the 1850s.[4]

Apprehensively, I joined these long-gone souls in 2015, unpacking boxes in the half-light of a January morning. And, within a few days, I knew this chilly basement kitchen — somewhere akin to a workshop, a place to seek and foster ideas — would give me exactly what I needed.

~

As an adult, my experience of 'home' had been uncertain and variable. Surging London rents meant precarious living throughout my twenties and some of my thirties. I stayed, for several years, at countless different addresses, either house-shares or tiny studios, whatever my meagre wage as a writer and bookseller could afford. Onto the doormat of two different addresses in south London that I particularly liked – a ground-floor Victorian flat in Brixton and a newly decorated studio in a converted school in Battersea – the same letter landed. The words, under a neat estate agent's logo, plain yet devastating: 'We are giving you two months' notice. The owner is selling,' or words to that effect.

Few things can make you feel so instantly lost and irrelevant. I had no choice but to politely accept the fact, and leave. I kept my self-pity in check by repeating to myself, *it could be worse.* After all, I had no children, no significant debt or real responsibilities, and I held a vague but lofty moral opposition to home ownership – who wants to be a slave to a mortgage? To pay such interest and to owe such a huge debt? To live with such threats to their freedom? My grandparents rented. My dad grew up in a rented council house. Why was I any different? Don't we all learn to subsist on what we have? And anyway, I believed this insecurity and transience was the price to pay for a freelance writer's life.

But I knew deep down, stronger than any righteous objection, that I never, ever wanted one of those letters again.

I accepted that London was beyond my means. It was irrelevant that my ancestral roots can be traced back to the southeast of the city, Penge and Crystal Palace having been home to my extended family for centuries, many of them living on the same street in terraced houses, all with identical narrow gardens leading down to railway tracks. Some worked as housemaids; others were night watchmen for factories. Some were survivors of war and London bombings. Some were sober, others drinkers.

In 2012, I left London for good. You know in your bones when it is final, and so for the umpteenth time in my adult life, I deposited my belongings in bin bags and boxes at Dad's house and booked a flight.

In Kathmandu, I drank gin and tonics in touristy Thamel and then tried to get a flight to the Tenzing-Hillary Airport (also known as Lukla Airport or 'the most dangerous airport in the world'), with a plan to join a group and hike to Everest Base Camp. Again and again, flights were cancelled due to bad weather. Unsure what to do instead, I went to a travel agency and bought a Biman Bangladesh Airlines ticket to Dhaka on a whim. Bangladesh was a country I had always wanted to see, having spent many months across the border in India backpacking over the years. On the flight, I had half a dozen business cards pressed into my hands by kind Bangladeshis looking out for a solo traveller. Only after landing did I discover that the small Nepalese plane had eventually departed just after I left, but on take-off it had hit a large bird and crashed, killing everyone on board, including seven Britons on a trekking holiday to the Everest region.

~

It was around this time that I began a correspondence with my future husband, James, himself a peripatetic news journalist. In one long email, written during a train ride aboard the Rangpur Express, from the north-west of Bangladesh to the capital, I described a night aboard the PS *Tern*, a dangerously overloaded century-old paddle steamer, steered by Captain Jahangir Alam, that had taken us through a river system called Cyclone Alley, and mosquito-heavy nights I had spent in the misty Chittagong Hill Tracts. We married two years later.

James gave up his London flat-share, and we moved to a remote sheep-farming community in the Yorkshire Dales, where we rented a large draughty farmhouse. Without upstairs heating, almost certainly haunted and not updated in decades, it did boast spectacular hill walking straight out of the kitchen door, plus a classic oil-fuelled Aga, as well as a huge Victorian black cast-iron range in the dining room. Then, with our new puppy, Darwin, a Yorkshire-born lemon-and-white beagle, we leapt north again, to Edinburgh, unable to face another damp Yorkshire winter spent sleeping in woolly hats.

Neither of us had ever owned property, nor did we know Edinburgh very well – only that it was architecturally compelling, well connected to trains and planes and had superb access to mountains. James had lived in Moscow, Oslo and Almaty, working for news desks, and together we were clueless on mortgages, contracts and solicitors.

We viewed ten flats but settled on the first one we saw. It was a bit scruffy, as past owners had not given it enough care or attention, but it had its own front door, unlike many tenement flats, and, spread over two floors, it felt spacious. All the walls needed plastering (and they still do, because plastering is probably the most boring and messy way to spend a lot of money), but the kitchen, taking up the entire basement – a world within a world – was where I knew life would happen. It felt right. We needed a home, the three of us, and I sensed that we had found it.

The previous tenants, two young male professionals in a flat-share, had used the kitchen as a sitting room, and the estate agent's photographs showed how they had arranged it. A chunky well-used L-shaped sofa sat in the middle of the room, where my kitchen table is today, and, in front of it, a flat-screen television on a low-slung media unit. There was little else. No pictures on the walls and no sign of cookware or utensils. The biggest walk-in cupboard, my future study, which would soon be wallpapered and filled with books, was a utility room full of old nails and hooks for tools bashed into the walls. The second-largest cupboard was a lonely storage place of cobwebs, but in time it would become my pantry. In the corner of the kitchen, by the single sash window, a tangle of ugly black wires dangled down ominously. They'd be ripped out first, we agreed. But, exuding stillness and calm, the room undoubtedly had something about it. And what it needed was for someone to make it a working, and welcoming, kitchen again.

After viewing the flat, whenever I scrutinised it in my mind, it was always the kitchen I pictured – especially the two dark oak beams bisecting the ceiling, which gave it a countryside feel not so different to Yorkshire. I began yearning for it: envisaging myself cooking there and filling the cupboards with my things. For someone so beset by restlessness, who'd spent so much time in transit, in hotels and in and out of insecure living arrangements, the idea of this particular kitchen to come home to was irresistible. The seed was planted, and the hunger grew. I put in an offer from the A65, as we drove back from Edinburgh to Yorkshire, and a few months later we moved in.

~

Quickly, we developed a system that worked. When projects took us overseas, Darwin, bless his brave heart, would be driven down south to stay with his 'Yorkshire cousins', who are in fact a generous and kind beagle-owning couple we are friends with. This arrangement became important as when Darwin turned a year and a half, our worlds became affected by the heart-wrenching bad luck of canine epilepsy. For dogs, this means occasional violent seizures, often late at night, and a carefully monitored timetable of medication. They had experience of such matters and a genuine love for Darwin, treating him as their own.

For the three of us, settling into our new flat, the kitchen immediately became a place to regroup and eat together. A room of greetings and partings, and the emotional intensity that comes with all that. 'The most crucial moments in the life of a traveller are often not his adventures in a faraway land but his departures and arrivals,'⁵ as the Moscow-born novelist Zinovy Zinik once wrote.

~

At first, Edinburgh felt like cold comfort. Missing Yorkshire, and longing for London and the future I would never have there, at times I felt intensely unmoored and lonely, unsure of myself and my surroundings, nurturing a sadness for friendships that would inevitably fall away with distance and time. But I was invested – and the challenge of moving anywhere new is to begin growing roots. The kitchen offered shelter and a cure, a place where hands are kept busy and the soul is fed.

I began to view Edinburgh as a correspondent would – but one in pursuit of home, rather than stories. I would go out with a fictitious notebook, extending my attention outwards, photographing the cobbled lanes, the wide Georgian streets of the New Town, the narrow alleyways of the Old Town, all under constantly changing northern skies. By listening and observing, I found out that oysters are dressed in gin at the Café Royal. I discovered that Edinburgh was once known for its oyster-parties, known as 'oyster-ploys', and that, under streetlamps, ladies would advertise their fresh oysters by crying out '*Caller ou!*'⁶ I read local newspapers at the kitchen table and revelled in reports of forty-foot whales returning to Scottish waters, of them 'playing' in the Firth of Forth and feeding on shoals of sprats. Such wonder, so close to home, less than half an hour's drive away. I watched clouds scud across the view of Fife from Dublin Street, saw how the Old Town, after a downpour, looked like a sepia-toned Piranesi painting. I learned how the Edinburgh Colonies in Stockbridge, with their unusual external staircases running down to the pavement, were built in the 1860s as homes for workmen escaping slum landlords.[7] I noticed how Arthur's Seat, Darwin's grassy domain, the place of a thousand or more dog walks, looked wholly different under gorse in mustard-coloured bloom.

At weekends, I would jog down to the port district of Leith – encouraged by its motto 'We Persevere', which is painted onto walls and pavements – for shopping, stocking up at a trio of supermarkets that I had quickly become loyally attached to: Akdeniz, the Turkish/Mediterranean shop (for pistachios, pul biber, dried limes, pickled lemons), Taste of Poland (for sausages, bread, kefir, dill) and PCY Oriental (for sesame oil, tofu, black vinegar, noodles).

To my southern English eyes, sometimes the city appeared as a strange living dream, with its statues, its spellings (meuse is mews, wynd is alleyway), its moody and fickle light and the constantly plaguing gusty wind, often present even on the warmest days. Robert Louis Stevenson, writing in his book *Edinburgh: Picturesque Notes*, commented on the gales: 'But Edinburgh pays cruelly for her high seat in one of the vilest climates under heaven. She is liable to be beaten upon by all the winds that blow…'[8]

Through the emotional investment that I began pouring into my surroundings, I felt I was somehow beginning to belong, and that somehow Edinburgh was becoming part of me in return. Because this slightly forbidding, slightly prim city – one of medicine, rubber, eccentrics, geology, wind instruments, surgeons, dictionaries, publishing and biscuits – absolutely exists, too, here in the kitchen, because it is a living thing, and it is a witness to history. It is old and it is part of the city's make-up.

And through its single basement window, Edinburgh comes drifting freely in, at all hours, its watery light and composed beauty, the voices of its residents and visitors, its sensibilities, ideas and atmosphere. Seeping in, uninvited but always welcome, and every time melting my heart a little like hot fat.

CHAPTER ONE

Winter Melons

Hunted by the cold, runners go jogging past the kitchen window. I can hear the heavy landings of tired bodies, but I can see only ankles and raw-looking calves. Dividing us is a subterranean courtyard, slippery with lichen and liverwort, and an arch of stone steps leading up to the pavement, lined by spear-headed wrought-iron railings. Dogs' tails and bicycle wheels go by intermittently, lives half-revealed for mere seconds, before they continue on through the classical harmony of Edinburgh's Georgian New Town, built from Craigleith stone the colour of clotted cream.

The morning's unblemished silence, broken only by the song of the robin, has disappeared, replaced by the afternoon's chattering and beeping of street activity and a certain pressure in the air promising a storm. It is building, building, under a severe sky, alabaster clouds now grizzled silver. Best stay indoors.

Darwin the beagle has slipped into the pantry, his claws click-clacking on the wooden floorboards, giving him away. He wants a carrot, for they are his passion. Poking about, under shelves lined with jars of dried limes, white peppercorns and sesame seeds, he begins his search by nuzzling a row of Kilner jars lined up on the floor, their empty bellies awaiting this year's marmalade. Next, he bothers a pile of papery banana shallots in a crate, his long ears dropping down to his muzzle, expertly trapping the particulars of various smells close to his twitching nose. Finally, groping in a wicker basket, he tugs a single muddy carrot out, trotting it triumphantly towards his doughnut bed at the other side of the kitchen. Curling up his body, he wedges the vegetable between his front paws, white, furry and bony, and begins gnawing greedily, his wet eyes surveying the room. In front of him is a dark oak rocking chair, and to the right, a white timber windowsill that speaks of the season: dumpling squashes in a pyramid, their ribbed green skin enclosing bright orange flesh; pots of woody wintry rosemary, none of the softer leafier herbs of summer; and two Christmas cacti, glossy and green, their flowers erupting from heavy stone pots like garish pink fireworks.

There is nothing grand about this kitchen. The walls, whitewashed in a sun-soaked taverna sort of way, are flaky and lumpy, and next to where I stand, my shadow hovering over a plastic chopping board, is a stainless-steel sink, then a hob and a cheap electric oven mounted between cream laminated cupboards. All were inherited from the previous owner. I moved in, and they were here. There are students, half my age, on this very street, cooking in far better ovens, and kitchens, than mine. But none of this is important. It is the things, the old things, on shelves and in corners, recalling specific atmospheres and places, that matter most. The silver sugar bowl from Mumbai, the bread stamps from Tashkent, the honey jar from Tasmania. Inanimate objects of modest value, precious and powerful, held in display niches of a wall-mounted cupboard. While I would like a new oven – gas! with real flames! – I tell myself that this kitchen is undoubtedly a more organic, and more soulful space as it is not done up, sparkly and new. Recycle, make do.

Less expense, more longevity, I tell myself.

Dominating the kitchen's back wall is a tall, dark, wooden dresser, weighty and heavily carved with a floral and geometric design, its nooks, shelves and cupboards filled with candles, cut-glass decanters and half-drunk bottles of Haitian rum, Polish Pan Tadeusz vodka and Ararat brandy. Bottles for the violet hours. And on the very top of the dresser sit two large decorative plates, propped up on display stands, golden and lustrous. Bought in Istanbul, they are hand-painted with ancient sailing ships on tumbling waves. Above them is an interior window the size of a porthole, but square, offering a glimpse of the gravestone-grey flagstone steps that curve narrowly upstairs.

Beside Darwin, now finishing his carefully guarded carrot, is another dresser, with the same dark patina as the larger one, but smaller, hip-height, a 'server' with a scalloped apron and turned legs, useful as a side table. Underneath it, an always-almost-empty wine rack. And at the centre of the kitchen, a large dark oak table, hexagonal and therefore good for seating people around, ringed by wooden chairs with leather backs and well-worn seats.

All this dark oak furniture, so rooted here as to appear as though it never could have existed anywhere else, was bought for not much more than an average day's wage at a barnyard auction house in the Yorkshire Dales surrounded by fields of sheep. 'Brown' furniture, the unfortunate-sounding label given to goods designed for Georgian or Regency townhouses, is démodé nowadays. Unfashionable and frumpy. Which is helpful as far as I am concerned, as it makes such solid and well-made pieces affordable to people like me. These warm wooden hues make the kitchen feel less cold, softening, if barely perceptibly, the draughts from cracks, gaps and single glazing.

The challenge is to make the kitchen as snug as possible, to defy the bleakness; to fill it with herbs, rugs, plants and the smell of baking until it is cosy as a nut.

~

Setting to work at the counter, next to the window, I have before me a slab of Bulgarian sirene cheese, briny and wet and similar to feta, a watermelon and a few sprigs of fresh mint. A deeply unseasonal salad-to-be, one to satisfy a craving, and a reminder that, eventually, summer will come. Pushing the large kitchen knife into the melon, I pull it down slowly like a weighty lever, through the granular flesh, cutting it into quarters and carefully taking it away from the white rind. Above me, a light bulb, one of an ugly plastic strip, quivers, sputtering its buttery light. Watermelon juice spills out beyond the borders of the chopping board, onto the laminated plywood counter. Bad light, sharp knife, slippery surface. Still, I go on cutting, squinting and breathing in the melon's weird hot-summer-night scent.

In Turkey, better cooks than me do not waste the rind, instead soaking the strips in water laced with pickling lime, then boiling it in sugar syrup for melon-rind jam. Sometimes, confectioners candy the rind into glacé sweets. So intense is the sugariness of certain Turkish melons that vendors pitch them to customers by calling out 'Sherbet, sherbet!'[1] Some of Turkey's finest, most-prized, and largest, melons are found in Diyarbakir, the de facto capital of the country's Kurds, in the south-east. Dovecotes there, especially by the banks of the Tigris River, where vine fruits thrive in the alluvial soil, hint at the location of melon fields. Nitrate-rich guano (manure) from pigeons and doves is said to heat and enrich the ground, thus adding to the uncommon sweetness of the often tiger-striped melons. Camels once brought these weighty fruits from the field to the city. There is much to learn about Turkish melons. In Mehmet Kâmil's *The Refuge of the Chefs*, published in 1844, there exists a bygone recipe for a sweet melon stuffed with almonds, pine kernels, rice and minced lamb,[2] reminiscent of the sort of fruity-savoury stuffed pumpkins of the South Caucasus. There was also a specific word for a 'melon thirst', kagunsamak,[3] now more or less forgotten. Why did the stuffed meaty melon, and the old Turkish word, fall out of fashion? Likely just time, whims and fads, nothing more. Today in Turkey, tiny unripe melons are sold for the purpose of pickling, and in villages melon flesh is boiled down to make molasses, a process more typically associated with pomegranate or sticky figs.

The watermelon I'm cutting, its skin waxy and smooth, did not ripen on the banks of the Tigris, nor is it esteemed. It was bought from a supermarket in Edinburgh and was imported from Spain. Others on the shelves had travelled from as far away as Honduras and Panama. It is an example of how we eat today. Thirst-quenching melons may be viewed as symbols of summer – think of novelty watermelon-shaped beach balls, icy melon sorbet and hydrating scoops of cantaloupe – yet they appear year-round in shops, though only ever a trifling selection, usually honeydew, galia and watermelon, maybe a mottled-skinned Spanish piel de sapo (toadskin).

The scent, though, is its own feast. In the cutting and cubing of it, more of its hard-to-pin-down ambrosial smell is dispensed, rising up like fresh-cut grass melding with cool iris. Batting away the temptation to eat a few coral-red wedges over the sink, I indulge, instead, in the anticipation of pleasure, imagining how, when I finally get to it, the melon's singular watery crunchiness – it is a cousin of the cucumber – and its copious juiciness will be sorbet-like on the tongue, as fresh and awakening as a glass of soda.

With the floral scent rising, this basement kitchen, underground and almost invisible to the world, becomes a doorway, and, soon enough, joining me at the counter are images, miniature mind-movies of a place far away – not Turkey, but Uzbekistan, land of the melon. I can see otherworldly piles of them, heaped up beside Soviet-built concrete bus stops, filling whole lanes of bazaars, gathered in huge mounds in fields. However, it is not the summer kind that I long for and reminisce over; it is the country's peculiar and mystifying winter varieties.

~

Snaking through Uzbekistan, from the border of Afghanistan to the capital Tashkent, is the multi-lane M39 highway. And it was there, one mid-afternoon in November, a few years ago, that I first encountered Uzbekistan's wintertime melons, fruits of rare and strange beauty. As the taxi inched through an unexpected gridlock on the outskirts of Samarkand, I gazed out of the grubby window as the city's fluted ensembles – mosques, shrines and mausoleums – grew smaller and smaller until the ribbed dome of the Gur-i-Emir, final resting place of warrior-ruler Timur, or Tamerlane, empire builder and 'conqueror of the world', receded out of sight.

A bone-dry wind drifted into the car, parching lips, but while Samarkand's air is arid, the valley surrounding the most famous city of Uzbekistan is wildly fertile, fed by the Zarafshan River, literally the 'strewer of gold'. When London-born explorer Douglas Carruthers wrote of it in his book *Beyond the Caspian* (1949), he noted that dazzling Samarkand 'stands high, tucked away under the foothills of the mountains, embedded in a veritable Garden of Eden, in a land literally flowing with milk and honey, where all the fruits of the earth seem to grow in profusion and to perfection...'[4] Such a verdant setting helped to make it not only rich, but also the best-known, and most romanticised, Silk Road city of all.

As the M39 stretched on, I noticed that every other car in front of us was stopping up ahead. Passengers were leaping out and heading off into a field, headscarves glittering as they went. Why? Once we got closer, it became clear. Melons.

'Stop the car! I won't be long,' I said, jumping out.

Stepping over discarded green and golden rinds, I followed the other travellers as they went picking through the piles of fruit, carefully inspecting, sniffing and hand-selecting melons to take home. Karim Qarshi, a melon trader in his fifties, was quick to introduce himself, explaining how during the melon harvest of autumn and early winter, he and half a dozen others set themselves up with single camp beds, topped with makeshift fabric canopies, where they rest at night. This allows them to remain alert and ready for sales at any hour. They stay on guard until the cold sets in properly in mid-November, overnighting in the heart of melon-bed land, in what is a melon-mad country. Karim talked me through his melons, some with skin smooth and yellow as butter, others knobbly and crocodile-like, the size of horse's heads.

'These are all winter melons. This one is called "old lady melon". It is very sweet, very soft,' Karim said, running his hand over the melon's tight folds.

Round as a football, heavy and full, its skin was ribbed like thick corduroy, its wrinkly stalk curved as a coat hook. Taking his knife, Karim carved a sickle moon from the seaweed-green melon, exposing, almost indecently, the melon's flesh, creamy as magnolia. In the middle, a tightly packed jelly-ball of seeds – unlike watermelons, which have their seeds scattered throughout – managed to hold its form despite the cut. From this strange melon came a uniquely robust fruitiness, mixing overripe pear with Bourbon vanilla. He held up the melon proudly, an example of the fruit in its prime, the cross-section of its seed house, glistening in the sunshine. In Uzbekistan it is the trader who decides when a melon is ready. There are no stickers ordering the buyer to 'ripen at home'.

He handed me the slithery wedge and I tried to unpick the flavours as grievous wasps landed drunkenly on the scattered rinds. First, sherbet. Then a little honey mixed with almond extract and, finally, pineapple and the smoothness of rum. Karim had a slab himself, and he *tasted* it. Biting into the melon's flesh, then holding it to his palate, then chewing and luxuriating in it, his eyes closed. I bought one and was generously given a second as a gift. Waving goodbye, he yelled the warning that melon traders like to dish out: 'Do not eat it in the evening!' Uzbeks believe the calorific melons are hard to digest and are therefore best eaten at breakfast. I got back into the taxi and put the melons on the seat alongside.

Uzbekistan's harsh continental climate – hot summers, cold winters – is just right for growing melons. According to one exporter I spoke to, 22,000 hectares of melon fields produce 400,000–500,000 tonnes a year. And, just as they are embedded in the terroir, the economy and the Uzbek imagination, they are entrenched in history and customs. Ancient Uzbek kingdoms would send forth their prized winter melons as much-coveted gifts. Wrapped carefully in cotton, or packed in snow inside insulating lead containers, they were sent by Uzbek nobility to China to impress its emperors, while other shipments would travel by camel caravan to the Abbasid capital of Baghdad or to Russian tsars and Mughal emperors.[5]

Melon madness badly affected Babur, descendant of Tamerlane, who longed for the incomparable fruit of his home-land when he was in India in the 1520s, paving the way for Mughal rule. In his memoirs, he wrote forlornly of there being 'no grapes or muskmelons, no good fruits, no ice or cold water, no good bread or cooked food in their bazars'.[6] In Uzbekistan, where he came from, there were melons with 'skin yellow and puckered like shagreen leather ... pulp four fingers thick'.[7]

Many who have tasted these melons have fallen under their spell: legendary Persian poets, various Great Game explorers and Victorian travellers. One of their earliest mentions was by tenth-century chronicler Muhammad Abu al-Qasim ibn Hawqal, who wrote a travelogue of his journeys through Islamic lands. In ancient Khorasan (historically extending over parts of Iran, Afghanistan and Turkmenistan), he noted that melons were prepared 'for export to numerous places of the world, and I do not know of any other place where such a thing might be possible'.[8]

A better-remembered traveller, the fourteenth-century wanderer Ibn Battuta, also stood in awe of Uzbekistan's melons. Undertaking a twenty-nine-year adventure as a pilgrim in 1325, a year after the death of Marco Polo, he recounted his 75,000-mile journey in his book *The Travels of Ibn Battuta*. As a literary fellow, and a wide-eyed gourmand, he sought hospitality with sultans and nobility, finding himself captivated by gardens, trees, recipes, aphrodisiacs, narcotics and even cannibalism. Relishing syrupy mangoes in Java and creamy coconuts in the Maldives, he also adored the sticky dates of Oman. But it was only the melons of Khwarizm (modern-day Central Asia) to which he devoted a special entry in his book: 'The melons of Khwarizm have no equal in any country of the world, East or West...'

Samarkand was singled out by Ibn Battuta for its 'bazaars, traversed by canals, and with many gardens. It abounds in grapes and quinces of exquisite flavour...'[9] and still today I do not think there is a city on Earth with a more evocative name.

~

When we were confined to our homes due to Covid-19, I would sit and conjure up my last visit to Samarkand, in 2019. Returning there seemed, suddenly, an impossible dream.

I would recall how, as the sun dipped and the clamour of the city began to sink with it, I wandered through the Shah-i-Zinda, an avenue of mausoleums dating back to the fourteenth and fifteenth centuries, filled with the tombs of Tamerlane's relatives. It was autumn and there were more overseas visitors than I had ever seen. It was the busiest month in a bumper year of tourism, and predictions were buoyant for the coming seasons. Nobody could have foreseen what was coming, and I happily lost myself in the desert-coloured brickwork and a sea of gleaming tiles, turquoise as a Maldivian atoll. Despite the earthquakes, and conquerors that had rocked and flattened it over the ages, and regardless of looting treasure-seekers and overzealous restoration, Samarkand was still sublime and unforgettable.

During lockdown, feasting upon such treasured memories was a way of getting through a period when even contemplating the idea of a walk at times seemed like radical thinking.

~

Darwin, lapping water noisily from his bowl, snaps me back to the task at hand, back to the kitchen. Rain is coming down now, in fat drops, flecked with white that looks like snow, or sleet. Violent wintry gusts squalling. With the weather 'in braw', as we say here, passers-by walk faster. I can see flashes of soggy macs and wellington boots, muddy trainers and solid hiking shoes. Rainwater, heading for the lowest ground, runs down the classical straight lines of the New Town, cleaning the uniformed architecture, lashing its bell pulls, cornices and fan windows.

'Winter is the oldest season,'[10] wrote the Irish poet-priest John O'Donohue. And it does feel that way, when we retreat to our homes and stay indoors, hibernating through short days and long nights – especially in Scotland, where the weather is rarely stable.

But despite heavy clouds, a feeling of contentment hangs in the air, coming from the kitchen's ability to be two things at once: to be an enclosed space that effectively opens up the world through taste and flavour and imagination. Nature comes in here. Pomegranate seeds on rice dishes, a strip of orange peel for a negroni, or a ribbon of lemon skin for a martini. A lime wedge for gin. A bowl of ripening pears. A jar of dates. Peaches roasted in rose water and stuffed with marzipan. Blackberries scattered on pancakes. Apricots cinched in chutney. Memories of melons, and the vine pergolas and fruit trees of summer, of prized Uzbek cherries carried in boxes across borders. The kitchen is an orchard.

~

Edging the window up an inch (a basement kitchen needs airing), the smell of roasting potatoes wafts in. Nearby, in other Edinburgh kitchens, cooks are preparing for Burns Night suppers. The immortal Scottish poet Robert Burns was born on 25 January 1759 and, in his honour, everywhere from the Northern Highlands to the Cheviot Hills, guests will arrive and there will be whisky on the table, a toast to the lassies, and clootie dumplings, cock-a-leekie, cranachan, crowdie, cullen skink, scotch broth, haggis (meaty, oaty, slightly spicy, slightly mythical), neeps and tatties. The national bard will, of course, be addressed with poetry, and the food blessed with the Selkirk Grace:

Some hae meat and canna eat,
And some wad eat that want it;
But we hae meat, and we can eat,
Sae let the Lord be thankit.

While Robert Burns never left Scotland, preferring to stay in 'the Land o' Cakes' (oatcakes), swapping Bibles with his lovers on silvery rivers and composing 'Tam o' Shanter', 'To a Mouse' and 'My Heart's in the Highlands', his relative Alexander 'Bokhara' Burnes (1805–1841) travelled far beyond. Involved in the Great Game, the nineteenth-century clandestine struggle between tsarist Russia and the British Empire, he served in the army of the East India Company and while journeying to holy Bukhara as a secret agent, its glorious fruit was not wasted on him. He marvelled at the 'never-ending employment of the fruiterers in dealing out their grapes, melons, apricots...' And made a special note on Uzbek melons: '...every cultivated spot groaned under the gigantic melons of Bokhara; many of which were also being transported in caravans of camels to the city.'[11] His memoir, *Travels into Bokhara*, chronicling Sind, Afghanistan and the khanates of Central Asia, became a bestseller before he was assassinated in Kabul, aged thirty-six.

Another Great Game traveller, Captain Frederick Burnaby (1842–1885), the British Army's swashbuckling balloonist, who stood six foot four inches tall and was said to have once carried a pony under one arm, also travelled to Central Asia and fell under the spell of its melons. In his 1876 book *A Ride to Khiva*, he wrote: 'The melons here have a fame which is celebrated all over the East. In former years, they were sent as far as Peking for the Emperor of China's table.'[12] Burnaby procured some seeds and tried, but ultimately failed, to grow them back in England.

~

It is possible that these British Great Game travellers were attuned to the delights of melons because of the fascination for them in the eighteenth and nineteenth centuries. Melons can, with some help, grow successfully in the British Isles and not that long ago there was a real desire and passion to try and do so.

A great chronicler of this fad was Gilbert White, born in 1720 in the county of Hampshire. An English gardener-naturalist and Romantic scientist, he was a storyteller too, keeping detailed notes in his *Garden Kalendar* and *Naturalist's Journal*. In the 1750s, White embarked on extensive experiments, growing recently introduced novelty melons in hotbeds under frames, with constant and gentle warmth generated by reeking horse manure. Meticulous in his documentation, he even noted the number of cartloads of decomposing dung donated by his neighbours: 'March 13th 1755 "Made a very deep & large Hot-bed for my melon-seeds; with seven cart loads of dung: thatch'd the edges of the bed without the frame." '[13]

The melons did eventually succeed, having weathered thunderstorms and floods, and during the summer of 1758 White allowed himself to relax, satisfied that his cantaloupes were 'delicate, dry and firm'. By September, he was ready to show them off, gathering friends around him in a building he had named 'The Hermitage', a little dwelling in the English countryside, for a celebratory melon feast. Gardeners today who look after White's estate, now open to the public, have carried on the tradition, growing two melon cultivars: 'Black Rock' and 'Petit Gris de Rennes'.

Further north, in Scotland, with its cool and wet climate, maintaining melon beds was extremely expensive, but with the introduction of hotbeds in the eighteenth century, local melons had become a possibility for fancier dinner tables. Prized as they may have been, well-to-do families could only eat so much fresh melon, therefore a need for preserving arose. Margaret Malcolm, a keen cook who lived two hours south of Edinburgh, in Langholm, kept a recipe book in 1782. In it, she recorded a recipe from a friend, Mrs Carnegie, for preserving melon. The fruit is 'boiled up' with ginger in sugar and then scented with lemon peel. Mrs Carnegie also suggested storage advice: 'To taste well of the ginger this sweetmeat should not be used for six to eight months, and will keep for years.'[14]

~

Cubing more melon, enclosed in the task, I can see that while the flesh is not yet mushy or hollow it will need eating promptly. Time is what matters most in a kitchen. Fruit and vegetables, bought as proof of the day, perspire, before cankering and full-on rotting. Plants and potted herbs dry out and wither.

Lemons decay, their sunny puckered skins turning to green-hued dust. Milk takes on a grey-ish sheen, good only for pouring down the sink. A kitchen, just like a garden, grove or melon bed, demands attention. Outside, the street is now completely deserted. Bad weather, getting worse, rain sheeting down. And as I finish constructing my salad of watermelon, feta and mint, I can feel Darwin's eyes scrutinising my back; his keen and expert nose has alerted him to the salty piece of bone-white cheese that I am crumbling and crushing with my fingers over a bowl. Even above carrots, it is cheese he likes best.

~

Uzbekistan's traders have many time-honoured ways of storing their cherished melons. Nearly all winter varieties spend time in a dark, cool, specially built shed called a qovunxona. Inside, strapped to the rafters with thick string or netting, they ripen in slow motion over the cold months, amassing maximum sucrose and becoming ever more melony. Matured that way, they can keep for up to eight months, making them available for most of the year and suitable to travel overland across vast deserts and steppes. To provide natural ventilation, the walls of a qovunxona are studded with saucer-sized porthole windows. A melon shed should be filled with clean, cool air, not the smell of melons. If their scent is present, they are already starting to turn. Before qovunxonas existed, farmers would shovel up snow or sand and bury their melons deep underground, where they would be insulated from the chill.

While qovunxonas may sound peculiar, they are not very different to the root cellars of seventeenth-century England: cool, sheltered undercrofts built for the storage of fruit and vegetables, which fell out of favour when electricity, refrigerators and urban living grew in popularity. Back then, the English seedsman Stephen Switzer (1682–1745) wrote of the fine delicacies and described the commitment required for the British melon grower, advising in his *Practical Kitchen Gardiner* that the gardener 'not fail to visit the melonry at least three times a day, morning, noon and evening'.[15]

~

The traders and farmers of Uzbekistan's melons know, very well, the true value of these fruits; how the act of really caring for them can, in turn, make us more mindful. Their reverence is evident in the names the melons are given – 'white feather', 'wolf head', 'golden eyebrow' and 'black lake', among others – and the sense of pageantry with which they are displayed.

In contrast to our Western tendency to import most fruit and expect year-round availability, the right fruit, eaten at the right time, in the right place, is incomparable. As Christopher Lloyd, the gardener-chronicler of Great Dixter, wrote in his book *Gardener Cook*, 'The difference in flavour between a fruit culled at exactly the right moment from your own tree and one picked weeks before becoming ripe for the sake of marketing has to be experienced to be believed.'[16]

You do not have to have your own fruit trees, so few of us do, but lost wonderment can be reignited in a single afternoon spent at a 'pick your own' field, or by sorting through brambles in search of blackberries. Or simply by slowing down in the kitchen, often a place of ceaseless activity, and thinking, really thinking, about the fruit in the bowl. Each encounter with an ingredient in the kitchen offers the chance to drift to lands elsewhere, or to reconnect with the past. Take fruit puddings, so long-lived and multi-generational that they cannot help but be full of memories: the plum pudding at Christmas, the summery peach trifle. When the mood takes me, and I find myself almost delirious with the vivid want of Uzbekistan's paradisiacal melons, I turn to any variety – and, by bringing it into the kitchen to eat, I can recapture again, with renewed wonderment, the exquisite experience of buying and eating them far from home.

~

After the storm, I sit to eat my salad, a dance of salty, sweet and cool. Crisp but also surprisingly warming, partly from the mint and partly from the reverie. And I am grateful to be here in this kitchen, both a respite from the world and equally a way back into it.

Mark Twain described watermelon as 'chief of the world's luxuries ... when one has tasted it, he knows what angels eat.'[17] And while I would not stretch to such a soliloquy for this particular melon, it doesn't matter because, whether rare or common, local or imported, Spanish or Uzbek, every melon is a kind of miracle in itself. This flesh-fragrant melon has more than served its purpose by unlocking the gates back to Uzbekistan, bringing forth good memories that, like provisions, have been tidied away, to be brought out at will from the store cupboard of the mind, proving that the real feast is within.

Watermelon, Feta and Mint Salad

This salad is far too elementary to require an actual recipe, but this is how best to put it together:

Cube half a watermelon. Crumble 150g of feta over the melon. Sprinkle with mint leaves. Dress with lemon juice, the best extra-virgin olive oil you have and some lemon zest or sumac. Serve at room temperature or slightly chilled, but not cold.

CHAPTER TWO

Russian Railway Pies

It is the beginning of March and three named storms, Dudley, Eunice and Franklin, have, in the past few weeks, brought blizzards and hurricane-force winds to Britain. But despite cancelled trains and shut schools, some routines remain. Firing from Edinburgh Castle, a distant boom shatters the kitchen's hush – it is the 'one o'clock gun', which discharges every day except Sundays, Good Friday and Christmas Day. Ships in the Firth of Forth once set their clocks to 1 p.m. by this 105-millimetre field gun, but today it is a useful marker for lunchtime.

Instantly, the streets are silent once again. All that is left is a limpid late-winter glow coming into the kitchen where, by the window, a single radiator is feebly doing what it can to warm the room.

On the hob, two eggs are bobbing in boiling water, steam puffing furiously, almost lifting the lid of the solitary saucepan. Nearly done, the timer tells me, ticking down from seven minutes. The eggs will be chopped and stuffed into dough, along with sauerkraut, mushrooms and caraway, to make pirozhki, small Russian hand pies. Fitting the palm snugly, they are easy to eat and easy to make. It is too cold to do anything but make pies today, a process good for warming up and unstiffening cold hands.

Scooping slippery sauerkraut from its jar into a sieve, I push the shredded cabbage down into the metal mesh with my fists to drain it of brine. A fermented whiff melds with the eggy steam, bringing forth the smell of Russia's stuffy wintertime kitchens. Today, Russian cuisine has begun to move beyond cabbage and caviar clichés, but not entirely. Cabbage forms the basis of the quintessential Russian soup, shchi, and its leaves are neatly rolled into 'little doves', or golubtsy, stuffed with pearl barley, mushrooms and dill. As the sulphurous smell builds and wafts, a soft, not unpleasant, melancholic feeling rises with it. The distinction between here and there begins to blur and, as the pirozhki ritual progresses, soon enough an imaginary Russian train pushes its way through the snowy taiga and into the kitchen.

Sometimes what we choose to cook mirrors what our soul misses, and sometimes the food we eat is a reflection of past routes taken. Pirozhki, combined with dramatic weather, connects me back to the winter of another year, 2016, and to Moscow. From there, with James, I had set off on a seven-day, 5,772-mile railway journey to Vladivostok, on the Pacific edge of Asia.

In my Trans-Siberian notebook – a cheap hardback with a brown faux-suede cover – I had made lists of things eaten. Scribbled in Biro, made wobbly by the train's lurch, it reads: rough-skinned gherkins, slabs of pork fat, plasticky-tasting Alenka chocolate, vacuum-packed Siberian pine nuts, black bread. Catalogued from the dining car: bowls of porridge topped with yellow butter, sour solyanka soup (with salted mushrooms, olives and sausage), salads of cucumber, red pepper and dill in sunflower oil, bottles of too-salty mineral water, Baltika beer and potato pirozkhi. Brought from home: chocolate digestive biscuits, Fisherman's Friend lozenges and oatcakes. Biscuits have always been vital for any adventure. Roman soldiers carried ring-shaped biscuits on campaign, Boer pioneers transported rusks in their wagons, and German emigrants to America lugged with them Bretzels, which became pretzels, as food historian Lizzie Collingham documented in her excellent book *The Biscuit*.[1] Aboard the Trans-Siberian, a miniature universe moving through the vast atlas of Russia, we travelled so sluggishly that there was much time to think about such things.

~

Cooking can be a mindful form of therapy, and it does for me what I imagine yoga or meditation does for others. Distraction slowly dissipates until all there is left is a single task, and then another, for which hands will do the work, until it is done. Sautéing, toasting, draining, coating, blending, browning, whipping, beating, spreading, cutting, reheating, brushing, sprinkling, filtering, dusting, mashing, whizzing, trimming, spooning, crushing, boiling, simmering, stewing, flaking, slicing, soaking, grating, steaming, pickling, frying, seasoning, sieving, mixing, salting, rolling, zesting, pouring, spatchcocking, or whatever. Happiness, so fleeting and impossible a target, is never the goal, but serenity is, and that is what immersive cooking can provide. Stress tumbles down and calm extends. Nagging voids and quiet torments are cut short, and restlessness – which, like hunger itself, is gnawing and achy – is pacified.

If I miss being overseas, or being in transit (and, as someone who is perpetually and hopelessly fond of the simple art of moving from one place to another, I do), then I cook until the antsy feeling dissolves. Because to cook is to create, and as with any creative practice, it increases 'flow', that pleasant state of being when you're fully absorbed in something. Cooking is an artistic practice where you are always pushing forwards, but sometimes, too, stepping back, assessing and problem-solving. And from this progress comes satisfaction and peace of mind, an equilibrium.

The kitchen is a testing room and a repository. Sometimes chaotic, sometimes disciplined. A place of new beginnings and dynamism, somewhere for interactive wandering and fascin-ation, with your mind roving about the project as you go. And it can be a scene of rebellion, too. The large glass of lunchtime wine, the recipe going joyously off-piste. Or one of rebirth: stale rolls demolished into breadcrumbs for coating fish, the discarded fish skin cut into strips for dog treats.

The kitchen has long been a place of submission and serfdom for a great many people, especially women. But it can also be a source of power, somewhere a timid hand can become brave.

~

Glugging milk and sunflower oil into a jug, I crack an egg into the mix and whisk. Then, into a large earthenware bowl, its raised-pattern exterior designed to provide purchase, I weigh out plain flour, followed by the yeast, salt and sugar. Next, making a well in the centre, I pour in the eggy-milk mix, spooning it round and round until the dough is shaggy, before pressing into it with my hands. Shaking the mass out onto the counter, I start kneading: slap, push, pull, slap, push, pull. It is annoyingly sticky, but I continue the effort over many minutes, taking breaks as I go – making a pot of coffee, watering the potted herbs, feeding Darwin his fish-skin treats – then adding a sprinkling of flour here and there, until the dough is soft, soft, soft and elastic.

Time and patience are what is required now. I cover the bowl and shut it away in the walk-in cupboard at the back of the kit-chen where the tumble dryer is generating heat. This is the only place warm enough in the kitchen to raise dough in winter.

~

'It's like the sea. Too huge to write about.'[2] So claimed Beat poet Lawrence Ferlinghetti of the 'Great Siberian Plain' when he embarked upon his own Trans-Siberian railway trip in February

1967. And it is not unlike crossing the Atlantic, say, by ocean liner, with the repetition and perceived emptiness of the environment, a wariness of fellow passengers and the titanic distances. Ferlinghetti continued, 'Nothing but birch trees like the froth on endless white groundswells – Sometimes thin lines of black forest on the horizon. Forlorn wood towns, rail junctions, with switchmen standing outside of sentry houses holding up woodsticks from which the signal flags have long since worn off – a horsedrawn sled or two...'[3]

As someone travelling for pleasure, as I was, you embark with good intentions of reading, and pacing yourself, but in the end you just stare and stare at the hypnotic horizon, eat all of the snacks carried from home too soon, and generally drink too much – glad to be there, forever toasting the journey. But that is not to say that it is a tourist train, for it is used by scientists, students, travelling salesmen, grandmothers and soldiers.

It is also true that, as with most epic excursions, memories of setting off, the highly anticipated starting point, are made strong, and cemented in the mind for life, partly by the power of nerves. That first winter's night in Moscow, with me wearing bobbly woollen tights under thick corduroy trousers (I had been warned by James, who'd lived in Russia, not to wear jeans as should they get wet they'd freeze and stick, potentially ripping skin from shins and knees), we sat in a café near Rachmaninov Hall, drinking beer and eating pirozhki still warm from the oven. Snow fell, enlarging the pirozhki's appeal, and adding to the café's cosiness.

I had never experienced such frightening cold. Opposite the concert hall a bearded man, in torn trousers and with wild hair, had passed out on a bench, one leg hanging down, the snow falling like icing sugar into his open mouth. Until I saw him twitch, I worried he was dead. Would he survive the night and, if so, how?

In the heated underpasses more homeless men slept and huddled. Some shouted angrily into the night. Women in belted fur coats went by in three-inch heels, despite the pooling, slippery snow melt. Grateful for the warmth of the café, I looked forward to returning to our overheated hotel on Bolshaya Nikitskaya Street. James said that a lot had changed in Moscow since he left: 'Nowadays, cars stop at pedestrian crossings.'

Never having spent so long on a train, apprehension and excitement had welled up until, on the morning of departure, it bubbled over, making me annoyingly talkative. This buzz was not in keeping with the old Russian superstition of prisest' na dorozhko, which, roughly translating as 'a quick sit for the road', demands that you quietly pause with your packed bags, in order to contemplate what lies ahead. For me, this level of composure was impossible at such a blood-tingling moment.

At Moscow's Yaroslavsky Station, with its stucco plasterwork of strawberries and birds promising summertime, we pushed past soldiers dressed in blue berets and camouflage fatigues, and worn-out looking policemen in black fur hats. From frigid platforms, trains were pulling away to Perm, Kirov and Tomsk. 'That life-quickening atmosphere of a big railway station where everything is something trembling on the brink of something else,'[4] wrote Vladimir Nabokov in 1936, during his exile in Berlin. And, in my cold kitchen, dough still rising, I think there is something Nabokovian about the pirozhki I am preparing, too. In his novel *Pnin*, Nabokov singles out 'hot pirozhki'[5] as a quintessentially Russian snack to be eaten by his expatriate Russian professor – although, famously, Nabokov was not much of an eater; dinner for him was often just a can of Campbell's soup.[6]

We found our train, then our second-class, four-berth compartment and bunks. The sky above Moscow was leaden, threatening more snow, but I was, at that precise juncture, perhaps the happiest person on Earth. To be on a shared adventure, with new landscapes constantly unfolding, and revelling in the promise that soon the world would be compelling and juicy once again. Exactly on time, our train, the Rossiya, departed.

Our provodnitsa (conductress) made an appearance, checking tickets and handing out clean, neatly folded bedding. She had pirozhki to sell, so I bought four and set them on the table by the window. There is something about food wrapped up neatly in brown paper bags that offers satisfying reassurance – the knowledge that, whatever happens, you will not go hungry.

For the next three hours we had the cabin to ourselves; after that, it would be a shared experience the whole way.

Passengers, in their standard issue grey and red Russian Railways sandals, flip-flopped back and forth to the samovar at the end of the carriage for hot water. I sipped tea from a podstakannik, a glass held in an ornate metal holder, but quickly realised that what I actually needed, as we bumped along, was a mug with a lid. Under the two fold-down bottom bunks, heaters belched out hot air until it was stifling, while outside, a bleached-out white sun shone, torch-like, illuminating church domes sprinkled with gold leaf and huge housing blocks. I sat glued to the window as we went by picket-fenced dachas and Siberian huts with their painted shutters and log piles, the accumulated snow on some so thick that they looked fit to collapse. Birch trees slid by on either side of the tracks. This motion picture of banks of snow and taiga then repeated, as if on a loop, and once again our attention would be tightly held. It felt less like running away, this railway escapade, more like running *into*.

In our carriage we were the stranger guests, with most other foreigners choosing to take the Rossiya in summertime. I thought about the singular oddness of sleeping and sharing food with a revolving set of passengers. How best to meet this moving realm, with its parallel engagements and undercurrents of suspicion? It felt like stepping back into the early days of travel — a time before mobile telephones and cut-price airfares — with all of its uncertainties.

At the city of Vladimir, Mikhail, a businessman, and Yevgeny, a referee in the sport of bandy (similar to ice-hockey), joined us, shaking our hands in the formal Russian way. Soon it was dark and we went to sleep. When we woke up, a bathroom salesman who spoke some English had taken Mikhail's place. Yevgeny had also left. It was piercingly cold outside, -20°C or so. Every river we crossed was frozen solid. The next day, watery sunlight melted the patchy ice that had formed on the inside of the train windows overnight, creating rivulets of condensation. I unpackaged a pirozhki, ate it and decided on the dining car. The carriages along the way were flooded with cold light. People dozed on the angles of their arms, or played chess and picnicked on hard-boiled eggs and instant mashed potatoes, gnawing on pickles as if they were apples. Everything smelled vaguely of rotisserie chicken. I carried on through more carriages. Some passengers had hung sheets around their bunks for privacy and one snoring man on a top bunk had a seatbelt strapped over his belly to keep himself from rolling off. I was thankful for my silicone earplugs, and for not having booked berths in a cabin at the end of a carriage, which share a wall with the toilet.

Keep going, I muttered to myself. *Don't get your hand stuck to the frosty handrail between the carriages and lose a fingerprint.*

Sitting on a cherry-red faux-leather seat in the restaurant car, I peeled back a frilly yellow curtain and took in the wintertime beauty of the land. In the Urals, the hypothetical border between Europe and Asia that also divides Russia in two, the landscape was surprisingly diverse, polar tundra, taiga and forest steppe, meadows blasted by blizzards. I had heard that the local pirozhki are sometimes filled with herbaceous horsetail, which apparently tastes like celery and has long been revered for keeping remote villagers going during times of famine. In the summertime, bakers fill their cakes with northern berries — cranberry, cloudberry and serviceberry.

Persil-white, snow-covered timber mills and gingerbread houses rushed past. Snowflakes that hit the window shone like crystal. Sometimes the sun was a weak smudge in the sky, other times it became a wobbling red ball. It was closer to lunch than breakfast, but time had taken on a strangeness, and somehow mealtimes no longer mattered, so I ordered a bowl of kasha (buckwheat porridge), topped with a thick slab of cold butter.

As I lifted my spoon, the cook appeared momentarily, dressed in slippers and a velour leopard-print tracksuit, her tangerine hair curled around pink rollers. I remembered Ferlinghetti's observations about the food on board: 'A man in a soiled white coat comes thru the car every once in a while selling buttermilk in bottles, and other men come thru selling hot meat-dishes ... two Finnish boys in the diner get drunk on four bottles of champagne they buy to use up their meal-tickets.'[7]

I would have liked some buttermilk, I mused silently, or some ersatz champagne, but that was decades ago now and things have changed, though many of Ferlinghetti's impressions and questions still stand: 'The Face of Siberia has ice eyes and a beard full of icicles ... In order to arrive where I'm not, I must go by a way I have never been? ... Taiga and tundra flash by in the night, ghosts of shamans and tungus flash by over the landscape.'[8]

I sat back, listening to the rattling light fittings and comedic horns, the odd siren, long whistles. The calming clickety-click of the train, rhythmic as poetry, its tempo felt in my chest.

Given that the majority of dishes on the dining-car menu were always unavailable, it was surprising to later learn that Russia's railway buffets once fed passengers extravagantly well. As Alison K. Smith notes in her book *Cabbage and Caviar*, when the railways got going in the nineteenth century, 'food became part of the story of the journey'. She goes on to cite an English traveller of the 1860s, who, taking the train from St Petersburg to Moscow, understood that the leisurely pace (twenty hours then, just four today) was in part 'to accommodate long stops for meals'.[9] In 1901, British journalist and MP Henry Norman was less impressed and found the dining behaviour aboard wanting. 'As for a Russian's meal-times, he simply has none ... This habit of eating when you are hungry and eating whatever you may happen to fancy, instead of eating when the cook wills, and then only what custom severely restricts you to, is disorganising in its effects upon the refectory of the train.'[10]

For British writer, and gourmand grandee, Lesley Blanch (1904–2007), meals aboard the Trans-Siberian railway in the 1960s did not disappoint. In *From Wilder Shores*, she breathlessly wrote, 'And apropos the restaurant car, what about the meals? ... What did I eat? Caviar. Caviar? Yes, all the way. I turned in all my different meal tickets, renouncing round-the-clock relays of stew, fish, soup, and stew again, for caviar tout court. Caviar, tea, luncheon, tea and more honey at tea time, caviar, vodka and toast for dinner, with Caucasian champagne, the sort Alexander Dumas so unkindly described as epileptic cocoa.'[11]

Near the snow-clad town of Kungar, men bulbous in camouflage-printed coats were out ice-fishing in the middle of the Sylva River. Beside them, thin tracks made by animals led into thick forests of birch, aspen and poplar.

~

Back in my kitchen, thinking of beautiful snow-clad Russian forests, I feel a sense of unease looking at the sodden mushrooms strewn on a tea towel. News reports are coming in about Scotland's decimated woodlands, victims of the devastating winds that characterised the storm season. Storm Arwen, in particular, damaged thousands of hectares of woodland and millions of trees. Many entire forests, the sort I often like to walk through, are being turned into timber: mature beech trees, granny pines, ancient oaks, conifer plantations. Trees upended, with trunks split, turned to stumps. Damage not seen on this scale for decades. Our climate emergency will likely bring an increased frequency of such severe storms. The prospect is terrifying.

Outside, the wind is blowing more strongly, and a sharp cry suggests that someone has slipped over, their hands, I imagine, grabbing at the black railings, with their fleur-de-lis balusters and pineapple finials, that line the pavements of the New Town. I start dicing the mushrooms as small as possible, before mixing them with grated onions and carrots.

Darwin may be a silent witness to my cooking, but he is watching my movements with interest. Eyes fixed.

I throw him a carrot top and, satisfied he has won the battle, he lets go a canine sigh and leaps up onto the window seat to watch the passers-by and sniff at the Christmas cacti on the window-sill, their tubular flowers lit by Edinburgh's northern light. But soon I can sense his eyes on me once again, so I pour some milk into his bowl. Affection given so unquestioningly, always. Him to me, and me to him.

As the caraway seeds release their warm scent into the oily pan, the excited yells of schoolchildren flood in. Snowball fights. I listen, and watch Darwin's ears perk up at the hollering. Then I add the sauerkraut, the other vegetables, sugar and salt to the pan, sautéeing the lot with ample black pepper. Hearty, healthy ingredients. Ingredients to fight another cold day.

~

At Yekaterinburg, our new cabin mates Tatiana and Alexei boarded, with a picnic bag the size of a washing machine, which they casually slid under the fold-down table. Inside was black rye bread, a brick-sized hunk of salo (pork fat), several litres of vodka and a crate of beer. Alexei was thirty-two, a staff sergeant in the army, and dressed in a fur-lined leather jacket. A crucifix swung above his grey vest and a military sentry ring glinted on his left hand. His wife, Tatiana, was rosy-cheeked and cheerful. As darkness swelled outside, Alexei disappeared to the dining car, where he procured some glass beakers. 'Russian champagne, it is Valentine's Day!'

And so it began.

After the sweet fizzy wine had been drunk, the door to the cabin was pulled shut and locked and Alexei slid his bag out from under the table. Knives and plates were offered around, the black bread and salo, and then the vodka, each shot packing the kick of a mule. In the traditional way, we drank until the last drop of the bottle. The vodka was cheap, but it did not matter because vodka does not require top-notch references. In no time, we were committed drinkers, the four of us. Alexei tried on James's tweed hat. We took drunken portraits. Each shot was chased with a slice of the greasy, smoky, home-cured pork fat, because there is no better partner for vodka. At one long stop, we all leapt onto the frigid platform, wholly black, except for the pallid glow of the station lights, to smoke, the icy north wind assaulting our throats with force on each cigarette suck. I remembered reading somewhere that if the train moves off and you get left behind, then the thing to do is find the station master, who will possibly get your bags unloaded at the next station for you to then catch up with them by taxi. A horrifying thought in the freezing-cold darkness, but less so with a head full of vodka.

Back in the cabin, more vodka was sloshed to the brim of shot glasses decorated with the sideburned face of Alexander Pushkin. With no self-restraint left, there was a tacit complicity between us. If I tried to refuse, Alexei would suck his teeth in disapproval and pour regardless. The fiery vodka coursing through us was a buttress against the extreme cold, the distance and the creeping tiredness.

This camaraderie fostered a sensation of togetherness and companionship, a social collectivity that Russians call sobornost. As we continued on, we drinking cousins, time lost meaning, but then no one on the train ever seemed to know the hour of the day, nor did they seem to care to. By 6 a.m., three or four bottles later, the cabin was swimming. Lulled by the cradle-rock of the train, we all dozed off. When we woke at lunchtime, sour-mouthed and sallow-faced, to thick falling snow, the air around our heads smelled of warm feet and armpits. There were no showers on board and fresh sheets were given out just once, upon boarding.

~

Pearly light poured through the frosty, pock-marked window onto the pull-down table, highlighting the sober truth that not an inch of space had been spared. Our clammy cabin had been tolerably clean before, but now it was woeful and seedy.

The Pushkin-faced shot glasses rolled about on their sides amongst breadcrumbs and chewed crusts. Knife blades were slick with pig grease. James's Russian dictionary was butter-flied open, face down on a smeared plate. A whole medley of grimness, almost like a crime scene. It reminded me of an image I had seen somewhere, surprisingly similar despite the inter-vening years. In the photograph, under a thick rug, a man lies asleep on his bunk. He is shirtless, his chest pale as skimmed milk, his hair auburn and spiky. Beside him is a table filled with empty bottles, packets, napkins and jars. Through the train window, Siberia is unmistakable. The man in the photo is David Bowie, and he had also slept it off aboard the Trans-Siberian, back in 1973. Along with the man who had caught him unawares, pho-tographer Geoff MacCormack, they had drunk beer and wine with Russian soldiers belonging to a construction unit.

The morning after necessitated emergency biscuits and I can generally be relied upon to supply these, partly because I grew up in 'biscuit town'. Until 1972, Reading, where I was born, was home to the red-brick Huntley & Palmers factory, founded in 1822 by Thomas Huntley and once the world's largest biscuit manufacturer. By 1874 the factory was churning out 12,600 tons of biscuits a year, with trade bolstered by the town's convenient location, on the Avon Canal between London and Bristol.[12] Today, Reading is no longer known as 'biscuit town', but the town museum houses the factory's memories in the Huntley & Palmers Gallery. On show, alongside a stash of Captain Scott's biscuits, is an African thumb piano made from a recycled tin. The *Reading Standard* once claimed that 'Himalayan shepherds would trade a week's supply of sheep's milk for a Huntley & Palmers biscuit tin.'[13]

Edinburgh, my current home, was also once a biscuity place, with its steam-powered factory belonging to McVitie & Price, a company that grew out of a bakery in Rose Street, and the former premises of Crawford's Biscuits in Leith, now an arts centre. As I unwrapped the packet, I thought of travel writer Bill Bryson, who recognised the chocolate digestive as a British treasure in his book *Notes from a Small Island*.[14]

~

Rumpled and with weighty limbs, it dawned on me that I had entirely missed Omsk, Siberia's second city. Fyodor Dostoyevsky hated Omsk, my guidebook informed me, as you would if you had served a four-year sentence there for 'political crimes'. In *Buried Alive*, he recorded his trials. Worse than the beetle-infested cabbage soup – 'my fellow-prisoners evidently thought that they imparted an additional flavour' – was the lack of privacy. 'I began to realise that in prison life there is something harder to bear than the loss of freedom or hard labour in fetters, and that is the impossibility of being alone even for one moment.'[15]

The train clattered on. Villages appeared marooned and immobilised by banks of crisp snow breast-high against houses. Trees were laden with hoar frost. All of it blinding, dazzling. I imagined packs of wolves and Arctic foxes roaming through the forests. Soon all the biscuits were gone, and in their place was a bizarre feeling of physical exertion, brought on by the constant movement and the vodka. With tigerish appetites, James and I returned to the dining car to order bowls of solyanka soup. The rhythmic clanging of the spoon against the edge of the soup bowl was like the knocking of the train on the tracks, and suddenly, as I fed my parched and weary mouth, it was all too much. The hangover was like a dead weight and, to my surprise, I found myself longing irresistibly not for Omsk or Tomsk, but for the familiarity and normality of a wet Sunday afternoon in Leith.

We said goodbye to Alexei and Tatiana, who, facing hangovers paired with family obligations, grumpily disembarked, leaving us to the evil odour of our cabin. Neither of them had ever left Russia, they told us, and to them this was just another journey through a giant slice of the world's biggest country. I watched them trudge down the platform until they disappeared in a heavy mist of snow.

~

In the kitchen, the cold season is everywhere: in fruit bowls, knobbly quince, winter citrus and pomegranates; on shelves, pears in syrup next to candied chestnuts in jars. Decanters of whisky and bottles of rum stand ready for drinks, along with sugary cranberry cordial heavily laced with cinnamon.

A litre of frozen sea buckthorn juice, fiercely orange, as orange as marigolds in full bloom, is defrosting in the sink.

Sea buckthorn grows along the coast on sand dunes in Britain, but it is rarely used here – unlike in Russia and Central Asia, where it also thrives, and is offered as a standard addition to hot tea in cafés. Legend hints that warrior-rulers and conquerors such as Genghis Khan and Alexander the Great, who stormed across the steppes of Central Asia and Mongolia, tanked up their armies on the berries, and perhaps their horses, too. Sea buckthorn's Latin name, *Hippophae rhamnoides*, means 'shiny horse', and some historians suggest that in ancient times, after a battle, when the horses were left to graze, they would come back with glossy manes, having feasted on sea buckthorn.[16] Others link the name to the mythical flying horse, Pegasus. I know all of this because of my sea-buckthorn-foraging neighbour, Kirstie Campbell. After hard years spent as an aid worker in Sarajevo, Iraq and Gaza, she has successfully turned her harvest of these superfood berries into a business in Edinburgh. While she was in Pakistan, coordinating logistics after floods, a commander of the National Disaster Management Authority mentioned sea buckthorn as a food source, spurring Kirstie to draw a line back home to Scotland where she knew it flourished (though it is a non-native plant). Today, with Teal the springer spaniel at her heels, she scours nearby coastal dunes, painfully separating the golden berries from vicious inch-long thorns.

~

As we sped through more time zones, days became distorted. That the train runs on Moscow time the whole way adds to the confusion (it would be Moscow +7 by the end of the journey). Eventually, even the stations had wintry names. As we pulled into Zima ('winter' in Russian), it was almost -30°C outside, and snow had compacted on the platforms to form an ice-rink.

By this point, giving up on standard time, James and I had fallen into our own rhythm. Each afternoon, as dusk gathered, we would go to the dining car to drink Baltika beer and chat with Olga, the lonely provodnitsa, who was usually holed up in her cabin with a microwave. She told us that when the train terminated at Vladivostok, she would return straight away to Moscow, allowing no time for real rest. Outside, a lone dog dashed down a short, deserted railway platform and past a round-shouldered brown log house, its roof smothered in thick snow, giving it the appearance of an iced Christmas pudding. Other small timber houses were so engulfed by fresh snow that they appeared like ships sinking into a white sea. It was difficult to believe, staring into the whiteness of the taiga around Usolye-Sibirskoye — known as 'Siberia's salt shaker', as this is where rock salt is mined — that summer would bring abundance: forest berries, milkcap mushrooms, edible ferns and crops of rapeseed, rye, oats, barley and buckwheat.

~

Finally we reached Irkutsk, in eastern Siberia, where we broke the trip for two nights. We gingerly walked down the platform on black ice, in the half-light, passing people dressed in black fur hats and black leather jackets. As we checked into the Hotel Victory, across the street we saw men sweeping the rooftops to stop them collapsing under the weight of snow. The short days went by in a blur. There was dinner at an upbeat Italian restaurant called Figaro, where we celebrated with what seemed to our newly humbled palates like impossibly indulgent food and drink: mango and pumpkin-seed salad, salmon risotto and a bottle of good Italian wine. Lining the streets were baroque and Art Nouveau buildings with lacy wooden shutters, cornices and window aprons. At Lake Baikal, covered with three-metre-thick ice strong enough that cars drove across it, we met migrant workers, mainly Tajiks, selling the layered, pilaf-like rice dish called plov to tourists. And at the market we tried golomyanka, little chubby fish with 40 per cent fat, and omul, so powerfully smoked that I could only manage such high fishiness paired with the familiarity of golden discs of the Central Asian bread called non, which the plov cooks were also selling.

Back on board, Irkutsk lingered for many miles, as virtually every passenger boarded with bagged-up omul; and as they picnicked on the greasy fish, the heaters did a sterling job of transporting the pungent, kipper-like smell throughout the carriages. We rattled on towards Chita, with its merchant mansions and Labrador tea trees that blossom pale purple in the summer, trudging back and forth to the dining car, where we drank black coffee that tasted of cigarette ash.

~

This railway adventure was, in many ways, an exercise in decelerating – quite literally, as we journeyed more slowly at times, it felt, than carts dragged by oxen – and of being disconnected. Mobile signals were often non-existent, and I found myself grateful to be forced offline from the digital world. Sucking up time and attention, constantly leaching it away, our anti-physical online worlds disperse activity so effectively that it can be tough to do anything properly. When our train halted at smaller stations, hardy children sometimes stood in the snow with their parents, waving and watching us go by. Then, almost too soon, Vladivostok. A city after countless villages. The final stop.

'I felt as if I had always been on the Trans-Siberian,'[17] Peter Fleming (brother of Ian Fleming, creator of James Bond) glumly wrote, and it did feel that way as we extracted ourselves from our overheated compartment to step falteringly into the weak afternoon light. With the breeze stinging our faces, our lungs gratefully sucked in fresh air – at last! – cold as glass. Crunching through the snow and swaying slightly, as if sea-sick, across the icy platform paved with Japanese clay tiles, we agreed that it might have been only seven days on the train, but it felt as though weeks had passed – so much had been said, seen, shared and drunk. Now, with Japan to the east and North Korea to the south, even the regional flora had changed, to sea kelp, ginseng and lotus, no longer what we think of as typically Russian.

The journey was over, and we felt transformed by it. Our next journey would be by aeroplane, back to Moscow in a day's time. So far east had we come that the flight would take nine hours.

~

Recalling this journey now stings because of what Russia has increasingly become. On 24 February 2022, eight years after illegally seizing Crimea, Putin launched his unprovoked 'special military operation' against Ukraine, in reality a sickening full-scale invasion that soon became the biggest attack on a European country since the Second World War. Sweeping sanctions were imposed on Russia as missiles rained down across Ukrainian towns and cities. Mariupol looked like a vision of hell. A missile hit Kyiv's television tower, located opposite the Holocaust memorial site of Babyn Yar, where, in 1941, German SS troops massacred thousands of Jews. Nuclear attack was repeatedly threatened ('I am not bluffing,' Putin said, straight to camera). During the first year of the war, thousands of Ukrainian civilians were killed, millions were internally displaced and millions more crossed borders seeking refuge. Hundreds of thousands of Russians fled to former Soviet states, countries they can enter without visas, fearing conscription and martial law, or simply to look after their businesses. James reported on the Kremlin's activities from Edinburgh, and then from surrounding countries impacted by the war: Kazakhstan, Moldova, Estonia, all places with connected stories to tell. As I chaired panels of Ukrainian and Russian writers at cultural institutes in London and elsewhere, the premises of equivalent organisations in Ukraine were being shelled: the Ivankiv Historical and Local History Museum, the Soviet-built Slovo ('Word') apartment block in Kharkiv, originally constructed to house Ukrainian writers. Curators at Odesa's Fine Art Museum began stripping the walls and plinths of its irreplaceable artefacts, its staff reportedly hiding art in basements. At the Kharkiv Art Museum, director Valentina Myzgina was quoted as saying, 'It looks like we have to hide Russian paintings from Russian shells.'[18]

In the kitchen, when James and I were together, we spoke of little else, both of us in shock at the mounting casualties and Russia's fast march towards full-on fascism, terrorism and genocide. My heart ached for Ukraine, a country I admired and adored, especially the Black Sea port city of Odesa, where I had spent a happy time researching and writing not so long ago. During Russia's horrifically misjudged war we are reminded that anything is possible; that the violence wrought via bombs and bullets aims to destroy even more than Ukrainian people and buildings; that it intends to decimate Ukrainian culture and history, threatening the country's very existence.

Ever since the invasion, I keep thinking of another Russian train journey James and I took, a few years after the Trans-Siberian, this time from Kazan to Yekaterinburg. On that trip, in the dining car, an unsmiling man, possibly drunk, dressed in a black turtle-neck jumper, said to us, loudly and pointedly, 'What do you both *want* from Russia?' At the time, I had no idea how to answer this probing question and I recall that we ignored it, brushing the man off. But I know what I would say to such an enquiry now, should a Russian ever ask it: for Russia's army to cease stealing Ukrainian land; for Russian soldiers to stop murdering Ukrainians.

~

Punching down the risen dough, I divide it, then roll out sixteen rounds, spooning the cabbage-y filling onto the centres. Then, bringing the sides up around the filling, I pinch and pleat, sealing tightly and shaping as I go. I let the pies rise once again, before brushing the tops with egg wash and sliding them into the oven.

They are not a chapter-and-verse recreation of the real thing; they are, instead, 'a version of' pirozhki, irregular in shape, size and quantity of filling. And as I eat the first one, my fingers warming, I feel two things: modest pride in the pies made well, and a slight gnawing guilt for having brought Russia, at a time like this, into the kitchen.

But the kitchen is a portal to a hundred different places, people, times and experiences and I acknowledge that next time, just as it doesn't have to be pies, it doesn't have to be Russia either. I look to Darwin for comfort. He lies on the floor beneath the oven door, curled up like a cinnamon bun, softly snoring, his paws flinching in dream.

Russian Hand Pies

Do not let winter pass without attempting a batch of these little pies. I like to eat mine warm from the oven with unorthodox sides and condiments – a salad of pickles, along with pots of sour cream, mayonnaise and tomato ketchup for dipping. This is an adaptation of Darra Goldstein's classic recipe in her excellent cookbook on Russian food culture, *Beyond the North Wind*.[19]

MAKES 16

1 beaten egg, for glazing

FOR THE DOUGH
250g plain flour
7g fast-action dried yeast
½ teaspoon fine sea salt
½ teaspoon caster sugar
115ml whole milk
1 medium egg
1 tablespoon sunflower oil

FOR THE FILLING
1 tablespoon sunflower oil

1 teaspoon caraway or
  dill seeds
1 medium onion, grated
1 medium carrot, grated
80g chestnut mushrooms,
  chopped
130g sauerkraut, drained
2 hard-boiled eggs, chopped
small handful of finely
  chopped dill
small handful of finely
  chopped parsley
sea salt flakes and freshly
  ground black pepper

For the dough, put the flour into a large mixing bowl, then add the yeast to one side, the salt and sugar to the other. Whisk together the milk, egg and sunflower oil in a jug, then make a well in the flour and pour in. Mix until you have a shaggy dough. Turn out the dough onto a lightly floured surface and knead until the stickiness is gone, 10 minutes or so. Cover with a damp tea towel and leave to rise in a warm spot for at least an hour, or until doubled in size.

Meanwhile, for the filling, warm the oil in a large frying pan, add the caraway or dill seeds and fry until their scent is released. Add a generous pinch each of salt and pepper, along with the onion and carrot, and sauté for 5 minutes, then add the mushrooms and keep sautéeing for another 2 minutes. Remove from the heat and allow to cool.

In a large bowl, combine the sauerkraut, hard-boiled eggs and herbs, then add the cooled sautéed vegetables, adding more salt and pepper to taste. Combine the filling well.

Line two baking trays with baking parchment.

Cut the risen dough into quarters. Working with one at a time (and keeping the dough you are not immediately using covered with the damp tea towel, to stop it drying out), divide the dough quarter into four again, then roll each piece into a 10cm round. Add roughly two tablespoons of the filling to the centre of each round, then bring the sides of the dough up to enclose the filling, pinching and pleating along the top to seal. Once all the pies are assembled, let them rise again for 20 minutes in a warm place.

Meanwhile, pre-heat the oven to 200°C/180°C fan/gas 6.

Pinch closed any splits in the risen pies, then brush with the egg wash and bake for 20–30 minutes, or until golden.

Nice eaten warm, but equally good at room temperature, they'll keep in an airtight container for a couple of days.

CHAPTER THREE

Snow Falls on Sultanahmet

Carrying his bowls of yoghurt or pudding, neatly stacked in crates, a roving salesman goes crunching through snowfall towards Istanbul's Sultanahmet Mosque. Wrapped in a heavy woollen coat, heading past the baths of Roxelana, his modest appearance is set against the magnificence of fluted domes and slender minarets.

At my kitchen table, looking at the glossy black and white photograph, with its wintertime melancholy lifting off the page, it is impossible not to feel the cold, or sense the sort of silence found only in snowy surroundings. This photograph, capturing Istanbul's heart-stopping beauty in winter better than most painted or poetic attempts, was taken by a young Austrian, Othmar Pferschy (1898–1984), who arrived in Istanbul on the Orient Express in 1926 and stayed for forty years. Featured in an issue of *Cornucopia* magazine,[1] the image is in the rückenfigur ('figure from the back') style, where a person is seen from behind in the foreground of the image, as a stand-in for the viewer. You gaze at the photograph, wondering at it, and then, for a few seconds, you find that you yourself *are* the wandering, snow-flecked salesman, willingly stepping into the shadowy light and Istanbul's chill.

Still wrapped in thick woollens during the day, and pyjama-ed early at night, I notice that the smell of winter is everywhere in the kitchen. Seville oranges, marmalade, brandy, whisky, nutmeg, ginger, Stilton. Early in the morning, sneaky frosts cover the courtyard with a sparkling white sheet, a reminder that winter is not yet ebbing away, not at all, though the sun is beginning to draw down a little later.

As evening gathers around the city, I am poaching fruit for Turkish hoşaf, an infusion similar to compôte. When ready, the hoşaf will be served at room temperature in a glass bowl, so that its glow can be seen. And, importantly, it will be eaten with a delicate spoon.

I have some vintage silver Uzbek cutlery, but a true Turkish hoşaf spoon ought to have a bowl of mother-of-pearl or tortoiseshell, and a very thin handle set with gems. The sort that fed sultans at Istanbul's Topkapı Palace, where the kitchens had a dedicated hoşafçıbaşı (chief hoşaf-maker)[2] because a hoşaf would crown the end of each and every meal. My spoons, too cold, too metallic-tasting, are not quite right. The art of hoşaf is as much about the spoon as its preparation. I cast concerns away and instead wallow in the heady rosy-lavender-ish fragrance that is rising from the pan on the stove. Intense and intoxicating, it offers a pleasing foretaste as the dried apricots, chewy as toffee, and whole jet-black prunes carried back from Istanbul bob in the simmering sugary water.

This spoonable, fruity concoction is an attempt to feed the heart what it misses, and to bring some colour to the table. And it is an edible tribute to Istanbul, city of infinite hoşafs, unquestionably at its most alluring in winter, when devilish fog swirls around the Bosphorus and the excesses of summer have long gone.

Istanbul's colder months are when seasonal delights of tantalising curiosity come to the table. Plump anchovies butter-flied on toast, teeny wild 'lamb' chestnuts collected from Black Sea forests and glasses of thick, fortifying boza, a pudding-like fermented millet drink that is hawked in the streets by men swinging pails, calling out '*Boza, booooooooooooooo, boza!*' My good friends Noriko and Coşkun, who live in the city's business district of Levent, sometimes send me night-time videos of their local boza vendor. Blessed with a particularly melodic call, he often strolls beneath their balcony, as late as midnight and in all weathers, not unlike the salesman in the Pferschy photograph.

Nudging the kitchen door open with his apple-shaped head, Darwin brings with him the smell of wood smoke entangled in his fur. He stares at me, looking small and puppy-ish. Like many dogs, Darwin has a great ability to change his mannerisms and personality to turn a situation to his advantage, but some things remain constant. His ability to sleep at any time, in any position, in any situation. His indifference to most other dogs, and even cats (but never foxes). His habit of checking every room before everybody settles down to sleep for the night. A body clock you could set your watch by. Maybe he'd like a chewy dried apricot. I put one on the floor and he snaffles it noisily and gratefully, his brown eyes already asking for more. My heart swells, and I stroke him.

~

Winter is when I reach for my passport. If through autumn, I have been at home a great deal – taking root, until it feels like the entire cargo of my writing desk is pushing down on my shoulders – then I pack my feelings into a suitcase and go to Istanbul, and I stay there a short while until I feel right again. I have no desire to chase the sun. I want Istanbul in the cold, not the city in summer with its all-night noise, and all-night traffic jams, and the drip, drip, drip of air-conditioners pissing onto pavements. Crude, melting sunsets. The sheer vanity of it all, the gym-toned, the tanned and the self-adorned. Everyone desperate to catch a Bosphorus breeze. How exhausting it is to meet a new day when it is already thick and syrupy with heat. No. It is far better to drink your coffee, or red-hued Turkish tea, wrap up, grab an umbrella or, better still, a hat, head outside and suck in the crisp, chill air. Give me fickle weather, rain-lashed post-war apartment blocks, poorly lit alleys, gloom circling about minarets, nocturnal cigarette smokers huddling in doorways, white-mist dawns and pea-souper afternoons; the impossibility of taxis and the cancelled ferries, which force another meal, another drink, a longer stroll home. And the fog. The purple fog, blue fog and white fog. Film noir fog. How I love the sheer romance of it; disorientating, dominating, concealing and revealing. The city's 'flaws', more obvious without the golden champagne fizz of sunshine, only make it feel more real, binding you to it far more durably, more relentlessly. Summer and winter are so very different that it is sometimes hard to marry the two in one city. Rain bouncing off the Galata Bridge. Clouds swirling about skyscrapers. Snow falling on Sultanahmet. Breath billowing white in the cold air. That is my Istanbul.

~

Chopping charcoal for braziers, the chestnut sellers were already out on street corners as daylight broke weakly over the Golden Horn. I walked briskly through the biting cold down to the docks at Karaköy, descending the steep lanes around Galata Tower filled with breakfast carts, delivery vans and lightbulb sellers, past greengrocers selling fruit: mandarins from the Aegean coast, pears from Ankara and miniature apples from the Black Sea city of Amasya. Dogs in packs, and skittish cats, were already busy bothering rubbish and chasing each other. As I ambled along, I mapped out a route in my uncaffeinated mind for a perfect day of doing nothing more than eating Istanbul's wintertime delights, over on the Anatolian side of the city.

By the docks stood a cart selling freshly baked simit. Breakfast. I handed over some coins, sesame seeds scattering to the floor as

I paid. Then, following a man carrying a tray of scalding tea ready-poured into tulip-shaped glasses, I boarded the ferry for Üsküdar, the bready simit pressing against my hip like a promise.

If Istanbul is a city of a thousand villages, then each has its own emotional season too. Exuding a certain solemnity, a sobriety and gravitas, Üsküdar feels like a wintry place, one with too much heft behind it – an ancient history of religious piety, Sufi lodges and fourteenth-century tombs – to be considered summery. It is refreshingly subdued, even during the highest days of August.

Aboard the ferry, weather had forced all life – the ship spotters, seagull feeders and accordion players – inside. Sitting in our collective body heat, wind ruffled the water that carried us, along with freighters, oil tankers and cargo boats. Windows blurred with rain. I wiped away the condensation with my sleeve, in the unlikely hope of witnessing a pod of dolphins, as I had done once before on this same stretch of water – there and then gone, as if a daydream – but all I could see were grey waves pushed by a strong wintertime current. The waterline, melding with drizzle, then haze, then sky, made it seem as though we were floating in mid-air. I sipped my tea, and once warmed up, went outside. Wind held the mobbing gulls and I squinted into the far distance, where the city's first suspension bridge straddles the Bosphorus, bringing to mind a fragment of British history.

When the bridge was opened in 1973, drawing more than a million onlookers, it had taken 400 workers and 35 engineers over three years to complete it. An engineering masterpiece, its construction was overseen by legendary builder of bridges Bill Brown, also known for his design of Edinburgh's Forth Road Bridge. 'A bridge, which is not only a bridge across the Bosphorus linking both parts of Istanbul, not even a bridge between two continents within Turkey, but a bridge to link people and nations as well,'[3] he said of it at the time. Initially, not everyone was sure about this continent-joining feat. In *A*

Traveller's Alphabet, the 'bard of Byzantium' historian Steven Runciman, friend of Freya Stark and Patrick Leigh Fermor, wrote: 'I cannot in my heart approve of the great new bridge across the Bosphorus ... No man, I think, should join continents God has put asunder. But in the misty light it had great beauty.'[4]

Returning to the cabin, I stared out across the waves, yawning, until, almost too soon, the crew began to flit about, signalling our imminent arrival. To the tune of a ship's siren, Üsküdar's two majestic waterside mosques, built by Mimar Sinan, chief imperial architect to multiple sultans, panned into view through the mist. A mooring rope was thrown around a bollard, sending skywards pearls of water, and the ferry juddered to a halt. We had come to Üsküdar.

~

The old harbour was once the gateway to Chrysopolis, or City of Gold, as it was known to the ancient Greeks, the starting place for many routes east. In his iconic book *Strolling Through Istanbul*, reprinted umpteen times, John Freely describes the dock as mystical sounding: 'In Ottoman days it was known as Square of the Falconers and was the rallying place for the Sacred Caravan that departed for Mecca and Medina each year with its long train of pilgrims and its sacred white camel bearing gifts from the Sultan.'[5]

The market behind the square today is busy with male-dominated enterprises: scrap metal, fishing kit and kebab sellers. But if you know something of Üsküdar, then you know that arriving there is to cross into a district forged by potent femininity. Several of Üsküdar's mosques are connected with all-powerful women. Tying a headscarf under my chin and taking off my boots, I walked into the Mihrimah Sultan Mosque. Set by the docks, it often goes by the unassuming name of iskele ('jetty') mosque, and its exterior, heavily cast in stone and lead, gives few hints of the vibrancy inside, or its remarkable story.

The mosque was built for the seventeen-year-old Princess Mihrimah, favourite daughter of Suleyman the Magnificent, who later commissioned her own great mosque at Edirne Gate. She was said to have had tiny feet, and in muddy weather would wear traditional pattens, wooden platforms some eight inches high, matching her elevated social standing, and inlaid with jewels.[6]

On entering, all seeing eyes are drawn skywards. First, to the stained-glass windows shining like an assortment of boiled sweets – sun or no sun – bright as fireworks. Then, to the dome where, appearing almost weightless, simple mosque lamps hang from a circular metal frame. Muslim or not, observant or not, it is impossible not to discern, in the presence of such a sublime aura and visual splendour, a feeling of solace and divine nourishment. It is a place not only to pray, but to think and be inspired.

Spiritual sustenance of another kind saved many lives at the old Selimiye Barracks, not far away, where Florence Nightingale, the 'Lady with the Lamp', resourcefully tended the sick and dying during the Crimean War in the 1850s. At times, more soldiers were dying in the filthy British military hospital at Scutari, as Üsküdar was called then, of typhoid, cholera and dysentery, than from injuries. A peculiar war, at a fervently religious time, it was one that saw Britain and France, together with Ottoman Turkey, fight Russia in the Black Sea, over whether French Catholics or the Russian Orthodox Church had rights to the keys of the holy places in Jerusalem.[7] The wider goal was all too familiar today: to limit aggressive Russian expansion into Europe.

~

At the kitchen counter, I splash a little more water into the simmering hoşaf pan and begin contemplating multitudes of other possibilities: cardamom-laced hsoşaf with apples and cherries (par-boiled and therefore more likely to float elegantly), bubbled in apple juice and freshened with a squeeze of lemon. A pink-hued quince variation with a little cinnamon. Simple prune, rich and dark. Apricot and orange blossom, with golden sultanas boiled with a spoonful of honey. Small, slightly unripe pears, peeled, then brought sweetly alive by heat and sugar. Whatever is in season or, in times of scarcity, dried fruit. Carried away by ideas, I rip off the pointed end of a baguette and dip it into the thin bubbling syrup on the stovetop. *Almost there*, I say to myself.

~

Lying behind the grandeur of the docks is Kanaat Lokantası, a well-loved esnaf lokantası (tradesman's cafeteria), furnished predominantly by its food. Headlining the restaurant, as you step in, are sparkling glass counters presenting a rich treasury of heavy puddings: candied quince halves with dug-out middles filled with kaymak (clotted cream) sit beside rice puddings, milk puddings and Noah's pudding – a dish said to have been concocted from the last provisions remaining on board when the Ark landed.

Everything in the room is as clean as it is white: white cuffs, white chefs' hats, white crusty torpedoes of bread sliced up ready in a basket on each table, next to plastic cups of Turkish mineral water with tear-off lids, like you get on aeroplanes.

Waiters, all male and all with cigarette-stained voices as thick as honey, slide between tables keeping watch, ever-efficient and with age-old courtesies, but also with an enthusiasm tempered by melancholy, as is the way in traditional Istanbul, and especially in Üsküdar. The chefs, far more animated, extract drama from their stews of beans and entrails, and their rice dishes, including Uzbek plov, chicken liver pilav and chestnut tekke pilav – made with pine nuts and currants, and based on an old Sufi recipe. There is much delight to be had in surveying all this time-honoured food, laid out with care. The ethos of the communal canteen is here at Kanaat: present in the workaday, in the highly polished glass and chrome, and in the sense of sharing. And, whenever possible, food ought to be shared.

Slapping a round of tekke pilav onto a plate for me, chef Mustafa Erdin, from the Black Sea town of Ordu, advised that, 'Usually it is a side for a more meaty dish.' But I was happy to have it on its own, to appreciate the simplicity of perfectly cooked rice as a meal in itself. Ordering quince hoşaf for dessert, I took my plate and went to sit with third-generation owner, Murat Kargili, a Turk of Macedonian descent with a taste for the delicious. With sparkling eyes, Murat revealed some of the lokanta's mysteries with good-humoured charm. He told me that the chestnuts for the pilav come from Kastamonu on the Black Sea and, while they are buttery now, they will get softer and richer closer to spring, and that for new year's dinners, when some Turks eat turkey, his chefs make volumes of this seasonal chestnut pilav and deliver it around the neighbourhood. The lamb, chopped small and peppered through the rice, is delicate, quite different to the high-tasting mutton that tops the rice dishes of Central Asia. Murat knows this well, as he too has travelled to Uzbekistan and Turkmenistan, 'buying antiques', he told me conspiratorially. As we talked, he poured tea, brushing the table with his palm, and gently directed, ordered and watched, in the effortless way that longstanding proprietors do.

By the windows, a few solo lunch diners sat like waxworks, sunk into a state of full satisfaction, staring out at the busy street where Istanbul's characteristic scents – petrol, mud, leaves, oud, fried onions, cheap tobacco, simit, fish, cat stink – coagulated under a sky the colour of tin. 'Kanaat' means conviction or opinion in Turkish, and it is impossible to leave this place, under its famous green awning, cool-hearted or without verdicts.

Walking up Üsküdar's steep slopes towards another matri-archal mosque, warmed by pilav and the flame of conviviality, I wondered if the Ottoman chronicler Evliya Çelebi (1611–c.1684), self-proclaimed wandering dervish and world trav-eller, would have appreciated Kanaat Lokantası. As he was a gastronome and a rambler of Üsküdar, I like to think so. His notes, kept during more than four decades of journeying, and published in his ten-volume *Book of Travels*, mark him out, according to historian Simon Sebag Montefiore, as 'a writer who is a combination of Samuel Pepys, Falstaff and the eighteenth-century courtier Prince de Ligne writing in the Islamic world of the Ottoman empire'.[8] Çelebi certainly loved hoşaf, noting that in his lifetime Istanbul was home to 500 hoşaf shops. In 1668, he visited Ohrid, nowadays North Macedonia's trump card holiday destination, and feasted with Ohrid's Albanian lords. Served more than twenty varieties of hoşaf, he admits to 'almost becoming a martyr to overindulgence'.[9] Open to life's rhythms, and possessed with a ferocious appetite, this stroller of seventeenth-century Istanbul makes some tall assertions about the 'prosperous abode of Üsküdar', claiming that it had over 2,000 shops, a dozen caravanserais, countless dervish lodges, hundreds of vineyards and even more rose gardens. Important militarily, he emphasises, yet also mystical. Somehow, the gist of that lives on today.

Turning a corner, I arrived at Atik Valide Mosque ('Old Queen Mother's Mosque'), which does, with its pale stonework, glow like a 'dome of light', as Çelebi wrote. Commissioned by Nurbanu Sultan, the wife of Sultan Selim II (also known as Selim the Sot, or Selim the drunkard), and mother of Murat III. Once a concubine of Selim, Nurbanu built her majestic mosque up on Üsküdar's hillside in the 1570s and 1580s, the complex growing with her prosperity, until it was a small-scale town, a meeting point for caravans gathering for the journey east or crossing to Europe, with shops, medrese, a soup kitchen, caravanserai and slaughterhouses. Some historians claim Nurbanu Sultan was the illegitimate daughter of the Venetian Nicolò Venier, Lord of Paros (and, possibly, niece of the Doge of Venice) and that she had survived life as a slave and concubine but rose up during the Kandınlar Sultanatı ('Rule of the Women') era, a time when commanding women influenced decisions made by their male relatives.[10] Today, it is a peaceful place of plane trees, where mothers and children gather in the shady courtyards and men talk and run thumbs over their tesbih (rosary beads). Inside is a bewildering gilded marble pulpit and a panel of Iznik tiles, the sort you stare at until your eyes begin swimming in tulips.

~

Üsküdar goes about its everyday business, rather than courting visitors with cocktail bars and tourist menus — but that is not to say that nearby Kadıköy, considered far more secular than Üsküdar, is not also a place that promises unexpected delights, because it is. And perhaps that, really, is the key to travelling well, seeing familiar places anew, letting travel refresh the mind and place again and again. That, and taking whatever comes your way with a lightness of spirit. 'One can only really travel if one lets oneself go and takes what every place brings without trying to turn it into a healthy private pattern of one's own, and I suppose that is the difference between travel and tourism,'[11] observed Freya Stark, slightly haughtily — yet she is right. After the Second World War, when she began retracing the routes of Alexander the Great, she occasionally stayed at an ill-fated eighteenth-century yalı (a grand waterside wooden house) called Hekimbaşı Salih Efendi, painted ox-blood red and built on the Bosphorus for the head physician of three sultans. She described it in *Turkey: A Sketch of Turkish History* as somewhere owls visit, and where the 'family pours out with easy, faithful welcome'.[12] In 2018, a Maltese-flagged tanker crashed into this unique and irreplaceable building, brutally wedging itself into the yalı's waterside façade.

~

Stepping out of a taxi by Kadıköy's docks, only to be struck by a strong soughing breeze and lashing rain, I huddled under an umbrella by the Roma flower sellers, waiting for the weather to ease – which it did, almost instantly, leaving us with a spent grey sky.

Then, walking towards the Armenian Church of Surp Takavor, I strolled along with a shopping list of edible things. My first stop was the confectioner Cafer Erol, founded in 1807, with its gloriously kitsch window displays of marzipan fruit and vegetables in every colour. I approached with a sense of growing anticipation, worrying that they might have sold out, or stopped stocking the very thing I had come for. But there they were. Jars of candied chestnuts, gleaming on a shelf in a neat row. I picked up two pots and held them to the light of a window, examining the chestnuts suspended in syrup. I paid, then went outside to join a queue, under the shop's famous blue awnings where a cart had been set up, for a takeaway cup of boza. The server asked if I wanted roasted chickpeas and cinnamon sprinkled on the top, to which I enthusiastically answered, 'Yes, please.' With the colour and consistency of custard, it came with a plastic spoon. Ibn Battuta, the fourteenth-century traveller and diarist, once mentioned a 'fermented drink of the Turks',[13] which could have been boza. Evliya Çelebi, in typical number-crunching fashion, identified 300 bozahanes, or dedicated boza taverns, during his time. I paused before the first sip. It was sour from the fermentation, not too sweet, very slightly citrusy and as filling as soup.

Just right for wintertime, and supposedly good for the immune system too.

Sipping and spooning as I went, I was joined by a street dog who, almost as tall as my hips, quickly matched my stride. Solid and thick-coated, he had clearly been well fed by the market. Istanbul's city dogs tend to be more on the move in the cooler months, roaming during the day, then seeking shelter at night, often in the doorways of whichever fishmonger or butcher feeds them. A woman with slightly wild hair lobbed the dog a giant bloody bone that landed by my shoe. I looked at her, supping my boza. The dog sniffed the bone indignantly, decided against it, and we both moved along, weaving through the market past bundles of dried camomile, honey shops and glistening displays of horse mackerel, smelt and sea bass, the wet rain-lashed lanes empty of tourists, the dog still loyal at my side like his canine cousins, Turkey's famous kangal sheepdogs, who act as protectors of the flock.

~

In Edinburgh, the hoşaf, taking its name from the Persian, meaning 'delightful water', because that is exactly what it is, bubbles on. Fruit plumping up and bobbing in the pan: the apricots like wrinkly-skinned cheeks, the prunes like black onyx gemstones.

I think about the simple magic of it. How by taking a handful of dried apricots and prunes, then adding sugar, water and heat – and time, the most important ingredient of all – it becomes glorious hoşaf. There is such pleasure in knowing that a piece of Istanbul – sometimes out of reach, but never out of memory – can be poured into a small bowl to be enjoyed at will. Cooking, even in its simplest forms, such as poaching fruit, is a mental practice as much as a physical one. Meandering through the process, lingering over the alchemy, crossing over the threshold to other times and places.

And isn't that the most enjoyable part of what cookery is, dreaming otherwise?

~

I chose not to stray far from the port in Kadıköy, stopping at a branch of the confectioner Hacı Bekir with a café, somewhere I always visit. There, I stocked up on boxes of lokum (Turkish delight), in flavours of rose, pistachio, lemon and coffee, ready to be stashed away in the pantry at home for birthday and Christmas gifts.

The story of founder Hacı Bekir himself is interesting. Born in the Black Sea city of Kastamonu, he set up in 1777, near the Spice Bazaar, making lokum and akide (boiled sweets), then eventually became chief confectioner to the sultan. Before the First World War, there were ten branches of Hacı Bekir in Istanbul, with distributors in Europe and America. So successful was the business that his grandson, Ali, was chosen as confectioner to the Khedive of Egypt, owing to the success of their shop in Alexandria. In the Louvre, there is a painting of Hacı Bekir weighing out sweets for children; it was painted by Amedeo Preziosi, a Maltese artist who was killed by a stray gunshot while hunting and is buried in a Catholic churchyard in Yeşilköy, the southernmost European point of Istanbul.

Taking my seat at the back of the café, I spotted salep on the menu, a warm winter drink made from the powdered dried tubers of wild orchids, specifically *Ophrys speculum*, which has weird furry bumblebee-like flowers. I ordered a glass. Two steel shakers, one of ginger and one of cinnamon, were set down with the cup and I sprinkled both powders onto the drink, hot and dairy-tasting. It instantly reminded me of childhood, its subtle flavour not easy to nail down: vanilla-like, reminiscent of mastic, earthy, woody, smooth as velvet. The sort of thing you'd take to sip under the covers while reading a bedtime story.

Later, I read about what should have been obvious – that excessive collecting of such orchids, which kills the plant, has led to serious conservation issues for wild orchid populations. One website claims that 'a single cup of salep needs about 13 orchid tubers.'[14] Feeling guilty, I vowed never to have it again.

~

Back at the port I found better weather and, with it, chestnut sellers. In Turkey, chestnuts are not just for Christmas, or for stuffing; they are deeply ingrained in the culinary culture. To understand their hazy history, we have to go back two and a half thousand years to the commercially minded Lydians of ancient western Anatolia, said to be the originators of gold coins and the first to establish retail shops. During a fleeting dominion over Asia Minor, their capital was Sardis and, as chestnut trees flourished there, chestnuts came to be known as Sardinian nuts. Ancient Greek thinker Diphilos called them 'Sardis-acorns' and considered them nourishing and well-flavoured, though Mnesitheus of Athens warned that consuming too many encouraged wind. The Romans renamed the nuts castanea, prefiguring both the modern Turkish name, kestane, and their botanical name, *Castanea sativa*.[15] Today, many Turkish chefs are notably inventive with chestnuts, anticipating them eagerly, as we might asparagus season. They are tucked into cabbage leaves, dashed through lamb pilavs, mixed into helva and crumbled into ice-creams. But for many, simply roasted is best.

By the docks, I stopped to talk to chestnut sellers Fikret Gunar and his uncle Sabri Akkaya, originally from the Black Sea city of Kastamonu, where the choppy and humid mountain-sea climate fosters wild chestnut trees with their smaller, sweeter nuts. Between them, they told me, they have been in this spot, roasting chestnuts on their cart, with a mangal grill and some charcoal, for seventy-five years. From eleven in the morning to eleven at night, and not just in winter but right into spring, as chestnuts are often stored to extend their availability. 'Join us for tea,' said Fikret, sliding a warm chestnut into my hand. As I nibbled on it, they waved away Bursa's famous nuts, as proud Black Sea men might: 'Bursa's chestnuts just don't open as nicely, they're only good for candying.' Evliya Çelebi would have disagreed, perhaps, as he noted that Bursa's chestnuts were unrivalled in the world. But, as with all things edible in Turkey, where food is absolutely a way of life, everybody has a view.

Pocketing a paper cone of roasted chestnuts, I bought a ticket to the strain of a fog signal, to travel back to the European side, past the old Haydarpaşa Station and the breakwater where egrets and cormorants often gather.

Countless writers have tried to sum up Istanbul's appeal, but I think James Wilde (1929–2008), foreign correspondent for *Time* magazine for thirty-two years, had it right when he wrote, 'Istanbul is a city drowning in urban sprawl, but it is also a place where magic holds sway, where people continue to scribble three wishes on to scraps of paper and bury them under a flowering rose bush or throw them into the sea.'[16] I gazed out and dreamt of heading further east, where the snow was likely as high as a cow's belly, slowing right down the ordinary transactions of life and silencing cities and plateaus.

My annual journey to wintertime Istanbul is like an unfaltering love affair: one with a beginning but no end. After all, it is far easier to delight in a place, rather than a person, for ever.

~

The hoşaf, lit by a sickly puddle of artificial light, has created a stupor in the kitchen, and the windowpane runs with moisture. Stepping into the pantry for a little more sugar, I put my hands instead on a forgotten box of candied chestnuts dipped in dark chocolate and coated with neon-green pistachio dust. Noriko,

my dear friend, had given them to me in Istanbul the last time
I was there. Cracking the chocolate first, my teeth sink slowly
into the fudgy chestnut; it is a deeply indulgent and mouth-filling
treat. By eating it, I think once again of Turkey and, simultaneously, feel in my bones a warm and contented feeling of home.

Fragrant Apricot and Prune Hoşaf

There are infinite varieties of hoşaf and, given that in many cases
the fruit is dried, it is not dependent on the seasons. Terrifically
simple to prepare, hoşaf can also transform hard fruit that won't
ripen, such as pears, and goes very well served alongside rice-
based dishes such as pilav. It will keep in the fridge for a couple of
days, perhaps to be spooned onto breakfast yoghurt or similar.

SERVES 2 GENEROUSLY

50g dried apricots

50g prunes, stoned

1 cinnamon stick

1 tablespoon caster sugar

1 tablespoon honey

300ml water

Put all the ingredients into a small pan and bring to a boil,
stirring to melt the sugar and honey, then cover and simmer for
about 20 minutes, just long enough to fully soften the fruit.

Leave to cool and steep for half a day at room temperature.
Discard the cinnamon stick and serve, at room temperature, in
little bowls.

SPRING

CHAPTER FOUR

Better a Dinner of Herbs

Rain is rushing in from the North Sea, battering the wild greens and pot herbs and bathing the temple to Hygeia, goddess of health, who watches over the Water of Leith. The deluge, like birdsong or the distant buzzing of the very first lawnmower, is ringing in spring. A time of nervous and untrustworthy weather. Whole banks of wild garlic are glistening and reeking down by the River Tweed, there are buds on the trees and blossom is promising just up ahead. The land is dandelions and the sea is dulse.

Kitchens have their seasons. And in this subterranean world, hidden from rainstorms and eager winds, is a world of wheat, wine and herbs. Always herbs. Herbs with balm in their leaves and flavour in their throats. A harvest of herbs on the windowsill. Parsley, coriander, tarragon. Basil, of different varieties, Greek with its anise-clove flavour and 'Sweet Genovese' with its jumbo cinnamon leaves.

By the stove, I am chopping mint, coriander, tarragon, basil and parsley. The leaves and stems will go into a soup inspired by a region that taught me just what can be done with herbs, the South Caucasus – that is Armenia, Azerbaijan and Georgia. From springtime until winter, whole bouquets of herbs arrive ceremoniously to the table, sometimes so fresh that clumps of earth still cling to their pale whiskery roots. Vital as bread, drawing eyes and senses forward, they are the centrepiece of the table. Intensely fresh and fragrant, unbruised and unwilted, they are a meal, a feast. Vitamins after a long winter. Never an after-thought, a mere sprinkling, or worse, 'a pinch'. At breakfast, oozing omelettes filled with molten white cheese and blades of tarragon. At lunch, bulgur salad, always more leaf than wheat. Ice cream is mint, sorbet is basil, soda is tarragon. In warmer months, they are refreshing, health-giving and sanity-saving as the sun starts hammering down.

So today, in this kitchen of a hundred crossroads, to welcome the beginning of spring, I will bless this soup with a crop of fresh herbs.

~

By the chopping board, I have a memoir splayed open, its cover creased, spine cracked, pages dog-eared. It is Carla Grissmann's *Dinner of Herbs: Village Life in Turkey in the 1960s*. I like to have a book to hand when I am cooking, ready for when onions are steadily caramelising in the frying pan, needing just the occa-sional stir, or when the oven requires time to heat up, or like now, when the bulgur has come off the heat and is softening silently in its steam. 'Cooking takes my mind off everything but itself,'[1] wrote Sheila Kaye-Smith in her book *Kitchen Fugue*, and I agree, except for the friendly book offering quiet company. Essays are good. Poetry is better. Pauses during cooking give a chance to revel in a single line or to grapple with an argument, philosophy or stanza. But best, when cooking, is a favourite paperback, one that you already know well, so that you can fixate, pleasurably, on the author's style, or luxuriate, at leisure, on choice passages. For that reason, *Dinner of Herbs* remains within reach.

Carla Grissmann is a name that ought to be better known. She is remembered in certain circles for helping to safeguard and cata-logue the holdings of Kabul's National Museum of Afghanistan in the 1970s, but it is in the pages of her book, outlining a year spent in rural Anatolia in the 1960s, that her impressions and ideas best live on. Leaving behind a job at the *Jerusalem Post* when she was in her late thirties, and arriving at the tiny farming hamlet of Uzak Köy, she recounts 'non-stop meals' and sitting with the village women 'packed together on the floor in an incredible confusion of laughter and chatter, eating walnuts, apples, sticky pink and white candies'.[2] Her motive for going is not made clear, but the reasons behind her journey did not appear to trouble her hosts very much. 'Through all the months I was in Uzak Köy there was hardly a flicker of curiosity about who I myself was, where I had come from, what I had done before or was thinking of doing next.'[3] Though we do learn that eventually she took the bus east to Kabul.

Open-minded and forever curious, Carla fitted in surprisingly well in Uzak Köy, and was accepted despite being different and an outsider: '...at the time I was not really aware of the magnitude of their courtesy and kindness. I was not a Muslim, I was a woman alone, and these two facts were enough to warrant suspicion, disapproval and exclusion.'[4]

Her book succeeds not only because her prose is open-eyed and undulating and filled with vitality, but because she hides nothing and never glamourises, or trivialises, the lives of the villagers. And like many writers, she paid rapt attention to how things looked and tasted and she seemed to hold dear the notion, as I do – and I suspect you do, too – that food partly makes us what we are. She knew that food is not really about secrets and science but the sharing of it, and the firm belief that giving it to others is part of what makes us human, because food is so often deep-rooted in love.

This is how Carla wrote about food in the spring: '...the earth was slowly letting go. Minute yellow and pink crocuses had broken through ... The men were beginning to prowl through their gardens ... I got presents of eggs, still warm. I would find bowls of milk and yoghurt on my bed, and small damp fistfuls of tiny orange wildflowers left by the children.'⁵

She is at her best in the sections where you can really feel her ethereal descriptions, the passages where you are right there with her, in a landscape where 'Grapevines grow at random, lushly, spreading out their tendons like clusters of giant green starfish sprawling in the powdery earth.'⁶

It is not surprising that it was Carla who had translated Sybille Bedford's *The Legacy* into French, Bedford herself having been an extraordinarily fine gastronomic writer. Someone, like Grissmann, who wrote with her consciousness stretched to the fullest and who found food a key into other people's lives. 'My interest in how people lived was nourished quite literally by the food I shared with them,'⁷ Bedford wrote in *Jigsaw*, her partly autobiographical novel.

I know I would have liked Carla and I wish I had met her. I think, as I begin chopping tomatoes, that she would have liked this soup, too, its flavours hinting at Turkey and the South Caucasus.

Putting the book down and draining the remaining water from the bulgur, I can tell it is a little overcooked, but it doesn't matter as it is bound for soup. In my kitchen life I have learned to accept that I often get timings slightly wrong. I no longer sulk over scorched porridge, stale breadcrumbs or curdled buttermilk. Setbacks and failure are all part of a well-balanced kitchen diet and life. I have come to know this. And it makes me think about Carla's satisfying and assured title, taken from the Bible: 'Better is a dinner of herbs where love is, than a stalled ox and hatred therewith' (Proverbs 15:17). But it is another proverb that perhaps best sums up her well-travelled, well-fed life: 'a contented mind is a continual feast' (Proverbs 15:15).

Springtime in Turkey and the South Caucasus is idealised for good reason. Valleys are carpeted with wildflowers and the land is one of bewildering variety. Apricot trees start frothing white blossoms, soft green buds begin appearing on willow branches and the quince orchards turn pink with flowers.

And as soon as herbs come to life, imbued with the spirit of the green blooming hillsides, they are greeted and rallied to the table. Dill and parsley fill freshly griddled flatbreads – qutabs in Azerbaijan, jingalov hats in Armenia, gözleme in Turkey – often elevated by little more than a generous brushing of first-rate butter. In Georgia, coriander soup, thickened with potato, is served with dark rye bread. In Turkey, fresh mint is mixed freely with cucumbers, yoghurt and water, or with pureed broad beans. In Turkish, I am told, there is even a verb used for chopping herbs, kıymak.[8]

~

Darwin trots into the kitchen, panting, while managing to retain a haughty, almost regal expression. Immediately, he spots a large basil leaf that has fallen to the floor. Nudging it along, he picks it up in his mouth but then, disliking the taste, launches it into the air with his nose and paws, sending it up like a miniature paper plane, his soft ears flapping as he goes. A simple game, performed again and again. Oh, little dog, what a marvel you are.

It is hard to imagine domesticated Darwin as belonging to the same canine family as the working mountain dogs of the Caucasus. Throughout the seasons, they follow shepherds and farmers in and out of sheep-filled gorges and canyons, as protectors of the flocks. Come late spring, as the weather warms, these stately dogs go past wildflower meadows, plateaus of floral-smelling hay, freshly scythed, and settlements coming out of hibernation. Tarpaulins for ramshackle cafés are once again pegged up in shady glens and the first shashlik fires are lit. Rugs and flat-weave kilims – chemically dyed nowadays, but once coloured naturally with barberries, Georgian snow rose, madder and indigo – are draped over twiggy bushes and car bonnets for de-mothing.

In the pantry, waiting to awaken memories and flavours of Georgia, is a cache of things carried back from trips over the years: jars of neon-red adjika spice paste, packets of savoury Svan salt and small glass bottles of precious Kakhetian sun-flower oil, glowing yellow as buttercups.

~

Tbilisi, Georgia's capital, is a late-night, late-start city. The cobbled lanes on the left bank of the Mtkvari River, where I stayed on my last visit, were only truly quiet between six and eight in the morning, a time when many other capital cities are thrusting into rush hour. For that short window, racing cars that looped around the city all night suddenly disappeared, along with the under-powered vehicles that, spewing out cheap diesel, would scream with the effort of climbing up the steep backstreet right below my window. Silent then, too, were the barking dogs, the screeching cats, the random sleep-disturbing bellowers. As a resolutely early riser, I would loll in bed to the sound of noth-ingness, picturing mugs of rousing hot black coffee, tortured by the fact that few cafés open before ten o'clock.

Even though it was unseasonably hot – a fierce heatwave in spring – there were no joggers pacing in the cool dawn or strollers out with buggies. Few attempts were made to beat the heat by rising early. When the city did collectively drag itself up, the uncaring sun would already be pounding down, flattening the panting street dogs (or 'community dogs', as they are known) onto their bellies or bullying them into shady doorways. Heat compelled some men to roll their T-shirts right up to their nipples, while many older women wore sun-soaking black: funereal lace shawls, black half-calf nylon socks and black chiffon blouses. With my eyes screwed up against the sun, it was a relief to descend into the underpasses that cross beneath the city's main thoroughfare, Shota Rustaveli, named after the mediaeval Georgian poet who wrote *The Knight in the Panther's Skin*.

In these heavily graffitied subterranean tunnels, Tbilisians trade and eat. Tiny shops display touristy trinkets, religious icons, newspapers, puzzle books, cha-cha (a fiery spirit made from fermented grape skins), fancy socks and strings of chewy, nutty churchkhela sweets. Khachapuri (Georgian cheese bread) is sold, flavouring the stuffy subterranean air with the smell of dough and hot cheese, all mixed in with top notes of cigarette smoke and heady aftershave. And that is the scent of Tbilisi. If you exit in front of the Kashveti St George Church, where booksellers hawk old vintage hardback books and art catalogues ('But why wouldn't you buy this book on Pirosmani? He was simply our best painter!') you will see people crossing themselves three times in front of displays of rosary beads.

Eating and drinking well is partly what Georgia is, because food, nurtured by a sympathetic climate, is superior and plentiful. Dinners, far happier than breakfasts, go on and on, fuelled by amber wines, and it is not unusual for a summertime supra, or feast, to last far longer than the working day. As Rustaveli once so sagely wrote, 'Spending on feasting and wine is better than hoarding our substance.'[9]

On major streets, and along the skinniest of lanes, women wearing baseball caps and flowery vests sell onions, flavoured salts, berries and whole wheels of goat's and sheep's cheese, their rounds artistically branded by the tightly woven baskets in which they were set. And bundles upon bundles of fresh ferny herbs in shades of pine green, pickle green and pistachio green — a whole colour chart of green. Dill, tarragon, parsley and coriander, in contrast to raisin-coloured purple basil.

In restaurants, what comes to the table? First, wine and bread – in the shape of a slender Venetian gondola that has been baked in a round clay oven called a tone. The bread is crusty, but soft within, charred a bit on the bottom. Then, a dozen or more fragrant things. Rabbit soup made with walnut, pepper and garlic. Oyster mushroom and coriander soup. Beetroot quarters in sunflower oil and dill. Catfish in vinegar and coriander sauce. Bean stew and pickled vegetables. Chicken roulade in walnut sauce. Lobiani, which is a flatbread – possibly the finest of all flatbreads – filled with mashed kidney beans. Gebjalia, fresh cheese rolled in mint. Flowering coriander in hazelnut pesto and spicy green adjika. A whole stubby cucumber (peeled). Fermented forest jonjoli – samphire-like, tasting of capers and with bell-shaped flowers, harvested in spring – dressed with Kakhetian sunflower oil. Fried sulguni cheese, salty and chewy. Pink-hued Georgian trout. Tarragon panna cotta topped with blue cornflower. Matsoni, impossibly good homemade yoghurt, tart and cool, served with an inky and elegant black walnut preserve.

And heaps of herbs. Always herbs. Herbs are flavour, herbs are a whole salad bar; herbs are medicine, a salve. Invasive, weedy and rampant, like mint and goutweed, they are also pagan charms to attract friendship or fortune. Free-growing and bountiful, they have been survival food during the darkest periods of war, and verdant ornaments during the happiest days. And they are blessed by priests for the feast of the Assumption. The very best, though, the very finest, will go into the hands of Georgia's capable cooks.

Partner to herbs are tomatoes. In Georgia, as in Armenia, southern Ukraine and Bulgaria, they are often so fat and juice-filled that their skin simply ruptures under the sun. Capsules of flavour to be sucked on like strawberries. Carla Grissmann's village friends, across the border in Turkey, longed for such

gifts of warmer weather in Uzak Köy. 'Wait until the tomatoes come, they are red red red ... and the cucumbers and the
grapes and everything and everything ... We eat and we eat
and everything is good...'[10] she recounted one of the villagers
saying. The common language of food. Today, Turkey has sixty
different hybrid varieties of tomato, and many millions of tonnes
of them are grown annually. And not just commercially but in
any old pots or tins on windowsills and balconies. It is impossible to imagine a meal without tomatoes in the South Caucasus
and Turkey – and it is equally impossible, here in windy, cool
Edinburgh, to imagine growing them so casually, so freely.
A thought, I admit, which makes me deeply envious.

~

In Georgia, I had one weekend to go walking. Desperate to
escape the city heat, yet unsure which road to take, I persuaded
a friend, a committed hiker, to go with me. She suggested
driving up the Georgian Military Highway and, from there,
tramping about in the lower reaches of Mount Kazbek. Known
in Georgia as Mkinvartsveri, this extinct volcano is a place of
many folktales and legends, the most famous being that Zeus
chained Prometheus to its peak for stealing fire from the gods
and sharing it with mortals, and then sent a bird to eat his liver,
or an eagle to tear out his heart, depending on the rendition. Well
traversed today, historically Georgians considered climbing the
mountain taboo.

Leaving Tbilisi's murderous heatwave behind, we joined
hundreds of lorries heading towards the Russian border via
the winding highway, passing road signs showing distances to
the Russian city of Vladikavkaz in the North Caucasus and the
Turkish capital, Ankara. Mountains are natural barriers to trade
and transport, which makes this road as epic, in the truest sense,
as its name suggests. Once little more than a bridle track, it took

hundreds of soldiers to build it into a road fit for carriages in the eighteenth century. We noticed that the endless stream of trucks, mainly carrying fresh food from Armenia and Georgia into Russia, also showed the number plates and flags of Uzbekistan, Tajikistan and Kazakhstan. On seeing these clues, I wondered which countries continued to trade with Russia during Putin's catastrophic war against Ukraine, despite sanctions. Stalled in giant queues, some truckers were busy setting up for breakfast as we passed them. Generally, this did not mean a sandwich at the roadside. Large, well-practised picnics were laid out onto fold-down tables. Tea was freely poured from shiny kettles as meat, vegetables, bread and fruit were unwrapped from foil. Occasionally, in the distance, a lone horseman could be seen galloping across the land.

We drove on, stopping at a tiny bakery, signposted but hidden down a tight alleyway, to buy warm bread the size and shape of a skateboard. The road was perilous, with aggressive overtaking on blind bends, and just beyond Dusheti, known for its khinkali dumplings shaped like money bags, we saw the result: a truck on its side with a shattered windscreen, its load of flour billowing in huge mushroom clouds as cars sped past.

~

Three hours later, arriving at the alpine village of Juta – at over 2,000 metres, one of the highest settlements not only in Georgia but Europe – we laced up our shoes. Laundry blew about on lines and the air was far fresher and cooler. Men chatted quietly, with hoes or shovels in hand, their chests bronzed from the sun. I thought again of Carla's book, and her similar impressions of rural Anatolia: 'The genius of the countryside is one of solitude and silence – of summer insects and swelling fruit, a dog barking, a distant voice calling, muffled by the lustrous heat, remote on the edge of sound.'[11]

Leaving Juta behind, we began going uphill. With the altitude slowing us slightly, we went past the last of the houses, marching towards the dizzying and cinematic Chaukhi massif, its soaring wings of granite bursting vertically out of the earth, reminiscent of the Italian Dolomites. At the sight of herbs growing wild, we bent down and found what we believed to be a cousin of mint.

The well-trodden trails led through wide, emerald-green valleys, where the sun had not quite melted all the highland snow, and we gingerly crossed narrow but thundering rivers. Soon, Tbilisi's heatwave was forgotten. In fact, everything worrying or tiring was stripped away. We paid attention to our feet and the grand vistas and, as we got closer to the craggy peaks, it was the 'now' that mattered most. The moment, the path, the day. Above the snowline we stopped to eat a trail mix of dried blueberries and hazelnuts, to drink the salty mineral water of the hills and to peel the clementines we had brought along.

Mountaineers will always climb, and hikers will forever seek out new routes, but it is a fantasy that these remote valleys can ever really be known by outsiders. Geography only gives up so much. Here, with some of the loftiest villages as isolated as tiny islands far out at sea, culture and history is embedded in the gorges and rocks, just as it is elsewhere in books and museums. Located far away from the primary seats of power, old ways still live on, stories are handed down, and there remains a resolute independence. And a degree of clandestineness.

When we were tired, we simply came back down. Dodging an invitation from some friendly but very drunk men, we checked into a guesthouse in Stepantsminda, with Mount Kazbek, tinged pink with sunset, sawing into the sky above the little town. My friend knew a good place to eat, a simple outdoor café. And so, with a Caucasian mountain dog for company (a gentle giant, and far less expectant than Darwin at dinnertime), we ordered dumplings – khinkali and pelmeni – and soup. The soup was revitalising and rehydrating, thickened by white lentils and tomatoes, and with ample dill and parsley mixed through. Along with the strong-ish local beer, its green and black label showing the peak we sat under, the hot soup proved something of a sedative and soon our eyes were heavy with sleep.

~

The herby soup I am preparing in Edinburgh, on this rainy day, has the subtle flavours of the one eaten below Mount Kazbek, but with added bulgur, and green rather than white lentils. Stirring it, I decide it would benefit from some croûtons for crunch, and so, dicing a slice of white bread, I heat up butter in a small pan and fry the cubes with some salt until they turn a warm golden colour. Preferences for soup toast may differ – rye, multigrain, wholemeal, plain white – but everybody loves crispy croûtons.

~

The following day we walked again. Hiking through Truso Gorge, we followed a track lined with Siberian irises, raising their purple petals to the sun, and Prophet's Flowers, a relative of borage that is native to the Caucasus, their blooms strikingly yellow with maroon polka dots. Bubbling, iron-rich waters stained the rocks bronze, a tell-tale sign of the dozens of mineral springs buried underground. Butterflies flitted, wings shining orange and pink, past flocks of sheep and their canine guards.

~

Back in Tbilisi, but still mountain dreaming, I sat out on the street at a wrought-iron table by my hotel, plucking the choicest fruits from a gnarly mulberry tree whose fat old roots had burst through the pavement, buckling it dangerously. The wall beside me was snow white with creeping jasmine and the heady scent, along with the berries, was enough to slow down passers-by. Every other person paused, reaching up to help themselves. The street was named after the twentieth-century Georgian painter Elene Akhvlediani, a woman who so artfully captured Tbilisi's 'architectural bohemia' in her work ('Paris is beautiful, but Tbilisi is a real miracle!'[12]). Lined with elegantly peeling houses, complemented by wide colonnaded verandas and lacy wooden canopies shaded by vines and wisterias, it made for a handsome place to rest. Toasting my rambling efforts later that night in a garden nearby, drinking an amber wine and eating warm bread dipped into oil and salty red adjika, I heard a man practising his opera arias above the din of traffic.

In Georgia, singing, like food and wine, is to be indulged in at will. *Life is to be enjoyed*, Tbilisi seemed to keep on saying. Why the rush?

~

Tasting the soup bubbling on the stove again and again as it cooks, I sprinkle in more sea salt and white pepper, stirring it and allowing more time for the tomatoes to fully soften and collapse. Soon, it smells heady and rich. You know when a soup is ready by the way it smells. Carla knew this, too: 'The chicken suddenly smelled as if it were cooked, the apricots began to puff up and the rice started to look soupy. I felt a deep sigh well up from my lungs and a great wave of calm descend, as if the next thirty minutes were all the time in the world. The soup was also beginning to boil, and I blew on the hot chicken and on my fingers as I tore off the tough shreds of meat and put them back with the carrots. A boy came in with a loaf of bread...'[13]

Carla Grissmann died in her eighties, at home, in West Kensington, in 2011. One of her last interviews appeared in a magazine I used to work for, called *Steppe – A Central Asian Panorama*. When the journalist Hermione Eyre arrived to conduct the interview, she was saddened to find Carla wheelchair bound. However, pity was promptly swept away: 'I was never-theless pleased to discover that this did not diminish her zest: at 6pm sharp, she celebrated "cocktail hour", raising her fists in the air.'[14]

On reading Carla's work, it becomes clear that she well under-stood that joy – or paradise, even – usually lives right by us, but is all too often ignored or left unseen. It is hiding in the good-meaning things that exist in the everyday: in the mint crushed between fingers, in the glint of an ice cube, in a basket of warm bread and in the cracking of a walnut. In the abundant fruit tree, the shady bench, the overheard song and the greeting of a dog. In the bowl of well-made soup, slowly cooked, ready to make life a touch more pleasing, survival a little easier.

Springtime Soup with Bulgur, Tomatoes and Herbs

Modest and heart-warming, this soup can afford to go in its own direction a bit, so if you don't have green lentils, brown ones will do, and a red onion, or even a couple of shallots, will substitute for white onion just fine as well. The green chilli and preserved lemon are optional and, while they do broaden the taste, no one will complain if you leave them out. Do make the croûtons, if you can – they really are worth the little extra effort they demand.

*A note on bulgur: medium bulgur is ideal for soups such as this one; the coarse variety tends to be best for pilavs, and the fine is optimal for köfte.

SERVES 4

100g medium bulgur

2 tablespoons olive oil

1 large onion, finely chopped

2 cloves garlic, finely chopped

½ teaspoon fine sea salt

½ teaspoon white pepper

2 tablespoons tomato puree

700ml chicken or vege-
table stock

100g green lentils

10 baby plum tomatoes,
halved (or half a 400g tin of
chopped tomatoes)

1 teaspoon red wine vinegar

¼ teaspoon turmeric

¼ teaspoon sweet paprika

generous handful of soft
herbs (parsley and basil are
best, but dill and tarragon
work too)

quarter of a preserved
lemon, deseeded and finely
chopped, or grated zest
of half an unwaxed lemon
(optional)

1 pickled green chilli,
chopped and seeds removed
(optional)

FOR THE CROÛTONS (ENTIRELY
OPTIONAL)

2 slices of bread, cut
into cubes

1 tablespoon butter, or a glug
of olive oil

sea salt flakes

Put the bulgur into a saucepan and pour in enough boiling water to cover, then place a tea towel over the pan, clamp on a lid and leave to steam for at least 15 minutes. Try a couple of grains to check if it is cooked – it should still have some texture.

Heat the oil in a large casserole or saucepan over a medium heat and sauté the onion until soft and golden, then add the garlic and stir until its pungency has died down a bit. Stir through the salt and pepper and the tomato puree, followed by the stock and lentils. Bring to a boil, then simmer until the lentils are cooked but retain some bite, about 10–15 minutes, depending on the size of the lentils. Add the tomatoes and cook just to soften slightly.

Stir through the vinegar, spices and herbs, along with the preserved lemon or zest and green chilli (if using), then check the seasoning and let the soup bubble for 5 minutes more.

Meanwhile, make the croûtons if you fancy them. Heat the butter or oil in a small frying pan, add the bread cubes and a light sprinkling of salt flakes and fry until golden all over.

Remove the soup from the heat, adding a little hot water if you find it too thick, and stir through the bulgur. Ladle into bowls, scatter the croûtons over and serve at once.

CHAPTER FIVE

Baltic Symphonies

A discreet spring fever has descended upon the buttoned-up New Town. Coats have been dispatched, though not put away for good. Coming through open windows is the sound of musicians blowing into wind instruments – notes from flutes, clarinets, saxophones and sometimes even bagpipes are straining over the rooftops. Tentatively, couples are sitting out on tenement steps, mugs of tea and paperbacks in hands, sunbeams on cheeks. The hours of the day are a little longer, the atmosphere a little headier.

Blooming next to daffodils in parks are tulips in a wild rainbow assortment of colours, with fringed, curved and lily-like petals. On the trees are clouds of white, red and pink blossom, and in the woods, now newly neon green, banks of bluebells are bolstered by the right balance of sunshine and rain. A time of earthly gifts.

With sunshine pouring into the kitchen, the first true, luminous warmth since winter, I begin noticing details anew: a small shock of pleasure at the vibrancy of the blue dye woven through the Afghan rug; the bleeding colours of the purple, red and yellow ikat fabric, with its ram's horn motif, that covers the window seat.

Next to the pantry, wedged on a bookshelf among my mostturned-to cookbooks, the radio's gold dials are gently glinting, though pouring out of its grille speaker is depressingly dark news: the cost-of-living crisis and war crimes being committed by Russia against Ukraine. There is an acute contrast between the horrors being reported and the hopeful cookbooks that surround the radio, with hundreds of ideas between their pages for Turkish meze, Polish pierogi and Indian rice dishes. Positive, colourful, optimistic books. Treasured, because they have taught me how to cook over the years. In my study, a tiny room just off the kitchen – decorated with wallpaper of shingle, fishing boats and lighthouses – is the overspill, where hundreds more cookbooks and food-writing titles are piled into stacks. I turn the radio off, but the lingering worry of the news stays on.

~

Taking a loaf of dark rye bread, I begin mapping a course back to the Latvian capital, Rīga. I want to roughly re-create what I ate there one time, specifically a singular pudding that I thought about for days afterwards. I had eaten it at a restaurant in the Old Town called Milda, a rare place that manages the near impossible, by being both very good and unashamedly touristy. It is where you are first served the Latvian classic dish of 'grey peas'. The colour of marbled slate, they are combined with punchy things to ginger them up – that is, onion, salt and tiny cubes of heavily smoked bacon, all of which makes the bland-sounding peas decidedly moreish. A mackerel tartare with blueberries and beetroot might be next, followed by a version of sausage and mash – Latvian black pudding with sauerkraut, fried potatoes and sour cream. But the best thing arrives last. Bread soaked in dark beer, with dried fruit, spices (cinnamon heady and dominant) and honey, topped with a cloud of cream and a scattering of berries. In Latvia it is called rupjmaizes kārtojums. Served in a glass ramekin, it was like trifle crossed with a Christmas pudding, and once I had tasted it – so unlike any other bread pudding I had eaten before – I could not shake its rich fruity flavour from my mind.

92

When I first visited the Baltic's trio of countries, Estonia, Latvia and Lithuania, in the early spring of 2020, before the world shut down in response to the Coronavirus pandemic, James and I drove along the coastline. Starting in Rīga, we travelled north to Parnü (Estonia), then south to Jūrmala and Liepāja (both in Latvia), and on to Klaipėda (Lithuania), before heading northwards again back to Rīga.

Snow glittered on sand and driftwood lumber, and there was barely any visible life at sea. No rhythm of swimmers in the surf, few ships in the water. The air was sharp and clean and salty, and the waves were whipped with winter's final efforts. Immediately, I noticed how, on many sections of the coastline, there was hardly any beach infrastructure or furniture, just a handful of huts, benches and changing screens. This suggested that, come summertime, when the sun beats down and the crowds roll out their towels, there would not be much clutter spoiling the view. Most restaurants, bars and cafés, the worst generators of commotion and rubbish, were set back from the seafront, encouraging cleanliness and quiet.

The pale coast is starkly dramatic, and that is enough. Yet, unlike the Balts and Slavs who arrive in their thousands to enjoy this seaside every summer, other Europeans have been slower to catch on, faithful instead to the more familiar Mediterranean, with its palms, wine and warm air.

Wilder and greener than those sun-bleached southern shores, nature felt close along this stretch of the Baltic Sea. Sand dunes met inland lakes, which met marshes and pine forests. Everything, everywhere, was teetering on the edge of spring; closing the door to a dark, reclusive winter, and with the luminosity of an almost-still-light-at-midnight summer still ahead.

~

In the kitchen, as I slice and then crumble the rye bread, I begin to wonder why: why, when travel is generally so accessible today, do we still revere some cuisines and destinations but not others?

The flavours and food of the Baltics, generally reasonably priced and rich with variety and imagination, can often rival Nordic cuisine (which influences it), yet it is not held in the same esteem. I can still taste the sea buckthorn cheesecake I ate in Klaipėda – the whole berries set in jelly on top, their sharpness slicing through the full-fat cream cheese – and the snow-white fillets of pike perch, caught in Pärnu Bay, baked with butter and capers. The exceptional farmstead dairy produce – in particular, herby butters packed with the power of meadow grasses and flowers. Smoked sprats, cloudberry jam, and bread as nut-brown as the soil. And I think of the birch forests we drove past and how, at this time of year, Latvians would be out tapping the thin white trees to bottle the nutrients stored in their roots that each spring filter up through their trunks, carried by the rising sap, like magic.

Nowadays in Baltic cities, chefs are only slightly swayed by global fads and are busy, instead, overturning outdated ideas about what their regional food is, while honouring what local people have been good at for centuries – that is, carefully kept traditions of pickling, fishing, fermenting, mushroom foraging and berry picking. The old Soviet greyness and its scarcities, which once inflicted kitchens, have been long shaken off. And while dining out is not an obsession, as it is in some bigger cities, there are plenty of excellent places to eat just like Milda, where the food authoritatively speaks of the land and the sea.

~

Pouring dark beer over raisins and sultanas to soak them for the pudding, I begin pulling up memories of a more recent trip to Rīga, remembering how James and I had gone cycling out of the city, along railway tracks, past apple trees and oaks, and onwards to the spa resort town of Jūrmala, with its wooden mansions — all towers, coloured-glass verandas and decorative trusses. Marvelling at how easy it was to swap the cobbles of Rīga for the beach, as pine-infused, head-clearing sea air filled our lungs and we pedalled over wet glittery-grey sand, right up to the waves.

On the journey out to Rīga, food had filled my thoughts long before we arrived, at just past midnight, on a cheap flight from Edinburgh. I kept picturing Rīga's cafés, its cake shops, beer halls and bistros. Such longing was evidence, to me at least, that we were coming back to a city that knows how to feed people, and with strong, memorable flavours: sprats, smoked cheese, pickled garlic, horseradish, sauerkraut and dark, heady herbal liqueurs tasting of birch, ginger and liquorice. But there is, of course, far more to the Latvian capital than its stomach.

~

When I first saw him, through a half-open door, I gasped a small gasp. Then, self-consciously whispering *There he is!* to myself, I stepped slowly across the threshold and into the room, my eyes locked onto his thumping form. So smooth, so round. Quietly majestic. Solid, though not big in stature, Cūka, or 'Pig', is sculpted from speckled granite and, with a heavy brow and ears that hang down in perfect triangles to his upturned snout, he stands quite alone, on a plinth elevated above smart parquet flooring inside the Latvian National Museum of Art. Effortlessly dominating his surroundings, he unintentionally begs his beholders — and there are many, for he is the museum's star attraction — to break the rules and stroke his back, round as an archer's bow. The gallery acquired Teodors Zaļkalns' porcine sculpture back in 1937 and, in a way, 'Pig' tells the story of

Rīga's interwar years and the development of one of the greatest food markets in the world.

Rīga Central Market is in the Maskavas ('Moscow') district of the city, literally on the road to the Russian capital, which suggests it is located far away – except it isn't, at all. The market hall is merely twenty minutes by foot from the stately rooms of the art museum, and its hangars are so enormous that slices present themselves to you, like calling cards, from various cobbled corners of the Old Town. You really cannot miss it. Anticipating pleasure, what I was hoping to find inside the market was a field guide to the Baltic's natural larder. I pictured richly stocked lanes of gilded-looking fish, clumps of neon berries, slick pickles and the sorcery of burping ferments fuelled by healthy bacteria. Things born of nature feeding off the dead; mulch and soil, yeast and bacteria, giving new life. And the market itself? Would it be quiet or dynamic? Seedy or tidy? A place of piety or plenty? Who would buy what, and when?

Outside the looming market halls, the sky was hard and grey, and the chill air quickly puckered any exposed flesh. Scarce glints of colour came only from the neon signs on the front of buses advertising their destinations: Tallinn and Parnü in Estonia, and smaller towns elsewhere in Latvia.

Zaļkalns, the sculptor, had early plans to erect a giant version of 'Pig' at the market, some say as a symbol of Latvian bacon, but the funds were not there, so instead we have the smaller prototype version, just 80cm long from tail to snout, in its palatial gallery setting. Food is art, food as art. *How good*, I thought, *would it be today to be greeted by a giant granite pig at the market? And what would his message be to us? Watch your consumption? Beware capitalism? Remember me and mind your waistline?* I felt for Zaļkalns when I later learned that not only had his giant market installation been cast aside, but he had lost out in his submission to design Rīga's Freedom Monument, too.

But pig or no pig, the monumental market is utterly striking in its gigantic uniformity. The Zeppelin aircraft hangars that the market lives in were originally built by the German Army out at the Vainode Air Base, during the First World War. Later, between the wars, planners in Rīga, in need of a large market for a rapidly developing city (the one by the nearby Daugava River having become too small and unsanitary), saw these ginormous constructions as pieces of modern engineering waiting to be repurposed. In the winter of 1922, Rīga's City Council decided to go ahead, with works continuing for eight years. Once dismantled, various sections were reused to cover the market, and pavilion buildings were constructed, using six million bricks and 2,500 tonnes of iron.[1]

Today, Zeppelin airships – large, yellow and cartoonishly innocent-looking, not unlike giant skyward-facing melons – are the symbol of the market, and there are a few painted onto interior panels to give the impression of them floating above the halls. Something with the capacity to destroy entire towns now represents somewhere that nourishes and feeds people.

As I walked into the first of five giant hangars, pages of my notebook, already spattered with wine-glass rings and berry-juice stains, began to fill up with words capable of provoking strong feelings of love and hate: fried eel, Baltic shrimp, black bread, lingonberry jam, Baltic herring, birch syrup, fermented kvass, wild cherry leaves, crayfish, fruit wines, hemp butter, blueberry soup, flavoured salts from Georgia, pigs' snouts and ears.

And I immediately spotted something I had not noticed at monster-sized markets elsewhere: handwritten name placards for the pickle vendors – proof of the deeply personal within a huge, collective and public space. This made it easy to start up a conversation with Mariya Karavacka, who plunged happily into her subject. Born in Yekaterinburg, Siberia, and married to a

Rīgan, she explained, in Russian, that she had been in this spot for thirty-five years. Her neighbour, originally from Belarus, chimed in to add that she'd had her stall for only a little less time, thirty years. Mariya's display was completely tethered to her world, and to routines both past and present. She told me that her son now helps her to grow and pickle her cucumbers, tomatoes and carrots, and they work together as a duo: hunter-gatherers of their Latvian garden, just outside the city, and the dark forests beyond – where nature, forever providing, is constantly in a state of change through the clearly defined seasons of the Baltics.

'Here, try this,' Mariya said, handing me a midget bullet-shaped carrot.

Biting into it, the carrot was, initially, simply crunchy and sweet, but soon after came a hot-sour wham at the back of the throat. Looking down into the tub from where this fiery slug had come, I saw dozens of tiny livid-red chillies and black peppercorns bobbing in the brine.

Then, taking a hand out of her pinafore pocket, Mariya lifted up a whole head of pickled garlic, the bulb dripping and glistening with a waxy sheen. 'Would you like to try this? Many Germans buy pickled garlic from me and carry some home.'

I declined the offer with thanks, my tongue still slowly pulsating from the fieriness of the carrot, curious to know if she thought I was a Berliner.

On each of Mariya's pickle jars was a handwritten label showing the date it was sealed and advising the temperature it should be stored at. They are the absolute masters of the pickle world, I thought to myself, these women – just a few of the countless number of such sellers spread across eastern Europe, the Caucasus, Turkey, Central Asia and elsewhere in the world – dressed in smocks with pockets and standing sentry under spotlights that set aglow their handiwork. But each terroir, and each quirk of practice and method, makes every pickle unique. And just as the pickle sellers of Rīga Central Market have survived bullying regimes and true hardships over the decades, so too have their skills – which, born out of their heritage, are now wholly perfected.

What these pickle vendors, pillars of the market community, are offering you, for a modest price, little more than a few coins, is a piece of their world; their spirit of place, their history. What, really, could be finer than that? Or more generous?

Nearby, in the same hangar, stood a daunting number of counters all selling Rīga's famous sprats, in tins and jars, and other fish from the Baltic Sea: anchovies, rudd, bitterling, minnows, tench, ide, trout, eel, butterfish, pike, goby, shad, Baltic herring, garfish, pipefish, flounder, plaice, lumpfish. In repurposed tubs, scaly and strong-smelling dried fish sat upright and rigid, their silvery-brown heads poking up above the plastic, as though still sucking in air. Another stall showcased white honey brandy that had been fermented in copper pots and 'filtered through forest moss'. Dried herbs, not considered alternative medicine but rather a continuation of Latvia's long-held belief in natural remedies, were presented alongside bottles of sea buckthorn juice and whole heads of sunflowers. Wholesome and remedying; elixirs for a long and healthy life. Wild thyme to cure dandruff. Nettles as 'a rinse' to conceal grey hairs. Common wormwood to promote a healthy appetite. Yarrow to cure tired livers. Linden blossoms to ease nervousness. Camomile for mouthwash. Buds, leaves, barks, seeds. Unusual or common, I studied them all – all the tiny details, busy reflecting the Baltics, busy showing how interesting ordinary life is.

Taking a detour into the next pavilion, past cakes for festivities, and bread for every day, I sat at the Herrings and Dill café, ordering bite-sized snacks of baked eel, anchovies and sprats piled onto squares of neatly buttered bread. I thought of the

Latvian street photographer Gvido Kajons, and his affecting black-and-white photograph of fish drying on a washing line, among bed sheets and towels, outside a block of Soviet-era Latvian flats. Fish is *the* prized ingredient of Latvia. Business hotels offer Rīga sprats for breakfast, on rye bread with soft cottage cheese. If it is true that the table is the best reflection of a nation, then here, sprats are it: strong, salty, reliable, steady, healthful, affordable.

Opposite the café, Uzbek bakers at the Registan stall pulled fresh non bread, round and golden, out of a tandyr oven, an unexpected delight that I eyed with interest. Uzbek food is popular in Latvia: an edible link to the past, when Latvia and Uzbekistan — countries that could not be more culturally and climatically different — were part of the same 'union'.

I left the market just as the sun came out, making the usually grey Daugava River sparkle. The river, which once formed the backbone of Rīga's economy, would historically have been filled with Lithuanian, Russian and German cargo boats during the summer navigation season. Records from the twelfth century show that these vessels were bringing salt and herring from the west; from the east, flax, fur and hemp. Wine was often used as payment, and excavations have uncovered city-council wine warehouses dating back to the thirteenth century. In 1939, there was a spectacular discovery: a single-mast ship, made of oak and pine and designed for high seas, unearthed at the ancient site of Rīga's port.[2]

~

One of Rīga's greatest joys, Central Market aside, can be found on Jēkaba iela (street), right by the city's grand government offices known as the Saeima: it is V. Ķuze, a konditorei rare in its refinement, with the atmosphere of a Viennese café and the appearance of a stage set. Named after the chocolatier and businessman Vilhelms Ķuze, it is cosy, welcoming and peaceful — a bulwark against the trials of modern life. And it was there, on my first visit to Rīga, sitting by a window shaded with lace, sipping hot black coffee and eating a choux pastry no bigger than a wine cork, that I said to myself, *No other café in the world could be better for three o'clock tea time.*

Offering a flavour of the era before the Soviets and the Nazis occupied Rīga in the 1940s, it has vintage wooden cabinets and a polished black-and-white tiled floor. Flanking the back wall is a piano, forever awaiting its pianist, and in the centre of the ceiling, a giant Art Nouveau chandelier. Behind the counter, pinafored staff tie ribbons around boxes of chocolate truffles and arrange slices of rhubarb and honey cake. On the shelves are bottles of cognac and whisky for those who need to warm up, or have their jitters rubbed off.

There is no chilly air-conditioning or loud music, nor are there machines noisily crushing ice or whizzing smoothies. To plug in a laptop would feel wholly inappropriate. Usually, there is quiet jazz playing, or old French songs by Joe Dassin (his classic 1975 hit 'Et si tu n'existais pas' lives on in the taxis and cafés of the Baltics and the South Caucasus). On the polished walnut tables, sugar comes in a china pot, not a sachet, and it sits with its spoon on a lace doily. The customers are generally older, tending to sit in pairs, and they talk to one another, rather than into mobile phones. On the walls hang framed black-and-white photographs that tell the story of the old V. Ķuze factory – and of this well-liked businessman, whose motto 'Work like a horse and rejoice like a king!' could not save him from the Soviet cruelties that eventually came for him, as was the case with so many others in Latvia.[3]

Born in 1875, Ķuze was a teacher, a prudent businessman and the owner of a wildly successful confectionery business. He began in 1910 with a pastry shop and, up until the First World War, he employed sixty-five workers and had four outlets in

Rīga. Then, during the war, when many Latvian companies were evacuated to Russia, he opened a modest factory in Moscow in 1916. But the following year, after severe sugar shortages, came the Bolshevik ban on private businesses, and so his Moscow company was nationalised. Undefeated, Ķuze returned to Latvia in the early 1920s, restored his biscuit factory, resumed his sweets and caramels business, and bought more premises.

By the mid-1930s, his workshops were producing over 5,000 kilos of sweet treats a day, including over 500 varieties of waffles, biscuits, chocolates and candies, such as cat's tongue biscuits, chocolate brazil nuts, candied chestnuts, drunken cherries, coconut 'thistles' and other sweets with curious names like 'crayfish necks', 'green pike', 'harvest blessing' and 'bonza'. Containers were exported from Rīga to London, Paris, Stockholm, Cairo and Sydney, and the business was buoyed by the graphic artist Arturs Duburs, a visual thinker of great taste who was commissioned by Ķuze to design distinctive pictorial advertising and packaging, which soon became instantly recognisable. Conveyed in classic Art Deco style, the imagery appeared regularly in major newspapers and magazines, and was displayed at international exhibitions. By this time, Ķuze employed over 500 workers and was running a three-storey factory, served by a fleet of vans. But he was not just a master confectioner and businessman; he was also known for looking after his employees – the factory had a canteen, a choir, an amateur dramatics group and even a football team.

Then, after successfully navigating so many hurdles, tragedy. In 1940, during the Soviet occupation of Latvia, confectionery factories were nationalised and incorporated into the system of the USSR. Ķuze was kept on as a director, using his family's three-room apartment as his base – but, in the summer of 1941, having looked after his staff so well and toed the Soviet line as best he could, he was arrested and deported to Siberia with his family. And there, in the early autumn of that same year, he died in a Gulag in Solikamsk.[4]

Today in Rīga, if you walk to Tallinas iela, in the Grīziņkalns neighbourhood, and head down the quiet street of Artilērijas iela, you will come to number 55. And on the façade of this cream Bauhaus-esque building, you will notice a memorial plaque. This marks the place where Vilhelms Ķuze once lived – as it says in Latvian, underneath his unmistakable bespectacled face. And in the air, as an unintentional but fitting tribute to him, is the almost heavenly scent of sweet baking that washes over the surrounding streets from the nearby Staburadze factory (itself unmissable, with its purple mural of cupcakes).

On my last day in Rīga, I returned to V. Ķuze and its obliging charm, for refreshment of both body and spirit. On leaving, I found myself paying attention anew to the city, which is what a good café, one that has soul, is capable of. I reflected on the city through the seasons, imagining how it might look under snow, compared to the reawakenings of springtime, as the grey bare trees burst into blossom.

Part of what I find so pleasing about Rīga is its modest size and scale – very similar to Edinburgh – and its cacophony of wooden and Art Nouveau buildings, 800 or so of them. This combination makes the city a unique and harmonious place to walk around. Few high-rises mean that churches, rather than money-orientated skyscrapers, act as way-markers: there is the thirteenth-century Lutheran St Peter's Church, whose metal steeple, over 100 metres tall, acts as a beacon; and the huge neo-Byzantine-style, golden-domed Nativity of Christ Orthodox Cathedral, the city's major religious landmark. The Soviets occupied and rebranded it more than once, sawing down crucifixes and melting the bells, converting it into a planetarium called the Republic House of Knowledge, and an unruly café called the God's Ear.[5]

Inevitably, Russia's full-scale invasion of Ukraine has been felt deeply in the Baltics. The misery of Putin's soul-sickening war is impossible to ignore anywhere in Europe — but especially in countries such as Latvia, which knows all too well the consequences of Russia's diabolical threats. In Rīga, since the start of the war, Soviet signs and statues have been torn down and Ukrainian flags put up. Armies have been stridently preparing. When I visited again recently, high-ranking military from Britain and the US were staying in my hotel, media and dozens of soldiers in tow, if any more of a reminder were needed.

~

In the kitchen, I continue with my task of trying to mimic Milda's dainty bread pudding — one so deserving of an encore, even if it is born of my own efforts. It will be my memento, my souvenir from Rīga, based on a list of ingredients I scribbled down as the waiter told me how the chef had prepared it.

As I start to layer the pudding, I notice that the kitchen is gently reverberating. Darwin, underneath the table, one ear hanging over a footrest, is warm and fast asleep. He dozed off earlier, no doubt feeling victorious after snaffling a stray blueberry that rolled towards him. Now, with his wonderfully strong canine snoring, he is demonstrating that sense of satisfaction to the world.

Toasting the almonds, and then freshening the top of each serving with extra cream and berries, I am grateful to know of this pudding, for it is simple and good. And as its smell, so richly reminiscent of Rīga, rises in the kitchen, links between there and here become less severed. Memories become less fragmented and more whole, and the sounds of the city even become audible: cars on cobbled lanes, clattering bistros, trolleybuses zapping past misty parks; couples chattering in Latvian, English and Russian as the curtain rises at the opera. As I make and eat this pudding, I find myself once again part of the city.

Dark Beer and Rye Bread Pudding

Rupjmaizes kārtojums, as I tasted it in Rīga, was a surprisingly light pudding with a texture not unlike overnight oats. Sharp, sweet and moreish, it gave me the idea for this pudding – which is a little, if not a lot, like the real thing. The scent of cinnamon and cloves gives it a Christmassy feel, and therefore it could work well served at the festive table. You will need individual glass ramekins or small dishes to serve the pudding in; the quantities here can be easily multiplied if you're making it for more than two.

SERVES 2

110g mixed dried fruit, such as cranberries, sultanas, prunes
½ small cinnamon stick
1 clove
150ml dark beer, porter or stout (or enough to soak the dried fruit)
60g rye bread

1 teaspoon brown sugar
a handful of any fresh berries (I like blueberries and raspberries)
140g extra-thick cream
15g flaked almonds (optional)
2 tablespoons mixed seeds (optional)

Start by making the compôte. Put the dried fruit, cinnamon stick and clove into a bowl and cover with the beer. Leave to soak for a couple of hours until the fruit is plump. Fish out the cinnamon stick and clove, then drain and set aside.

Crumble the rye bread, tip it into a frying pan and dry fry with the brown sugar, stirring the whole time, just for a few minutes until the bread is lightly toasted. Leave to cool.

Reserve some berries and cream to use for decoration later, then assemble the pudding, working in layers. In the base of each ramekin, start with a layer of the bread, then spoon in some of the soaked fruit and some fresh berries, followed by a layer of cream. Repeat until you run out.

Toast the almonds and seeds (if using) briefly in a hot, dry frying pan, then decorate the puddings with the reserved berries, a final layer of cream and the nuts and seeds.

For best results, leave to chill in the fridge overnight before serving.

CHAPTER SIX

Journey Food

My blood always quickens inside the pantry, in this narrow store room that forms the heart of the kitchen. It is a shop that never closes; a place of ingredients, all carefully unpacked and arranged, that have travelled from far away to here. Silent powerful things, things that are patient but ever ready, all restlessly suggesting what they will become once exposed to a little heat, water or oil. Pink onions to be pickled in cider vinegar, white flour that will be transformed into bread, red lentils that will become dal.

Unlike the pantries featured in interior design magazines, mine has no bespoke timber or marble finishes. It is, instead, a simple walk-in cupboard with pockmarked walls. And on its six shelves, painted white, the cycle of life is evident: eggs, nuts, seeds, spines, bones. A collage of primeval things born of nature, speaking of the land: oats, bark, leaves; and the sea: dulse, anchovies, mackerel. Things, now in tins and jars, that have absorbed the power of soil, oxygen, water and sun. And pickled things, suspended in time: mushrooms and cucumbers, noble-looking white asparagus spears erect in brine. Herbal and floral vinegars, sweet and fruity. Soot-black Persian dried limes, snow-white coconut milk, Sichuan peppercorns, Scottish heather honey, Japanese bonito stock, Turkish lokum, dried Polish mushrooms. A flavour atlas of the world. And in tightly sealed containers, different flours – plain, wholemeal, gram, buckwheat – safe from mites and weevils, creatures that have been known to crawl into the pantry, through cracks in the old walls, on many tiny legs.

Above the shelves is a framed watercolour of two peach-coloured crabs, a wedding gift, and hanging below, on a series of hooks, are little wooden-framed portraits of Indian saints and gurus that I bargained for in New Delhi, wrapping them carefully before stowing them in my backpack. Squatting on the linoleum floor are two willow baskets, filled with root vegetables – potatoes, swedes, onions and carrots – each muddy specimen so intensely nourishing, life-giving and miraculous, yet considered so ubiquitous and 'everyday' that they are rarely admired.

As a storage space, the pantry is practical, but there is nothing ordinary about how it makes me feel: comforted, yet animated. Yearning might come from the last spoonful of mulberry jam, a preserve that conjures up the sticky summertime pavements of Turkey, Uzbekistan and Georgia, so often splattered with the dark juice of the berries. Black sesame seeds suggest glazed flatbreads – made well enough at home, though never tasting as good as those pulled out of a clay tandyr oven in Central Asia. Nostalgia stings from the nuts collected on the forest floor of the largest walnut woods in the world, in Kyrgyzstan, and from the vacuum-packed pine nuts bought at a Siberian supermarket. The forest is under threat from climate change, and Siberia has changed now, too, not least because of Putin's dire decisions.

Accordingly, in this kitchen alcove, my hands treat everything with the sort of care, love and respect that a librarian affords rare books. When I am home, I am in there daily, dusting and readjusting, shuffling and sorting. Labels are soaked from glass jars, and new ones are penned and stuck on as the stock is rotated and replenished: ground ginger makes room for cloves, whole nutmegs replace dill seeds. Pots upon pots, stacked on top of each other, as if in an apothecary.

~

At the kitchen counter, I am making vegetarian pasties, ready to take hill walking. Trickling olive oil into a frying pan, and sliding in chopped shallots, finely sliced garlic and a few slivers of preserved lemon, I sprinkle over sea salt and stir until the shallots start to soften and the garlic tempers. Next, into the pan go three handfuls of spry herbs and greens, then more salt and pepper. I put a lid on to let it all unhurriedly wilt down. The pastry dough, enriched with yoghurt and olive oil, and with warming cumin rubbed through it, is in a ball in the fridge, waiting to firm up before it is rolled out.

To the right of me I notice a shadow. It is Darwin. He wants a tinned sardine, and he is blocking the pantry door with his furry body. As soon as I open it, he'll jump up and dart in, quick as a hare. It is a game we play. As I cook, he is watching my eyebrows for signs of expression, and my hands for clues of what I might do next.

Crumbling feta for the pasties into a bowl and adding ricotta, I stir the greens in the pan, encouraging them to further soften. Darwin eyes me more eagerly now, losing patience with his sit-down protest, searching for a twitch of recognition, the promise of me coming closer to the pantry door. On seeing none, he lets out a defeated sigh. Not yet, little dog, not yet.

As I work, through the kitchen window comes the dirge-like drawl and nasal hum of bagpipes, most likely coming from a wedding party at the nearby church. The music brings to mind a piper I have come to recognise, dressed in his kilt, long woollen socks and Glengarry-style hat, who is sometimes positioned by Waverley railway station, in front of the gothic Scott Monument. He is there in all weathers, emotion dictating the sound, the pace, the volume. Stirring like no other instrument, bagpipes are the sound of the Highlands here in Scotland, but also of other towering tablelands. I have heard them playing across the remote rolling brown hills of eastern Turkey – Black Sea Turks are keen pipers – the sound carrying a far distance on the wind.

Lately, when arriving into Waverley, pulling a suitcase behind me as Edinburgh's craggy castle pans grandly into view, I have become aware of my eyes welling up and my heart responding to the lone piper playing. Maybe *Highland Laddie* or *Row Me Home to Islay*. It has become the soundtrack of returning, of coming home to Edinburgh. And I feel at that moment, as is a musician's aim and a listener's want, that he is playing just for me.

~

In need of a rolling pin and some cumin seeds, I edge towards the pantry door, sliding Darwin, who is now feigning indifference, and his grass-stained paws, aside. Then, as I enter, quick as a flash, he is in too, immediately manoeuvring himself into his best and neatest canine sitting position, tucked under a shelf, eyes locked hard onto me. '*Oh, Darwin!*' I say, and he grunts from the back of his throat in reply. Peeling back the lid from a tin of sardines, I take a small fork from my apron pocket and begin poking at a plump fish. With the tines successfully dug into the reeking flesh, I pull the fish slowly out, and then lean towards him as he opens his soft mouth in anticipation, showing me his bottom row of tiny perfect teeth. Ever so carefully, he takes his win – without touching the fork, as he's been trained to do – and triumphantly retreats towards his bed, leaving me alone.

Wiping the pantry floor clean of Darwin's sardine drips, I am reminded of two items so seldom used that I immediately feel a hot stab of guilt at the sight of them.

One is a heavy steel pasta maker with an awkward-looking hand crank. It is dragged out once a year tops, when I will spend hours first pressing the dough, then hanging the long uneven strips on the back of dining chairs, only to erupt into a fit of swearing as they gradually tear and fall to the floor, before I promise myself never, ever, to make my own linguine again.

The second rarely used pantry item is a wicker picnic basket with woven handles. Taking up considerable room, and having gathered more cobwebs than outings, it silently shames me into thinking about all the wholesome things it could be stuffed with, if only I could be bothered: sausage rolls, small apples, cheese and chutney, roast chicken in foil, sloe gin, hot black coffee and cans of ale. Things that taste better eaten outside under sun and clouds, good for appetites made stronger by fresh air. This basket, certainly the most sentimental and overly optimistic thing in the pantry, is a means to take the kitchen, and its material items — enamel plates, forks, spoons and knives, miniature salt and pepper shakers, sturdy wine glasses with too-thick stems — out into the countryside. A park, a sandy bank, a glen, a shady valley, an outcrop of rock, anywhere that plays into the romanticised picnic myth. Nature itself is merely a stage set, and the weather is urged to play along, too — to be tame, predictable and placid, never wild or erratic. For picnic-goers, all must be harmonious and obliging, and altogether less threatening than the city escaped from. Suitable for niceties is light-hearted conversation on a thrown-down rug, a game of cards, the musicality of a portable radio turned low. Oh, sweet double-dealing nostalgia. Because it never is quite like that, is it? Instead, there is a row, or wasps, or rain.

Art is partly to blame for picnic fantasies. Especially popular in the nineteenth century, renowned picnic masterpieces include Claude Monet's *Luncheon on the Grass* (1866) and James Tissot's *Holyday* (c.1876), both twee imaginings of wealthy leisure-seekers lounging about on the grass, enjoying the moment, with shade or water for coolness. Then there is Francisco de Goya's earlier oil-painting *A Picnic* (painted between 1785 and 1790), which also shows an idyllic landscape, but one in which something has gone horribly awry. Empty bottles of wine are strewn about, and the party appears plastered and upset. One man has collapsed and is cradling his face in horror or shame. That is more like it. Far more believable. And so, for now, the basket stays put.

~

My 'picnics' are, instead, what I call 'journey food'. Taking a large Tupperware box that fits inside a small backpack, I fill it with no more than four or five things. What goes in? Apples, Fisherman's Friend lozenges, oatcakes, a wedge of cheese and pasties. Always pasties, the ones I am making now. Because few things travel better, so neatly packaged, as they are, in their own pastry shells, snug in the hand and therefore easy to eat on the move. They are taken along on hill-walking days, beach strolls, dog walks and car rides, and are carried to airports. And there is one particular recipe, by the food writer Rosie Birkett, that I am a devotee of. It is called 'Zero-Waste Allotment Veg Pasties',[1] and I have followed this recipe more than any other in my cooking life. I change them up a bit, as Rosie suggests her readers should do, forgiving as these pasties are. This time, along with a mass of spinach wilted down on top of pink-ish shallots, there are chickpeas.

Rolling out the cool pastry until it is no thicker than a pound coin, then cutting and shaping it into four large rounds, I spoon the filling into each circle and fold them over into half-moons, crimping the edges with a fork and brushing the top with egg-wash. Then, a generous sprinkling of salt flakes, nigella and cumin seeds. Putting them onto a baking tray, and back into the fridge, I will wait for them to 'set' a bit before sliding them into the warm oven. Less fiddly to eat than quiche, more capable of holding onto fillings than sandwiches, they are just as handy for eating on a bicycle saddle or train seat as on a patch of moorland. There is a reason why – despite so many alternative offerings – the railway station pasty shop still exists.

What a long way journey food has come. In *The Scots Kitchen*, by Florence Marian McNeill, first published in 1929, there is a suggestion for a 'hiker's special', which is oatmeal combined with salt and pepper, to be mixed with water from a stream 'until thin enough to drink' – a bit like a wild savoury oat cocktail or smoothie. 'This quenches thirst and, in the words of Robert Louis Stevenson, "provides a good enough dish for a hungry man, and where there are no means of making fire, or good reasons for not making one, it is the chief stand-by for those who have taken to the heather".'[2]

~

Further afield, what kit and rations travelling writers, and adventurers, chose to pack, and what foods they gathered overseas, is telling not only of the age in which they explored, but also of their standing and character, the climate and terrain. Bibles, penknives and champagne span continents and eras, but modern explorers have swapped Rolexes (Eric Newby's famously ended up in a bubbling vat of stew, as recounted in his classic 1958 book, *A Short Walk in the Hindu Kush*) for cheaper Casio watches, and meals are often dehydrated nowadays, rather than tinned. Menstrual cups, rescue beacons, water purification devices and satellite trackers are today's other essentials.

A contender for most famous travel snack ever is the bar of Kendal Mint Cake that was carried by Edmund Hillary, which he shared with Sherpa mountaineer Tenzing Norgay as they climbed Mount Everest in 1953. Confectionery was rationed in Britain at the time, but the team secured plenty after a supportive shopkeeper and his staff pooled their own ration coupons.[3]

When Clärenore Stinnes, daughter of the German tycoon Hugo Stinnes, set off to circumnavigate the globe by car in May 1927, she left Frankfurt equipped with sand ladders (used for driving across desert-like terrain); Lord, her black Gordon Setter; and three Mauser pistols. With a top speed of 53 miles per hour, progress was sluggish, and the climate fluctuated wildly. In Baghdad it was 54°C; on Lake Baikal, in Siberia, it dropped as low as -53°C. As she travelled, Stinnes added three evening gowns, 128 hard-boiled eggs and a bottle of vodka to her cases. Having covered almost 30,000 miles, she arrived back in Germany twenty-five months after setting out.[4]

For British yachtsman Sir Robin Knox-Johnston, who in 1969 became the first man to sail solo and non-stop around the world aboard his boat *Suhaili*, there was the luxury of space and he used it well, loading up with 120 cans of lager, several bottles of whisky and jars of pickled onions. Strong ingredients for a spirited sea picnic.[5]

Author Lesley Blanch devotes an entire chapter to the art of picnics in her book *From Wilder Shores*. On a lonely hillside in Turkey she recalls a graveside gathering and how 'mourners enjoy the departed's favourite food ... in quiet communion with the lost and loved.' Lesley had many ideas about dining al fresco but principally she liked it to be as far away as possible from 'the uninspiring cold chicken and Thermos flasks which nestle so smugly in the well-equipped picnic-baskets of convention'. Her picnics, quite unlike the quaint and sappy outdoor parties of England's groves, were not always successful: once she warmed up a bottle of vintage claret by skipping 'across the moors mulling it in my bosom' only to discover that there was no cork-screw. But Lesley was a superior journeywoman, and a superior eater. 'Travelling widely and eating wildly' was her motto, and she was fond of impromptu roadside feasts. 'Generally local foods, eaten by the wayside are more interesting than anything served in hotels or restaurants en route. In lands still considered "under-developed" (in today's patronising phrase) – life is still geared for the nomad or passer-by. No need to take much of a picnic basket along the Golden Road to Samarkand.'[6]

Blanch's first culinary travelogue, *Round the World in Eighty Dishes*, was published in 1956, coming out two years after the end of Britain's post-war rationing. It was the era of Queen Elizabeth II's Coronation and the Suez Crisis. Lesley's exuberant travel to such faraway shores, rendered in verbal Technicolor, would have seemed impossible to most. Like two other female writer-cooks of roughly the same era, Patience Gray and M. F. K. Fisher, she had an instantly recognisable voice. She was also, mostly, funny and frank, caring less for accurate recipes. 'Timidity and prejudice should have no space in the kitchen,'[7] she wrote.

Whether in Mexico or Egypt, the Balkans or Yemen, mealtimes were the lifeblood – and often the goals – of her adventures: food was culture, then code, and, finally, trophy. The ultimate memento that she'd then re-create back home or en poste with her diplomat-novelist husband, Romain Gary. It is not hard to picture her, out on the great plains of Hungary, or on the outskirts of Samarkand, wielding gifted silverware that she had ingeniously identified as ideal for picnicking – that is 'christening-present sets of spoon, knife and fork designed to start the toddler off in style' – carried in leather cases. Prone to anthropomorphism, Lesley believed these bijou sets 'enjoyed such exotic outings after years of high-chair nursery ennui'.[8]

Competition for Lesley, in terms of travelling modishly, and with gastronomic aplomb, would come in the form of writer Sybille Bedford. Here she is describing which foods she chose to pack on a train journey with a friend, from New York on their way to Mexico, in *A Visit to Don Otavio*: 'Whenever I can I bring my own provisions; it keeps one independent and agreeably

employed, it is cheaper and usually much better. I had got us
some tins of tunny fish, a jar of smoked roe, a hunk of salami
... watercress, a flute of bread ... a bag of cherries and a bottle
of pink wine ... I drew the cork with my French Zigzag. The
neatest sound on earth.' Even a peppermill was packed, loaded
with 'truffle-black grains of Tellicherry'. Why Mexico? It was
1946 and the Second World War was over. 'I had a great longing
to move, to hear a new language, to eat a new food...'⁹

~

Other travellers are remembered more for the food they sent forth
from other countries. In the winter of 1915, the moustachioed
British-Hungarian archeologist Marc Aurel Stein – famous for his
controversial 'discovery' of hidden Buddhist paintings at the Caves
of the Thousand Buddhas at Dunhuang, China – opened several
Tang-dynasty-era tombs at the Astana cemetery, in the Silk Road
city of Turfan, with the help of a professional grave plunderer.¹⁰

Inside, they found pottery, frail silk, damask, gold coins, sheep
bones, grape stalks, a lacquered tray and silk shoes, all described
in Stein's book *Innermost Asia: Detailed Report of Explorations in
Central Asia*, But perhaps most intriguing is what they found in
an otherwise empty eighth-century tomb:

> No remains of any sort were found in it, except a large
> number of remarkably well preserved pieces of fancy pastry
> scattered over the platform which was meant to accommo-
> date the coffin with the dead. The remains of fine pastry
> recovered here are as remarkable for their variety of shapes
> as for their excellent conservation ... there are represented
> among them flower-shaped tartlets of different kinds with
> neatly made petal borders, some retaining traces of jam
> or some similar substance placed in the centre; bow-knots
> and other 'twists'; buns, divided cross-wise; cracknels' and

straws. More elaborate productions of the confectioner's art are the thin ornamented 'wafers' and the ogee-shaped open-work cakes with finely ribbed sprays of foliage. Some black grapes also were found here, shrivelled but otherwise in good condition.[11]

The pastries had been preserved by the dry and hot climate, and Stein later sent them to the British Museum, where they were catalogued, with photographs (it is worth viewing them online,[12] as they are rarely displayed), forming part of what he described as his 'haul' of artefacts. Such plundering is, of course, scandalous but these cookies are surely the ultimate journey food, travelling in a myriad of ways, starting with the afterlife and then crossing entire continents.

~

Closer to home, the first food columnist of *The Times*, Lady Agnes Jekyll, was, as her 1937 obituary in the same newspaper points out, a 'mistress of all domestic lore'.[13] But she was also a keen mountain walker and swimmer, and had all sorts of ideas on portable provisions, as she discusses in her excellent book *Kitchen Essays*, published in 1922: 'The birds have not a monopoly of migration in our restless age ... Travellers in these times are reverting to the old-fashioned habit of taking their journey food with them,' she begins, before noting that, 'Most cooks lack both the imagination and experience necessary for such journey requirements, and have thereby brought the home-packed hamper into disrepute...' While I would not subscribe to daintily packing my lunch 'in greaseproof paper with an outer wrapper of foolscap tied with fine twine', as she recommends, her suggestion of sandwiches layered with the 'thinnest gruyère' and bread spread with inventively infused butters, such as anchovies or olives, would impress anyone today, as would her Chelsea bun for 'the cold dawn', to be enjoyed with a Thermos of coffee. She neatly, and confidently, concludes that a traveller equipped with her suggested basket would find themselves independent of bother on their journeys, 'fortified against hunger and thirst' and 'immune to the extortions and insolence of officials'.[14] Though I cannot imagine there were many bureaucrats brave enough to swindle, or interrupt, Lady Jekyll.

~

Back in the pantry, surrounded by half-packets of lentils, buckwheat groats and orzo, I take down from the shelf a small fabric bag containing one of the world's earliest and very best journey foods: Turkish tarhana, the precursor of all packet soups. It is made from wheat flour and yoghurt that has been rubbed with herbs, spices and tomato paste (sometimes even dried cherries) and then spread out in the sun to dry naturally. Crumbled, crushed and sieved, it is left to dry again until absolutely all the moisture has dissipated. Tarhana can be stored more or less for ever, ready to be rehydrated and cooked at will, making it a highly portable convenience food. Traditionally made by seasonally nomadic herdsmen, today it is still used by shepherds who are away for weeks, or even months, in far-flung pastures.

Friends in the Turkish city of Safranbolu, Gül and Ibrahim Canbulat, once waved me off along the Black Sea coast with a kilo of tarhana. The tightly stuffed but thoroughly breathable cotton packet, the one I still have on a shelf, had scented my luggage with deep savoury notes for many weeks. 'You can forget it at the back of the cupboard for many years,' Ibrahim had advised, knowingly. And while pasties are unbeatable for the hillside, a bowl of warming and revitalising soup made with rehydrated tarhana is just the quick and easy thing to devour upon returning home.

Hillside Pasties

As mentioned already, Rosie Birkett's pasties, from her book *The Joyful Home Cook*, are my favourite 'journey food' by a country mile. I must have made them a hundred times and, while I cannot improve on them, nor do I want to change them a great deal, sometimes I like to add a few chickpeas and a bit more of a heat kick, courtesy of Kashmiri chilli powder. If kept chilled, they will be fine for a few days, though they are best eaten at room temperature.

MAKES 4

FOR THE PASTRY
200g plain flour
100g full-fat natural yoghurt
Scant 1 teaspoon fine sea salt
½ teaspoon ground cumin
20ml olive oil
1–3 tablespoons iced water

1 beaten egg, for glazing
1 tablespoon cumin seeds
1 tablespoon nigella seeds
sea salt flakes

FOR THE FILLING
1 tablespoon olive oil, plus extra for drizzling
1 large red onion (or 3 shallots), thinly sliced
1 garlic clove, crushed

a few slivers of preserved lemon (or grated zest of half an unwaxed lemon)
¼ teaspoon Kashmiri chilli powder
150g mixed greens (chard, spinach, watercress, kale) and soft herbs (lovage, parsley, dill, basil, tarragon), roughly chopped
100g tinned chickpeas (about half a 400g tin), drained
1 tablespoon lemon juice
75g ricotta
100g feta
Fine sea salt and freshly ground black pepper

Start with the pastry. Put the flour, yoghurt, salt and cumin in the bowl of a food processor and whizz until the mixture resembles breadcrumbs. Gradually add the olive oil and just enough of the iced water to bring everything together into a ball of dough. Wrap the dough in greaseproof paper and leave in the fridge to firm up for about 30 minutes.

For the filling, heat the olive oil in a non-stick frying pan over a medium heat and cook the onion, with a pinch of salt, until soft and glossy. Turn the heat down to low and add the garlic, preserved lemon (or zest) and chilli powder. Stir for a couple of minutes, then add the greens, herbs and chickpeas. Season with salt and pepper and add the lemon juice, then put a lid on the pan, or cover with foil, and let the greens and herbs wilt down for about 5 minutes. Remove from the heat and allow to cool.

Tip the contents of the frying pan into a large bowl. Stir in the ricotta and crumble in the feta, then combine it all well, adding extra salt and pepper to taste.

Line a baking sheet with baking parchment. Divide the chilled pastry into four equal balls, then, on a lightly floured surface, roll each one out into a 20cm disc. Heap a quarter of the cooled filling on one half of the pastry, leaving a 3cm border around the edge, then drizzle a little olive oil over the filling. Using your finger, wet the edges of the pastry with a dab of water, then fold the other half over and press to enclose the filling. Crimp the edges of the pasty with the tines of a fork and place on the baking sheet. Repeat with the remaining pastry and filling, then place the tray of pasties in the fridge to chill for about 10 minutes, or until firm.

Pre-heat the oven to 200°C/180°C fan/gas 6.

Brush the pasties with the beaten egg and scatter over a few cumin seeds, nigella seeds and sea salt flakes, then bake for about 30–35 minutes until golden and crisp.

SUMMER

CHAPTER SEVEN

Carried Away by a Cloudberry

On a wild patch of Scotland, somewhere above Glen Almond in the Highlands, I pushed upwards. Over blasted heath and spiky heather until, finally, several leg-straining miles later, a steady tempo settled in. Physical effort was being repaid with the rhythm of every stride, the trail made good by well-trusted leather boots, supple as second skin.

Walking commanded all five senses, until the stresses of life fell away completely. Step by step, moving away from problems and into nature, with its cloud-wrapped hills and stony knolls. Relief from the world. Harmony of mind. The rugged generosity of untamed scenery, appealing to the imagination and giving way to daydreams and gentle thoughts, momentary innocence, even. There were no anxiety-ridden ruminations, no troublesome commentaries. Weather and climate conditions were the only consideration. Changes in atmospheric pressure were duly noted, and thoughts occasionally were given over to the whereabouts of waterproofs or sunscreen, what had been packed in the rucksack and what had likely been forgotten.

In the course of a day, you might have fair-weather clouds, with little to hinder the view, or you might footslog it through a thick blanket of grey nimbostratus that will dim the scenery. Perhaps there will be a thunderstorm. Maybe you will outrun the rain. In Scotland, weatherwise, anything is possible.

Like cooking, hillwalking is both an activity and a way of life, and like cooking, it is a way to enter other worlds.

On this particular outing, with James and Darwin up ahead, a fine shifting mist hid the River Almond below, then revealed it again, like a stage curtain being tugged back and forth. Unusually, only a light wind whistled along the glen. All was summertime quiet. The city we had left behind thronged with tourists and August's overwhelming traffic. It was satisfying to be away for a while, with Edinburgh's raucous festivities out of sight and out of mind. We tramped separately and silently, enjoying the peace.

For several hours we did not pass another rambler, but on the people-less tracts creatures were plentiful, alert in the tall grass and spongy moss, before disappearing down holes at the sound of approaching boots. Hares skittered – all tails, all ears – never too close, but near enough to be seen. Gambolling past coal-coloured peat hags – giant hollows, with drooping mouths – they leapt like lemmings over the tops, scuttling down sharp hillsides, until they were gone. Under a watery sun, we went along trackless paths, with the miles adding up and up, over hills in shades of mustard-green and purple-brown, muted and soft as Harris tweed.

Then, as I was slowing down, my appetite forcing thoughts of lunch, the weight of my backpack reminding me of its savoury contents (that is, pasties, oatcakes and cheese), a single daub of neon brightness – shiny as a button, but almost certainly not man-made – snapped into view, hijacking my attention. Announcing itself in the heather, no bigger than a jelly baby, it lay just ten metres or so ahead. I knew I would lose it if I let my gaze wander, so I fixed my eyes onto its reddish-orange glow. I walked purposefully towards it, filled with hope. It couldn't be, could it? Surely not here?

Crouching down and digging my heels into a firmish patch of moss, I knew at once what I had found, despite never having seen one before in the wild. My heart began thumping. Without doubt, it was a single cloudberry – wrapped, like a gift, in a gauzy spider's web. Golden-red, the colour of cognac, and shaped like its cousin the raspberry, but with fatter, yet fewer, juice-filled drupelets, its solitariness hinted that its life had begun as a seed dropped by a bird; a fugitive out on its own, not part of a patch. Typically found in remote and scattered locations, cloudberries elude even the best and most hyper-local of foragers. So few in number are they, that they seem unreal – the fruits of mountain fairies or goblins.

Cloudberries are a distinct rarity in Britain, often more rumour than reality. I had never seen them in the wild in Scotland (though other walkers have), nor in the moorlands of northern England, where they are also reported to grow, each stem boasting just a single fruit. Notoriously hard to cultivate commercially – needing snow in the winter, followed by the right succession of damp, sun, rain and even fog – they grow mainly in Arctic and sub-Arctic regions, where wild fruit is scant and the summer sun never fully sets.

Yes! I said to myself, grinning maniacally as I sat down, disturbing into flight a white butterfly and a daddy-long-legs.

'*James, James – look!*' I called out, sweeping the satiny threads of the cobweb off, as he and Darwin came softly striding back across the boggy ground. As he sped up and got closer, Darwin's ears lifted magnificently in the wind, as if he was entirely pro-pelled and powered on by gusts.

Tiger-orange, and so dreamy and evocative of name, cloud-berries had been on my mind for years. The first time I ever came across them on a menu, rather than in a field guide, was in a bistro on Estonia's Baltic coast, in Pärnu, as a jam to accompany cake. As I was curious to try the preserve, the waiter agreed to bring me a spoonful, despite the cake being off the menu. Golden and precious as the amber torn from rocks at the bottom of the Baltic

Sea, it gleamed. But when I licked the spoon, I found the jam painfully sweet and frustratingly tasteless. Disappointed, I told James, across the table, that one day I would try a real cloud-berry – not cooked and steeped in sugar, but in a wild place where they grew. I doubted this promise to myself, but I had not forgotten it, even years later.

The compulsion, therefore, to pick this unexpected cloud-berry, so thrillingly close to home, was intense. Sitting on the quilted earth, I had to make a choice: eat it or leave it. It felt wrong to steal this freeborn fruit of the hillside, to wrest it from nature. But such swollen brightness meant it was eye-catching bait for all competitive eaters, and soon enough it would surely draw the attention of mouse or grouse.

Gently, I plucked it from its stalk, putting it into my palm and admiring its glow. I then photographed it and tossed it into my mouth. Thick, pale golden juice burst like a tiny rain cloud, tart as a lime and sweet as a peach on my tongue. Full-bodied. A trickle dripped down my index finger, caught just in time, too prized to go to waste. I let Darwin lick it.

The real thing, its brilliant sweetness, eaten miles from human habitation, acted as an intoxicating potion. Immediately, its taste unlocked the gates to other northern lands and, as the last of the sweet-sour flavour fizzed out on my tongue, overlaying images sped joyfully through my mind: birch forests, moun-tains, glittering lakes, snowy trains, windswept taiga. I lingered over that single cloudberry, cherishing it, more than caviar, more than whisky or truffles, more than anything else I had ever eaten, smoked or drunk before. Once it had gone, I felt only a little grief, convincing myself that the cloudberry – surely the ultimate 'taste of place' – was somehow a gift; I felt I had consumed its very northernness. It brought back the similar sensations of eating a pear in an orchard, a melon in a melon field, an apple in a grove, though nothing could really compare.

After that initial extraordinary flash of appreciation, came a quietude and breadth of soul. My mood soared, but in the most peaceful way. There, above Glen Almond, where a simple hill walk had turned fantastic, I felt a momentary but profound relief from our shattered world – the sort of soothing satisfaction sometimes found in the easy atmosphere of a warm kitchen when rain lashes outside, or the cool of a thick-walled church on a hot summer's day.

~

The further north you go, the stronger the fascination for cloudberries becomes. Out on Russia's late-summertime marshes and swamp forests, harvesters brave buzzing clouds of monstrous mosquitoes to fill their buckets with moroshka, or 'tsar's berries', stocking up on a winter's supply of vitamin C – these treasures of the tundra contain twice that of oranges. When Alexander Pushkin lay dying in the winter of 1837, following a duel with Georges d'Anthès just outside St Petersburg, he demanded moroshki, and his wife, Natalya, fed him tiny teaspoons of cloudberries she'd baked in a pie.[1] And the nineteenth-century ornithologist Henry Seebohm, who travelled to north-east Russia on a natural history mission to chart the migration of birds, recorded his observations in his 1880 book *Siberia in Russia*: 'The ice on the river split and disappeared, the banks steamed in the sun, and innumerable birds of all sizes and colours appeared within forty-eight hours after the first warmth. The tundra was found to be a moor, with here and there a large, flat bog and numerous lakes. It was covered with moss, lichens, heathlike plants, dwarf birch, and millions of acres of cloudberries...'[2]

In the realm of the NunatuKavut community in Labrador, Canada, families have traditionally collected the berries in birch-bark baskets, preserving tens of gallons by storing them in underground caches or seal-skin pokes. In Sweden, where the berries are called hjortron, Nobel laureates are served cloudberry liqueur by the king at black-tie dinners, and they are sometimes mixed with yeast, hops and water to make beer. In Finland, where they are known as hilla, they appear on €2 coins, and go into a sweet liqueur called Lapponia Lakka. In Norway, multebær are preserved and used to make multekrem, a Christmas dessert with whipped cream, while on the Lofoten islands they are made into wine. Norwegian royals often serve them for dessert at grand wedding banquets. In Scandinavia generally, people have fought over cloudberry harvesting rights, and there is an old rumour that circulates about an unfortunate forager who broke a leg while out gathering cloudberries – but, rather than give away their precise location, managed to drag themself some distance before signalling for help.

Cloudberry coordinates are usually kept classified. *Flora Celtica: Plants and People in Scotland* states that 'knowledge of good cloudberry patches tends to be a closely guarded secret among pickers.'[3]

~

Roald Amundsen (1872–1928), famous for being the first to reach the South Pole, kitted out his 39m (127ft) schooner *Fram*, three-masted and built for Arctic exploration, with provisions that included several hundred bundles of dried fish and over fifty dogs. The sled dogs, unlike the fodder-eating ponies used by British naval officer and explorer Captain Robert Falcon Scott (1868–1912), could better handle the extreme cold and ate whatever the men ate, namely seal and penguin. Controversially, the sled dogs also served as meat, butchered and fed to each other along the way, in acts of canine cannibalism. This system, of simultaneously feeding the expedition while lightening the load, was seen as critical to the success of the mission: 'I figured out exactly the precise day on which I planned to kill each dog as its usefulness should end for drawing the diminishing supplies on the sleds and its usefulness should begin as food for the men.'[4] Scott, whom Amundsen would beat in the race to the pole, saw this as deeply unsportsmanlike: 'One cannot calmly contemplate the murder of animals which possess such intelligence and individuality, which have frequently such endearing qualities, and which very possibly one has learnt to regard as friends and companions.'[5]

Amundsen was also aware of the dangers of scurvy. Though the cause of the disease – vitamin C deficiency – was not entirely understood at the time, it was generally known that it could be effectively countered by eating fresh raw meat, which Amundsen could stomach well. Previously, he had led the first expedition to sail the full length of the Northwest Passage, spending many months among the Netsilingmiut ('people of the place where there is seal') in the Canadian Arctic, eating as they ate and remaining healthy. Amundsen knew that berries and raw meat were key to survival. 'Scurvy, the worst enemy of Polar expeditions, must be kept off at all costs, and to achieve this it was my intention to use fresh meat every day,'[6] he wrote in *The South Pole*, published just after his successful expedition. He took with him plenty of preserved Norwegian cloudberries and bilberries, known antiscorbutics, and at the overwintering base camp of Framheim, the Norwegian ship's cook, Adolf Henrik Lindstrøm, served buckwheat pancakes topped with cloudberries. In his diary, Amundsen had this to say of his chef: 'He has rendered greater and more valuable services to the Norwegian polar expedition than any other man.'[7] Lindstrøm was awarded the South Pole Medal for his participation in Amundsen's South Pole expedition. Long before Amundsen and Lindstrøm, Viking explorers heading south to the Mediterranean had carried preserved cloudberries by the barrel-load on their voyages.[8]

~

Not long after the cloudberry jaunt, I climbed a Corbett, Beinn nan Oighreag, or 'hill of the cloudberries', in the Grampian Mountains. Scottish Corbetts, over two hundred of them, are mountains between 2,500 and 2,999 feet high, first listed by an Englishman named John Rooke Corbett. After his death in 1949, his catalogue was handed to the Scottish Mountaineering Club and Corbett's directory was published. The far more popular Munros, Scottish peaks over 3,000 feet, have been ticked off by fit and eager 'Munro-baggers' ever since Sir Hugh Munro indexed them in 1891. Corbetts are sometimes dismissed as 'old men's Munros',[9] but they are often spectacular and usually less crowded. Because Beinn nan Oighreag is considered a bit of a lump and, at 2,982 feet, falls just short of being a Munro, it rarely attracts walkers.

James and I had set off, with Darwin, leaving Edinburgh shortly after dawn. In my rucksack I had our journey food and, with great optimism, spurred on by the Corbett's evocative name, an empty Tupperware box, lined with kitchen roll as wadding for cloudberries.

The summer day was humid but dry and, after finding the starting spot for the climb, we set off. Tufts of sheep fleece flew about in the breeze. Down by the river a single deer antler, likely lost in a fight with a rival, looked both of its place and yet somehow completely out of place, museum-like and dead, thrown far from its body. Shadows of clouds moved over the side of sharp plateaus and the clefts of the valleys. We walked on and up into wide mossy uplands. Darwin was out front, leaping over mossy mounds and drinking from burns when the urge took him, his thirst coming from bashing through heather with his barrel chest, and the constant sniffing out of tiny mammal trails, his busy hound nose taking in as many different stinks and scents as possible.

Ascending the giant hulking hill of the cloudberries was a slog. It took marked concentration to keep going. *One foot after the other, one foot after the other*, I huffed to myself. We carried on up, determined, pushing on and on, forever up, over rough ground beset with holes, and through thick heather. Oh, for a track. But in Scotland what makes many of the wilder places so incomparably good to wander is that while they are typically mapped, they have not been tamed or marked. And for such uninhabited rugged loveliness, a price must be paid. I am not romancing this old landscape, which is justly aloof to us, because there is no need to. For me, nowhere beats Scotland for walking. At the top of the hill, wide views opened up, and the thrill of the vista and reaching the summit immediately returned to us all the energy that the trek upwards had drained away.

We came back down at a different angle and were met, in the foothills, not with cloudberries, but hundreds of bilberry bushes – tinier than cultivated blueberries, but still sufficiently sweet to eat raw. We had not expected them at all. Bending down among the purple and pink heather with my Tupperware box, I held onto the hope of spotting an orange glow among the bluer hues, but no luck.

The gathering of wild bilberries is notoriously slow-going because of the low-lying bush height and craggy terrain. I thought of the berry rakes I'd seen for sale online, called 'hand-harvester ladles' or 'picker scoops', their prongs spaced just so to allow the metal teeth to separate the fruit from the plant, combing the berries from the bushes, then depositing them into the attached box. With some basic wood carving skills I could make my own, a satisfying project. But lacking this neat-sounding tool, we relied instead on our fingers. Which is exactly how we found ourselves, for well over an hour, eating as many bilberries as we squirrelled away, our hands completely blue-inked. Only Darwin, occasionally bothered by wasps, seemed slightly bored.

As clouds began chasing through the valley – faster and faster, grey and heavy-looking – we could see that we had collected enough between us for a small pot of jam, and suddenly we felt rich. The bilberries were not a consolation prize for cloudberries; on the contrary, they also felt like an award or an offering.

Often it is the unforeseen and unexpected that shapes a hike and makes it memorable: breathing in the feast of piney smells in a dark forest, the sight of an eagle soaring on rising air currents, the satisfying squelch of bog underfoot. Though, so far, no hiking experience has topped that thunderclap moment above Glen Almond when I was carried away by a cloudberry. I remember it all so clearly – but I am, of course, far from the first to indulge such affections. When exploring watery Florida, well over a hundred years ago, the Scottish conservationist and botanist John Muir, born east of Edinburgh in Dunbar, in 1838, delighted in 'meeting so many strange plants' and, on seeing a single palmetto, 'standing almost alone', mused upon it in his book *A Thousand Mile Walk to the Gulf*, published in 1916. 'They tell us that plants are perishable, soulless creatures, that only man is immortal, etc.; but this, I think, is something we know very nearly nothing about. Anyhow, this palm was indescribably impressive and told me grander things than I ever got from [a] human priest.'[10]

Every walk is a discovery, and that is the beauty of it. You never quite know what you will get.

~

In the kitchen, the air is sweet and clammy. A large stainless-steel preserving pan sits on the hob and inside the hand-harvested bilberries are breaking down in the heat and bubbling in the sugar. Not over-ripe, the berries have a little pectin, but I am not expecting a firm set. I am hoping only for a little jelly-ness and, despite what my Scottish recipe books suggest, I decide against adding rhubarb, though I like the idea of its sourness.

Decanting the hot jam into a Kilner jar, I can see it will be ample to top morning porridge for a fortnight, though no more. 'Enough is as good as a feast', as the proverb goes. Mainly, it will be a reminder, an edible testimony, of summer-blooming walks through Scotland's wildest and finest scenery. Of rocks and rivers, of berries and insects, of sap and roots and trunks. Of us, so happily and freely hiking together, in a small team of three.

Blueberry or Bilberry Jam

This is a light, sweet, thin jam for spooning over porridge, overnight oats or yoghurt; it does not fully set, making it what my friend Diana Henry calls 'nearly jam'. Bilberries are a little more tart than blueberries, so you may want to up the sugar very slightly.

MAKES 1 x 500ML JAR

600g blueberries (or bilberries)

300g sugar with pectin (preserving sugar)

juice of 1 large lemon

Have ready a sterilised 500ml jar with a lid. To sterilise your jar, pre-heat the oven to 140°C/120°C fan/gas mark 1. Wash the jar in warm soapy water and rinse well, then place on a clean baking tray and heat in the oven for about 15 minutes. To sterilise the lid, boil it in a saucepan of water for 5 minutes, then drain and leave to air dry on a rack. Leave the jar in the warm oven until the jam is ready – it must go into a hot jar.

Put the blueberries or bilberries, sugar and lemon juice into a preserving pan or a large heavy-bottomed saucepan. Add a tablespoon of water, give it a stir (only once, as stirring lowers the temperature), then bring to a rolling boil and cook for 20 minutes. If any scum forms on the surface, skim it off and bin it.

With this softly set jam, you won't be testing for a 'set' in the traditional jam-making way, so keep a close eye on it. When it's ready, the sugar should have fully dissolved, roughly half the fruit will have broken down and the cooked fruit should have a thicker, jammier consistency than when you started.

Let the jam cool for 10 minutes, then carefully pour it into the hot jar and seal with the lid while it is still hot.

Once your jar of jam is opened, store it in the fridge, where it will keep for at least six months.

CHAPTER EIGHT

Soup and a Sparrow

The kitchen floor has warped, and August is why. Humidity, building over the weak Scottish summer, has forced a handful of the tobacco-coloured oak boards up into ankle-height inverted 'v' shapes. Every year it is the same. One summer morning we wake up, go downstairs and the kitchen has changed. It is an annual event, like the arrival of asparagus or swifts. Walking around is treacherous but to repair the pinged-up boards would be vastly expensive, so instead we endure them. A thermo-hygrometer sits on the dresser, logging the kitchen's temperature and vapours, providing clues. For dinner parties, we (half-jokingly) stick yellow and black hazard tape onto the humps so that nobody drunkenly trips. When autumn comes, and the central heating is turned on, they'll descend again, down, down, down, soundlessly as a slow puncture.

Sock-footed, I move about gingerly, preparing soup. Sliding over a hump, I grab a bunch of beetroot by its ponytail from the pantry and, dangling the bulbs over the surgical-looking steel sink, run the water on full. I start scrubbing with a vegetable brush until the beetroot's skin, clogged with soil, turns from crepey and ashen to shiny gothic purple. Then, with one hand I move a wooden chopping board onto the counter, and with the other I take a Japanese Santoku ('three uses') knife, with a deep flat blade, from the block. Off come the spinach-like leaves – not wasted but chopped into inch-long strips, along with the stalks.

With their skin washed, I grate the bulbs into a glass Pyrex bowl, my fingerprints turning crimson as the stubby ribbons fall in a heap, growing higher and higher, and a watery magenta puddle begins forming on the worktop.

I need to indulge a summertime craving, specifically for a chilled soup, and I can already tell I am a little short on beetroot, but cooking is a form of bartering and working with what you have, and I am too busy anticipating the taste — sweet, swampy, tannic — to care too much. Time will soon redeem: from raw to cooked, cold to hot, to cold again. Time converts everything.

It is likely that you, too, have *that dish*, something you once ate that has now, quietly but determinedly, acquired mythical status in your mind. Something surprising — but probably not *too* surprising — that you ordered somewhere else, away from home, saying to yourself at the time, *One day, I absolutely must have this again.* And then *that dish* regularly begins cropping up in a hungry corner of your brain, again and again. You day-dream of yourself eating it, recalling the dining table you sat at, the weather, your dining companions, snippets of the conversation. But it is also a bittersweet memory. Because you cannot recall exactly what the café was called where you had it, and you don't get to that city very often, nor do you know its streets well. And perhaps you cannot fully remember the name or the correct spelling of *that* dish, and maybe one of the flavours confounds you entirely no matter how many times you try to recapture it. Eventually, you accept you will probably never have *that dish* again, quite as it was. Maybe, you start to think, it was a one-off. And anyway, what is more important is not exactly what it was but how it made you *feel*. How it surprised you, or comforted you, or made you think, or yearn. For me, *that* dish was chłodnik, cold Polish soup, eaten in Warsaw a few years back — but more on that shortly.

Clicking his stubby claws over the uneven boards, Darwin eyes me before plumping himself down, soft as a rag doll, by the closed pantry door, beyond which are his longed-for crunchy carrots. Next time I open it, he'll be ready and in position. Smart dog, thinking ahead. From the speaker of the kitchen radio comes Mahler's *Songs of a Wayfarer*, filling the air with its striding outdoorsy soundscape. I turn up the volume.

Suddenly, waves of activity erupt outside. A group of men have stopped by the window, their long shadows stretching into the kitchen and their animated drunk-in-the-afternoon chatter rudely drowning out Mahler. Such voices and vibrations are occasionally heard in the early weekend hours, but they are here at lunchtime because it is August. The sounds of summer. Of festival-goers straggling from gig to film to comedy show. Venue names ooze sweat and firewater: Underbelly, Bedlam Theatre, Black Market, Nightcap, The Liquid Room, Necrobus, Brewhemia, Opium, Whistlebinkies. One neighbour has converted their sitting room into an art gallery and a nearby pub has become a music hall for violin sonatas. A big screen, showing crowd-pleasing films – *Clueless*, *The Goonies* and *Amélie* – has been erected in St Andrew Square, along with dozens of stripy green-and-white deck chairs. In August, visitors paralyse ordinary transactions of Edinburgh life, clogging up pavements, emptying ATM machines and booking out restaurants: a vital source of revenue for some, a cause of consternation for others. Either way, the whole city becomes collectively unbent for this month, drunk on the anticipation of intoxicated anarchy as each night goes on, unlimited and loose, bar keepers only locking up at dawn. Boundaries between realities, times, spaces and people blur. The unreal becomes real. In the morning, the city, litter-strewn and dirty, looks used up, reflecting back at us what it has seen.

The men walk away and the kitchen returns to its satisfying status quo. The radio plays on, and I slide Darwin two ice cubes across the floor which he chases and then detonates noisily between two pointed incisors before leaping up onto the window seat, a leafy halo of tumbling parsley above him. Sleepy, he slips down onto the cushion, and within moments his legs begin dream-twitching.

To get the soup right, I am relying on memory and imagination, rather than recipe – unsure of cooking times and exact quantities. My last effort, tasteless and bland, was quickly dispatched. 'Maybe', I had said out loud to no one, somewhat defeated, 'this soup needs to remain a myth.' But that wouldn't do. That wouldn't do at all.

A vital ingredient of cookery is hope, and I have an almost urgent need, on this unusually balmy day, to recapture the chłodnik. This time I am determined to get it right, to make it as gratifying here as it was there. And, at that moment, wiping my forehead as the beetroot slides into the saucepan, I can recall the soup clearly – and other things, ominous things, that I learned, and felt, during my first trip to Poland, a country of great and glittering light and severe and terrible darkness: oranges painted in oil on canvas and a postcard pinned to a wall, the sight of which shook my being and flipped my stomach to nausea.

~

I had left home at dawn, on a summer morning, just as the streetlights were clicking off and the New Town bakers were pulling their first loaves out of the ovens. Not even dog walkers were out, and newspapers and crates of milk were still waiting on shopkeepers' steps. But I didn't mind the unholy hour. Because whatever happens on a trip to come – all those unpredictable days stretching so deliciously out ahead, and the belief that new horizons will somehow give you what you need – few moments ever match the tingling thrill of the departure, and how that feels in the pit of your stomach. I have come to know this, and it is partly why, unlike most people, I like airports so much. Febrile with strange energies and alternative realities, an airport is a conundrum, both a blind alley and a way into the world; intriguing yet bland, a place where time and money freely slip. Everything is expensive, yet you soon find reasons to buy things you don't need, such as an overpriced tin of shortbread (a gift for someone) or an expensive cashmere shawl (because it will be cold on the plane). It is acceptable to toast the start of your journey, or to calm your nerves, with gin at breakfast. You are bored one minute, anxious the next. Wasting time but watching the clock. An experience, generally, that's all too easy to hate, I admit, yet nothing feels wholly real in an airport, and that in itself is kind of exquisite.

Arriving in Warsaw, stepping into its short leafy summer, I went straight out again, walking past the Nożyk Synagogue – opened in 1902, and a rare survivor of the war, owing to the Nazis using it as a warehouse – and then continued aimlessly on, zigzagging along wildflower-strewn verges that had sprung up by tram lines. I stopped outside a cigar shop, its windows reflecting Stalin's vainglorious gift to the city, the Palace of Culture and Science (strikingly similar-looking to the Seven Sisters of Moscow), then looped back to the city's Saxon Garden, where soldiers stand guard, around the clock, by the Tomb of the Unknown Soldier. Close by, at a café, I took a seat under a large beige parasol, excited to be in a new city, one that I had longed to visit.

I knew that the first meal would be the one most likely remembered in detail, and so I read the menu with senses heightened. The waiter poured my beer and recommended the soup of the day – a cold soup – and just then, a sparrow with reddish wings landed by me, its twiggy legs out of place on the pink floral tablecloth. Cocking its beaky head, and chirping, it flitted away briefly before determinedly landing back on the table, dive-bombing crumbs that had fallen from the wicker basket of dark rye bread. I liked this uninvited feathery guest and its stout body; its bravery made me smile. And I liked the cool beetroot soup – sweet, velvety, dairy-like and salty – that the waiter had placed before me. I was relieved to have his recommendation, too. Who wants a lot of choice in a café? It is stressful and it wastes time. Tell me what is good, and I will have that. The soup glowed pink in the bowl, the dill fronds spreading out like neon green capillaries. The texture was what made it, though, coming from the white brined cheese crumbled on top and the small grainy cubes of pear that had been stirred through. Pear! It was so delightfully unexpected. As I ate, I wrote down the likely ingredients in my notebook, aware that I was eating something memorable, knowing already that I would want to try and conjure it up again at home.

A single white cloud – appearing as a cross – hovered above me in the otherwise blue sky. And, at that very moment, I felt a surge of unadulterated happiness.

~

Energised, I strolled on towards Warsaw's National Museum, with a single painting I had read about in mind: Aleksander Gierymski's *Jewish Woman Selling Oranges*. Painted in 1880, it was stolen during Nazi Germany's occupation of Poland, and was retrieved years later after turning up at a Hamburg auction house.[1] Once returned, it underwent months of restoration. It is a famous painting, but nothing can prepare you for the moment you see it. It is hypnotic. The oil shines and shimmers, the colours changing in the light as you move your head to view the painting from different angles. Only by seeing it in the museum, hung on the eggshell-blue-painted wall, can you pick out the pinks in the woman's bonnet and feel the painting's eerie and persistent power. I have a postcard of it, and the image is flat and lifeless — nothing like the real thing, which has the chimerical intensity of a hologram.

In a room of many other Gierymskis, none of which are nearly as striking, it is a painting filled with stark beauty and great unease. First you stare at the textures of the woman's thick clothes, her deep russet shawl, her long sleeves and heavy skirt in beiges, browns and greys, then you examine the Warsaw skyline behind her, foggy, mysterious and cold. Her basket of gleaming orange fruits is a foil to the grey, ghost-like city backdrop, which appears to almost float in the smoke and gloom. And you start to wonder, looking at the details, where would those oranges have come from? Oranges don't grow in Poland. Is she a shop-keeper or a street vendor? Why is it oranges that she is selling? Are they intended for Christmas shoppers? What is in the other basket she holds, covered with a cloth? Is it empty, or are there other fruits in there? Is it the start of winter or the end? You stare at the basket, and then back to the woman's tired face, back to her basket, and back to the hollow stare. Her demeanour, unbearably tired and sad, exudes a sort of resigned hunger, more than the empty feeling you get between meals, more of a hurting hunger, a hunger born of never quite having enough. A hunger born of not knowing when you will eat next. You want her not to sell the oranges, but to eat them herself. And to eat them in peace and without worry. You think of the insecurity of life, the unpredictable horror of it, and your gaze wanders back and forth while the painting's power gradually unzips you — her nervous hands, her tired mouth, all taking their place in your head, to be etched there, possibly for ever.

What happened to Jews in Poland, a community that was part of Polish life for hundreds of years, does not feel like finished history. What are years, months, weeks, days, hours, minutes,

when such horrors have taken place? 'Let no one delude themselves that the Jewish issue would automatically be solved with
the departure of the Jews ... Jews might leave, but antisemitism
would remain,' wrote the Polish poet Edward Hołda in 1957,
his words today printed on a wall at Warsaw's POLIN Museum
of the History of Polish Jews.[2] And if you are Jewish, or if you
have Jewish connections, or merely an interest in the history of
humanity, or Europe, then to be in Poland is to exist a while in
this ongoing history and memory.

I am not Jewish. I have a master's degree in Jewish studies
and a Jewish ex-husband (who was an Eden, and whose name
I still go by), and I took part in a long period of Jewish conser-
vative conversion in London when I was in my late twenties –
and which I failed, right at the end, to complete. I suffered a
crisis of conscience whereby I just could not visualise, nor go
through with, the final step of the mikveh, the immersion to
achieve purity. I was brought up in an entirely secular house-
hold and I felt hypocritical, despite being so warmly welcomed
by my rabbi and his wife, whose house I would spend Sundays
at – learning about kosher kitchens, how dairy and meat is kept
separate with two sinks, two sets of cutlery and dishes – after
attending sabbath the day before. This I did most weekends,
while my friends partied in Brixton, where I lived at the time.
Somehow, I knew the waters of the mikveh would be a ritual too
far; the idea terrified me, and I was incapable of forcing myself
to go through with it. But today, out of respect for what I've
been taught, I still crack eggs into a glass bowl to check for,
and to remove, blood spots (Deuteronomy forbids consuming
blood, because blood is life), and the only snippets of prayers
I know are in Hebrew. Sometimes I regret, and feel guilty about,
not finishing the conversion.

Given all of this, I knew that Poland would present challenges
for me.

~

Leaving Gierymski's *Jewish Woman Selling Oranges* behind, outside I found the sun hovering high in the heavens.

In full-bloom Łazienki Park, with its follies, fountains and pavilions, I found Flora Café, an immediately appealing spot that had moved outside for the summer. There, in one of the inviting wicker chairs, under a thick slice of sun, I drank coffee and read a newspaper brought from home. Turning down the waiter's suggestion of szarlotka, Polish apple pie, I opted instead for a simple plate of seasonal fruit.

'Berries? We just have berries.'

'Perfect, thank you,' I said.

The berries arrived – a fruity hillock of blueberries, raspberries and strawberries – naked, without even a dusting of icing sugar, carefully piled up not on one plate but two. Sharp yet rich, each berry was a grenade of flavour, as complex as good wine. Guarding them from buzzing wasps, I could have eaten them for ever.

The crowd was older (notably, nobody scrolled on a screen), and most people greeted the servers with an ease that comes only from showing up regularly, time and time again, at the same café. Pushing down the plunger of a cafetière was the only exertion to be had, and the scrumple of newspapers the only noise to be heard. I liked to imagine that these affable routines played out most summer afternoons at the Flora Café.

~

Later, wandering past bakeries filled with babkas and bagels, and along streets of Brutalist apartment blocks, I stopped for dinner at the slightly musty Radio Café, owned by Stanisław Pruszyński, a journalist born in 1935 who worked for Radio Free Europe. I ordered what the café, close to the city's main railway station, is known for: homemade pierogi, filled with nothing but silky mashed potatoes and white cheese. The warm dumplings, of sportsman-sized proportions, arrived swimming in a pool of warm butter and fried onions, and were chased with ice-cold Polish lager. Right dish, right place – a satisfying combination. Over the next four nights, I returned every evening, rarely speaking a word except to order the same things: beer, dumplings and sometimes a bowl of thin, sweet beetroot soup. Simple, old foods, surviving whims over the centuries for good reason. There are better places to eat in Warsaw but by returning, and taking the same seat at the same table, I was able to gain a slender, if temporary, foothold. Eventually, to my surprise, I was asked to sign the heavy leather-clad visitors' book.

By the time I left Radio Café that first evening, darkness had come on and a woman, who I had noticed earlier, was still standing in the same position by the park, immobile as a mannequin. As I passed her, she leant into a saloon car that had pulled up to the kerb. Stubbing her cigarette out on the pavement, she got in and the car drove away. I pushed away a feeling of despair that you can sometimes sense at night, often close to railway stations, that if you let it, creeps under your skin, and stays there. The weather felt volatile and heavy, as though rain would come.

~

After a few days spent sightseeing, I joined hundreds of commuters weaving through Warsaw Central railway station, constructed as one of the city's flagship projects in the 1970s. A monster of a building, it is set mainly underground, with tracks stretching out like tendons to cities such as Lublin and Łódź. Outside, election posters of Rafał Trzaskowski, the socially liberal mayor of Warsaw and challenger to president Andržej Duda, flapped in the wind. The run-up to the presidential election of 2020 had been fraught, with a stark rural-urban divide to the fore. Duda, proffering his own singular blend of right-wing populism and strict Catholic values, had eventually won. I bought my ticket and boarded the train to Kraków.

We eased out of Warsaw, in a train carriage that was clean, cool and quiet, the scenery turning surprisingly quickly from glass and steel to pastoral, all pretty streams and lakes and woodlands. I thought back to the painting, and what had happened later to Poland's Jews who'd been murdered here, not only in the infamous and well-organised death camps and ghettos, but also in fields and forests like the ones outside the train window. I had not at this stage made up my mind as to whether I would visit Auschwitz, which is a 'day trip' from Kraków. I had assumed I would go at some point in my life. I had visited Jewish museums and cemeteries in many cities and I had led Jewish friends to Jewish places of interest in various places. But I already felt uneasy about going.

As we pulled into Kraków, I recalled a neat line I had read in a walking compendium that quoted the flâneur Charles Baudelaire (1821–1867): 'What peculiarities one finds in big cities when one knows how to roam and to search.'[3] And while I like to think that I do know how to roam and search in whatever city I happen to find myself in, I had not expected what I found in Kraków to undo me as it did. Nor for the shock to come from something so seemingly harmless and small.

~

I was met in Kraków by a familiar figure, Adam Mickiewicz (1798–1855), poet and hero of Poland. Liberating Poles from Russian control was Mickiewicz's greatest aim in life, and today he stands cast in bronze in the main square. Over the years I have found his statues and busts all over Europe: in Lviv, in western Ukraine; in Burgas, on the Black Sea in Bulgaria; and in Istanbul, at the house where he spent his final days. On

Christmas Eve, here in Kraków, I was told, florists decorate his statue with sprays of flowers. Today, his body lies next to Polish monarchs at the city's magnificent Wawel Cathedral in the 'crypt of the national bards', his spectacular white marble tomb carved with wheat sheaves.

Leaving the main market square behind, I followed a faint smell of lavender and sausages to Kraków's 600-year-old market, Stary Kleparz, where stalls sold tiny paper cups full of Poland's incomparable summer berries: gooseberries, raspberries, strawberries, cherries, most grown north of the city in family gardens. Somehow, colours felt more vivid: the façades, the trams, the parks. And sound more vibrant: voices, clattering cafés, spouting fountains. All because everything was new to me. Unfamiliar, and therefore invigorating.

With a cup of berries in hand, I headed to Kazimierz, the city's old Jewish quarter, with its pebble-dash buildings and mezuzahs nailed to doorways. I had read dismissive accounts of Kazimierz that portrayed it as a sort of 'Jewish Disneyland', a place of Yiddish dramas devoid of Jewish actors, and where clichés abound: a carnival of fiddlers, schnitzel, and wine from the Golan Heights. A place lost to time. It is hard to square an attempted revival of Jewish identity and history in Poland, even a fragmented one. Those that died are for ever lost. I have spoken to Poles who begrudge their history, and those who refuse ever to set foot in Auschwitz because it is too painful. The crushing weight of what happened in Poland – the pogroms, the horrors of the Holocaust, the communist regime of the 1960s which launched a hateful anti-Semitic campaign – is also shaped by what is happening today under the current rightist government, and in the nationalistic marches that take place annually on the country's independence day, attracting the far-right (some of whom set off red flares that fill Warsaw's streets with smoke, and chant slogans such as 'pure Poland, white Poland').[4]

But I did not find Kazimierz to be a theme park. It has too many bookshops for that. And too many pilgrims. In the cemetery behind the Remuh Synagogue, Kraków's smallest, I watched a group of Hasidic men gather to stand before a handful of tombstones that had survived the Nazi occupation. At an Israeli-themed restaurant, which served excellent hummus, posters advertised the Jewish Culture Festival that had recently taken place, one of the largest of its kind in the world.

Though its streets do purposefully exude a 'once upon a time' atmosphere, and there are kitsch elements, I think there is a real reason to, if not exactly celebrate it, then to acknowledge that Kazimierz does pull off what it sets out to do. And that is to commemorate. To make you think. At its very centre, the Warsaw-based Nissenbaum Foundation – founded in 1983, with the aim of rescuing testimonies and Jewish heritage in Poland – has built a 'place of meditation' to encourage passers-by to stop and remember the Polish Jews of Kraków who were murdered by the Nazis. And plaques on buildings offer clues, too, such as the one at 42 Józefa Street, which, in Hebrew, English and Polish, tells us that in 1810 a study group called 'Setting time for Torah' met there.

When I visited, my ears pricked up on hearing the London accents of a large group of Jewish teenagers, who bunched past me on their way to the outstanding Galicia Jewish Museum. This does three things really successfully: it remembers the victims of the Holocaust, it educates both Poles and Jews about their own histories, and it challenges stereotypes found elsewhere in Kazimierz. It is easy to be sceptical about the klezmer bands, the 'Jewish caviar' and 'Passover cheese' for sale at the cafés; far harder to remain unconvinced by memorials and museums which trace and commemorate Jewish lives and culture, and which draw such large numbers of visitors eager to learn and honour.

I thought back to Warsaw's Jewish Cultural Centre (JCC) on Chmielna Street, a simple square building in a courtyard, where I had turned up for its quietly celebrated Boker Tov ('good morning' in Hebrew) brunch. The menu was vegetarian, and there was a Kosher certificate from Rabbi Schudrich proving that the kitchen keeps strict kashrut laws, so that anyone can join in at their kibbutz-like communal tables. There are often more people than seats, I was told, and everything from the kitchen is used up in the most resourceful ways: cooking water from carrots makes a base for tomato soup, herb stalks are dashed through falafel, and fruit peelings go into the compôte. The egg salad was the best I had ever tasted, so rich with mayonnaise and spicy with pepper and parsley, and the potato salad with red onion was moreish, so too the tvorog cheese scattered with pomegranate seeds. Of course, Jewish culture should not always be reduced to nostalgia, or attached to tragedy, and it felt like the JCC, with its brunches and workshops and gatherings, held a genuine hope for a new, if small, Jewish Poland.

~

A faint smell of drains and tobacco followed me as I walked down to the Vistula, Poland's longest river, and towards the enamel factory once owned by Oskar Schindler (1908–1974), the man who saved the lives of hundreds of Jewish workers, and who was later immortalised in Steven Spielberg's block-buster film *Schindler's List*. But curiosity drew me instead into MOCAK, the giant modern art gallery next door.

Inside, I went past much abstract art I did not understand, stopping at a single postcard, framed in perspex and mounted on a huge and otherwise empty white wall. I moved closer and saw that it depicted an old-fashioned and serene-looking dining room. Just how bistros should be – with pristine white tablecloths, tavern-style dining chairs and paintings of landscapes hanging on the wall. An inviting room in which to eat, unfussy and calm. But only when I leaned in further to read the tiny type of the artwork label did I learn the absolute horror of it: that the tavern was in Auschwitz, and that it belonged to the Schutzstaffel, or SS, the self-described 'political soldiers' of the Nazi Party, headed by Heinrich Himmler.

As my eyes returned to the image — an actual 'wish you were here' postcard to be stamped and mailed — it jolted me physically. The sheer horror of the mundane, the ordinariness of terror. I felt sick, but I kept looking at it for clues, or symbols, a hint somewhere — a pistol, a leather boot, a stylised eagle — but there were none; it was simply a handsome dining room. I know that Nazis were 'ordinary' people, that they danced, had parties, started families, all the while being murderous. It was partly my reaction that distressed me. That I had got the postcard so wrong, that I had imagined myself dining there, that I had momentarily wanted to sit in such a room. Behind me, as I stared at the postcard, a film showed three generations of an Australian family dancing to the Gloria Gaynor song 'I Will Survive' in front of the infamous Auschwitz rail tracks and the 'Arbeit Macht Frei' sign. Artist Jane Korman filmed the video with her three children and her father, Adolek, a former prisoner at Auschwitz.[5]

The gallery and the postcard set my mind feasting on dread. It was right here, in 1941, that Kraków's Jewish population was marched to, and walled off in, what became known as the Kraków Ghetto, during Operation Reinhard, the Nazi plan to methodically murder all of occupied Poland's Jews. The postcard, a depiction of the utmost civilised behaviour amidst the most appalling cruelties imaginable, had been hung there, isolated and surrounded by white space, in order to draw the viewer in closer and closer, to shock and provoke. And it had succeeded.

~

At a café in downtown Krakow, I aimed to clear my mind, to steady it with something simple and nutritious. I took a seat and ordered poached eggs, salad and bread. But as my hands moved across the table, to my napkin, to my glass, I soon noticed the shaker-style chairs and the white tablecloths. Too close to the room depicted in the postcard. Stress began sublimating onto the food, and horror seeped in, contaminating the café. Weird images started flashing through my head. Alfred Hitchcock. That foul scene in *To Catch a Thief*, where a cigarette is stubbed out in the yolk of a fried egg. Hitchcock hated eggs.[6] Accidentally dropping a bread roll to the floor in my distress, I suddenly felt intensely lonely. I needed to talk about the postcard but there was nobody to tell — the sometimes-miserable fate of the solitary traveller.

I pushed my plate away and tried to distract myself with thoughts of Poland's celebrated milk bars, proudly egalitarian and culturally significant. How, back in Warsaw, I had sought out Bar Mleczny Rusałka in the eastern district of Praga, and had been intrigued by its no-frills service, its wood-lined walls and apple-green tablecloths, all virtually unchanged in decades. How I had managed, in faltering Polish, to order tea and soup, the older woman serving behind the counter scowling slightly at my efforts with Google translate.

Now, instead of offering reassurance (that not everything in the world is endlessly updated), such places made me think of the Korova milk bar in *A Clockwork Orange*, with its moloko and 'old ultra-violence'. I thought of Nadsat, the bastardised language Alex and his droogs used, melding Cockney rhyming slang, Russian (Anthony Burgess had learned Russian ahead of a trip to Leningrad in 1961), Shakespearean English and Romany.[7] It all swung in my ears. The white-suited boys off to 'tolchock some old veck in an alley'. The words mixing with the Polish chatter in the café. I could see the kitchen from my table, and I looked there for the familiar, for the rhythms of cooks working together, focused on creativity, nourishment and care. But I saw only their sharp knives and then catastrophised about poison in the mushrooms. The postcard, it seemed, had turned my mind.

Most of us are not proficient at processing the weight of our shared horrors – of wars, natural disasters and the endless current of human barbarities, the worst things that man can do. As one war erupts, another becomes a frozen conflict. Headlines scream economic disaster one day, environmental catastrophe the next. And, as creatures existing in a state of almost permanent crisis, our self-protection techniques usually amount to denial, repression or wilful ignorance. How do we learn to live with these things if we don't speak of them? If we mainly choose to look the other way?

~

The kitchen sweats the season, air close as summer. The windowpane, running with condensation, turns the outline of those going by – legs, buggies, dogs – wavy and soft-edged. Licking and slapping the sides of the saucepan, the grated beetroot is now soft in the stock and so I flick a teaspoon of sugar into the pan to bring out its sweetness, then I pour the lot out into a giant ceramic mixing bowl and let it cool before moving it into the fridge to chill.

Darwin, emerging from his warm animal sleep on the window seat, sighs deeply into his paws, and is thrown a couple of stinky dried sprats from a packet, which he chews loudly. Sated and softer, he gazes up from the basement to the sky's drifting sheepskin clouds. A bumblebee comes in to bother him, buzzing lazily through the open window, attracted by the potted herbs. I usher it gently out. The previous day James and I had walked Darwin in the Scottish Borders, trudging beneath thick clouds from Cairn Law and Broad Law, and then stepping over dozens of dead bees by the Megget Reservoir. An upsetting sight. Summer losses, I later read, can be down to the failure of requeening after a beekeeper's hive has swarmed.

Later, taking the bowl out of the fridge, I blend the beetroot mixture, whisk in kefir, squeeze in lemon juice and stir until the soup turns cherry-blossom pink. Feathery dill fronds spread out around the cubes of pear and the crumbled white cheese. In Poland, I had eaten wildly inventive dishes – fennel granita with orange foam, vegetarian sausages made from black lentils, buckwheat and sunflower seeds and pickled cabbage butter – but it was this soup that had become *that* dish. Cool yet comforting, refreshing and surprising, it is just the sort of thing to turn to when appetites wane in summer. It had, quite unknowingly, helped to cement my love for Poland and Polish food (I have since returned again and again to eat and wander).

Now the soup, so flavoursome that it creates a hunger for itself, helps me repossess my visits to Poland; it makes me think of the horror, the beauty, the truth. Of what we choose to ignore, and what we choose to remember. And it makes me think of a quote, often printed on museum merchandise in Poland, from the historian Marian Turski, one of the few living survivors of Auschwitz. Attending a memorial at the site seventy-five years on, his primary message for the rest of us was a simple but compelling reminder: 'Thou shalt not be indifferent.'[8]

Myth-status Chłodnik

Mythical, because this is not true Polish chłodnik, but I have experimented with all sorts of quantities and ingredients, and this is as close to my memory of the heavenly Warsaw soup as I can get. It is at its best eaten outdoors on a warm summer afternoon.

SERVES 4

500g beetroot, with stems
   and leaves
1 tablespoon rapeseed oil
750ml vegetable stock
½ teaspoon granulated sugar
250ml plain kefir
Juice of half a lemon
1 large conference pear, cored
   and cubed

60g feta (or other crumbly
   white brined cheese)
small handful of finely
   chopped dill, for
   scattering over
sea salt
freshly ground black pepper
   (optional)

Wash and finely chop the beetroot leaves and stems, then set aside. Scrub the beetroot well – no need to peel them – then grate.

Heat the rapeseed oil in a large saucepan or casserole over a medium heat. Add the beetroot, including the stems and leaves, stirring to coat everything in the oil, then add a pinch of salt and cook for 5 minutes, stirring occasionally, just to soften the beetroot. Pour in the stock and bring to a boil, then stir in the sugar, cover and simmer for 30 minutes.

Remove from the heat and leave until cool, then chill in the fridge. Once the soup is cold, use a hand-held blender to blitz until smooth. Next, whisk in the kefir and lemon juice and check the seasoning.

When ready to serve, stir through the pear, crumble over the feta, sprinkle over the dill and grind over a little black pepper for a dash of heat, if you fancy it.

CHAPTER NINE

Cheap Thrills

It is the morning after a dinner party and the haar has come, creeping in overnight as we merrily ate and drank. This North Sea mist, its name smacking of thick salty breath, arrives only rarely, usually during the warmer months. And today, paired with the silence of a Sunday, it has stripped everything of colour and form, transforming Edinburgh into an old black-and-white movie.

Foggy headed, I have just returned to the kitchen, having stepped out to air Darwin. I walked more slowly than usual, feeling at sea amidst the nebulous haze. Each step felt muddled, movements of legs and feet heavier. I kept Darwin close. Then, as an experiment, I extended his retractable lead fully, and, sure enough, he momentarily dissolved into the murk, his upright tail going last into the haar before I reeled his fuzzy body back in again like a fish.

On usually busy Princes Street, a single pair of bus headlights crawled along towards us, blazing yellow discs cutting through the woolly light like those of a mobster's car. The clock at the top of the Balmoral Hotel was lost in the milky brume, the Scott Monument too. Cloaked were the flags above the National Gallery, the Saltire and the Union Jack. A man dressed in a heavy tweed coat crossed the road and then altogether vanished, phantom-like, into the pearly vapour. Such unusual weather is strangely stress-reducing, the miasma making sights and sounds muffled and non-urgent – and a hangover, with its sickly clamminess and mental dimness, welcomes such slackness, invisibility and withdrawnness.

As we slithered back through it, the air brackish and cool and the cobbles slippery, even the most ambitious houses of the New Town, those commanding Great King Street and Northumberland Street, sat veiled. How curious the city felt, almost dematerialised. All alabaster-looking, eerie as a death mask. A neighbour, who I feared we had kept up late with last night's antics, told me that the haar is not the same as Scotch mist, which is what envelopes the glens and does not come from the sea – and that it is not 'smirr', either, which is Scots for fine drizzle.[1] As soon as he sauntered off, I entirely lost sight of him.

~

Sitting down at the table – overflowing with last night's cutlery, glasses, flower vases, corks, napkins, bread baskets, bottle openers and matchboxes, evidence of people gathered around and sharing ideas – I think of how informal our set-up was, compared to Edinburgh's bygone dinner parties.

Eighteenth-century philosopher David Hume, lover of good manners, roast chicken and backgammon, returned here from Paris in 1769. He came back equipped with what he modestly called his 'great talent for cookery', treating his guests to a combination of French flair and Scottish traditions: 'I also make a Sheep's Head Broth in a manner that Mr. Keith speaks of it for eight days after, and the Duc de Nivernois would bind himself Apprentice to my Lass to learn it.'[2]

But it was the Ballantyne brothers, founders of the Ballantyne Press, who, in Sir Walter Scott's era of the late eighteenth and early nineteenth centuries, had the most elaborate tables, laid with turtle, venison, iced punch, turkey stuffed with truffles and perhaps an entire boar's head.[3] The dinners were likely gossipy – who was going where, whose luck was rising, whose was on the slide – and indigestion-inducing. At certain addresses around town, I am pretty sure they still are.

Sometimes, the kitchen deserves people, deserves a party.

But there is never any show-off cooking or culinary grandstanding during dinner parties here: just simple things that require some time, thought and attention. Guests are an honour. It is a chance to see friends and to see them differently, in your home, removed from daily pressures and the formality of restaurants. Why put stress and fuss onto such a positive opportunity with elaborate productions? The best dinner parties tend to be less opera, more choir. And so rather than plating up and serving everyone, and thus risking giving people things they'd rather not eat, last night I had put everything out, buffet-style, encouraging people to go back for seconds or thirds.

An arsenal of cold plates went onto the dark oak server to mingle together – plaited challah bread, sour-ish herring with apple, pickled mushrooms with thyme, purple basil and red grape salad. Leave a dish within easy reach of the table and someone will eat it. If anything is left, then that is probably a sign that it wasn't right. Casserole dishes of fluffy chestnut and sage pilaf and Polish bigos, rich with sausage, bacon and prunes, were kept warm on the hob. All quite straightforward. Darwin had positioned himself early as a noble assistant, only to be quickly resigned to his bed for the evening, from where he evaluated the scene, ever ready to corral anything that found its way onto the floor.

'Ponder well on this point: the pleasant hours of our life are all connected by a more or less tangible link, with some memory of the table.'[4] So wrote 'king of the gastronomes' Charles Monselet (1825–1888). And it is true. Enjoyable times around the table can help to quell despair.

Kitchen as host, kitchen as innkeeper.

Putting a neat full stop to the dinner party – where hours were counted in bottles of wine, and conversations revolved around everything and nothing – were thin cigarettes, smoked until the candles guttered.

Lighting someone's cigarette is a delicious move – it is intimate, of course, but also the first puff is the best. And if cigarettes are shared at the table, after a meal or over a drink, they can help make connections. As Oscar Wilde observed, in *The Picture of Dorian Gray* (1891), 'A cigarette is the perfect type of a perfect pleasure. It is exquisite, and it leaves one unsatisfied. What more can one want?'[5] Their fleeting bliss, their pointless extravagance. Cigarettes make time elastic. Gratification begins before they are lit, and endures long after they have been stubbed out.

Cigarettes also serve up memories and are just as capable as flavours or smells of doing so. Left out on the table, a single packet of Ararat Slims, with their elegant blue-and-white packaging, charts a road back to Armenia. 'A souvenir may make tangible some otherwise intangible travel experience,'[6] wrote the academic Russell Belk, an authority on collecting, in a 1988 research paper on possessions. And these cigarettes are named after Mount Ararat, the holy mountain that cements the Armenians' identity as the people of the Ark, descendants of the legendary founder of Armenia, Hayk (to Armenians, 'Armenia' is Hayastan – literally, 'Land of Hayk'), whose forebear was Noah. Strong and robust, they hold something of the country within their white papers. For me, all other brands now taste slack and disappointing, trivial in comparison.

The lingering mess at the table, proving the social aspect of the kitchen, will soon be tidied away, and the room will smell again of furniture polish, and spiced apricot biscuits. Baking is a hangover cure, with wholesome and redemptive steps to follow that are guaranteed to stave off the worst of the stomach-sinking sweaty fear that too much strong alcohol induces. Mind into focus, hands on the task.

Melt honey and butter. Stir in a few drops of orange blossom water. Combine ground almonds, flour, dried apricots, barberries and sultanas. These are the starting points of aromatic apricot cookies, and memories of Armenia: a heroic country of heartache, incomparable apricots and heavy smokers.

~

Mount Ararat is often shrouded by haar-like coiling clouds. When the poet Osip Mandelstam visited Armenia for several inspiring months in 1930, eight years before he was targeted by Soviet authorities and sent into the vast network of Gulags and camps, he described such a scene: 'I managed to observe the clouds performing their devotions to Ararat. It was the descending-ascending motion of cream poured into a glass of ruddy tea, dispersing in all directions like curly-puffed tubers.'[7]

For the Ukrainian storyteller-turned-war-reporter Vasily Grossman (1905–1964), who spent two months in Armenia in 1961, during a time of illness and marital woes, Mount Ararat was an ethereal sight, emerging 'out of the sky as if it had condensed from its white clouds and deep blue. It is this snowy mountain, this bluish-white sunlit mountain that shone in the eyes of those who wrote the Bible.'[8] As a Jewish outsider, and someone who had lived through the horrors of the Holocaust, the Battle of Stalingrad and the Holodomor (Ukraine's Terror-Famine, engineered by Stalin, which killed millions), Grossman found a sense of belonging in Christian Armenia. He was welcomed, finding Armenians, who themselves had been so fiercely persecuted, to be kind and compassionate. He wrote of his time there in *An Armenian Sketchbook*, which was eventually published in 1988.

Rugged yet harmonious, Mount Ararat sits in Armenia's historical lands. Now cut adrift across the border in eastern Turkey, it serves as a magnetic reminder of what has been lost, with the firmly closed border between the two countries adding to the attestation. Everything in Armenia is Ararat. Cigarettes aside, named after the mountain are baby boys, plains, provinces, villages, rivers, roads, the Yerevan Ararat Brandy Factory and a now-defunct airline; also, outside the country, an asteroid, an Armenian-language newspaper in Lebanon, an Australian royal navy ship and a football stadium in Tehran.

During the hot, apricot-ripening days of my own journey through Armenia, it was weeks before I saw Mount Ararat, with its cupola of snow. Then, finally, one day, the cloud vortex cleared, allowing me a view through a taxi window. The mountain appeared like an island in the sky. 'Our blue mountain, how blue it is!' said the driver in a chalky voice, describing exactly how it appeared, while echoing Grossman's sentiment.

Blue, the colour of smoke and the sky. Blue, the colour of heaven, the colour of the divine.

~

To try and comprehend Armenia – a country of great yearning, fortitude and melancholy – as an outsider travelling through its villages and over its hilly plateaus, is to undertake a series of adventures in attempted understanding. To pick up along the way whatever clues may reveal themselves in stray fragments of ancient culture, history and the language of the table, in a country where almost everything has meaning.

Viticulture here is so old that, in the fifth century BC, Herodotus wrote of wine being shipped to Babylon, carried in animal skins. Xenophon, marching through with his armies, noted the fragrant wines. Bread, called hats, is often lavash, the traditional flatbread, and when pulled out of the belly of a hot clay tonir it is, at that very moment, the best bread in the world. There is a thirty-eight-letter alphabet and a puzzle-like language, created by the fifth-century saint Mesrop Mashtots, who lends his name to the widest street in the capital, once called Stalin Avenue. Churches and monasteries appear in almost impossibly remote locations, in dense dripping forests, and on stark and pale mountain passes, safe from skirmishes.

Modern Yerevan, built partially of pink-ish tuff, a rock made of compacted volcanic ash, was shaped by the Russia-born Armenian architect Alexander Tamanyan – who is, according to his descendants, to Yerevan what Antoni Gaudí is to Barcelona. Tamanyan relocated to Yerevan to help rebuild the city when it was named capital of the First Republic of Armenia in 1918,[9] though as a settlement it is far, far older; recently, Armenians marked its 2,800th birthday.

Given the monumental suffering brought about by the genocide perpetrated by Ottoman Turkey in 1915, when at least a million Armenians perished after being periodically persecuted in both structured pogroms and sporadic attacks, Tamanyan wanted his architectural designs to symbolise the revival of Armenians and Armenia. Intrinsic to his plan was a desire for Mount Ararat to be a central feature of the city, and for buildings to be orientated towards it.[10]

Yerevan counts amongst its attractions a children's railway, one of the world's oldest Jewish cemeteries and a modernist chess house – built in 1970 and named after the Armenian grandmaster Tigran Petrosian (Armenia is a country that has produced very many great chess players). Inside, through decoratively carved wooden doors, are murals of chess pieces so engrossing, detailed and intricate that they rival the Bayeux Tapestry. Angels fly over bishops and knights, and peacocks spread their feathers next to priests and decorated stallions. Below the huge wall hangings are dozens of wooden tables with chessboards carved into their tops, and polished wooden floors covered with Armenian rugs. And not far away is Byron Street – so named because in 1816, Byron studied the Armenian language (with its 'Waterloo of an alphabet'[11]) at the Armenian Monastery on the island of San Lazzaro, in Venice, and Armenians have not forgotten this.

Few places are so deeply affecting to visit. This is partly because there is such longstanding pain, and partly because the suffering is ongoing. In autumn 2020, the year before I went there, another violent verse in the South Caucasus's long and bloody poem was written. A resurgence of the ongoing conflict between Armenia and Azerbaijan over Nagorno-Karabakh (or Artsakh, as the Armenians call it, because in medieval times Artsakh was the tenth province of Great Armenia) claimed 3,773 Armenian lives, while neighbouring Azerbaijan reported the death of 2,783 of its young soldiers.[12] When I was travelling around the country the following year, fluttering Armenian flags (the red band on top suggesting the blood shed by those defending their nation) on the roadside often signalled the harrowing sight of freshly dug graves. On one side of the headstone would be a portrait of the soldier dressed in civilian clothes; on the reverse, the same soldier in uniform, holding a gun. Far too many of them. The faces of youth that will never see manhood.

I stayed in Yerevan for the summer, taking all this in, having travelled there with James – who was covering an election that, thankfully, went off quietly, contrary to predictions. Afterwards, we left the city, free to explore.

~

In a hired three-door Lada Niva, a car almost unchanged since it first rolled off the Russian assembly line in 1977, we drove north, under the blistering noon sun, to Gyumri, Armenia's second city.

Muffling the engine noise was a CD of Armenian folk melodies, an ensemble performing the otherworldly instrumental
songs of the saintly scholar-singer Komitas Vardapet (1869–
1935), also known as Soghomon Soghomonyan. Komitas
has come to symbolise Armenian sacred music, as well as the
country's resilience. Greatly admired by other composers,
including Claude Debussy, he was an ethnomusicologist and his
skill lay in finding the links between everyday ritual and song.
He connected sacred music with folk music, seeing them as one
and the same, and he dedicated his work to birds, flowers, mountains and the breeze: love songs to nature, praises to God.

Having performed in Austria, Switzerland and France, in
Turkey he established a 300-member choir in Constantinople –
but it was there, on 24 April 1915, that he, along with other
intelligentsia of the Armenian community, was arrested and
forcibly relocated to Çankırı, close to Ankara.[13] Soon after, the
genocide gained momentum and Armenians were forced out of
their homes en masse and their property looted, as they were
banished and compelled to march into the Syrian Desert. Many
died from the heat, and many more were murdered out on the
scorching plains and in canyons. Komitas was brutalised but
survived, just. Severely traumatised, and rendered mute by his
experiences, he spent many years in French asylums, broken
by the ordeal. Today, as an intangible treasure of Armenia, his
songs are performed by orchestras worldwide and his statue
stands in Paris, Detroit and Montreal. The most important
instrument played in Komitas performances is the double-reed
duduk, carved of aged apricot wood.

Before Gyumri, we arrived at the town of Spitak, turning
off Komitas and stepping out into the full sun. The white Lada,
having taken us slowly over high passes, and on through cabbage
and carrot fields, was as overheated from the journey as we
were, its entire body speckled as an egg with sticky dead insects.

Spitak is not where it used to be. Late in the morning of Wednesday 7 December, 1988, at 11:41, a giant earthquake struck, splitting buildings in two, turning houses to dust and killing more than 25,000 people.[14] More than half a million were instantly made homeless, and nearby Gyumri was also flattened.

At the time, Armenia was part of the Soviet Union, and when Mikhail Gorbachev appealed for international assistance, rescue teams came from all over the world. In America, the Armenian community declared a period of mourning and cancelled Christmas celebrations. Inside Spitak's museum we were ushered around a display by two curators keen to show us how the destroyed town, an 'Armenian Pompeii', had been rebuilt at a slightly different location a few kilometres to the south-west, on account of seismological readings. It was one of the last large construction projects undertaken by the Soviet Union before it collapsed, three years later.

You wonder how much heartache one small, embattled country can manage. Dig, not very deep, in Armenia, and you will find pain. But, like the moving music of Komitas, equal to the pain is great holiness, generosity and beauty. And, thank goodness, more than a little humour.

~

In Gyumri, we stayed for a week in a former hospital, which had been established by the German Red Cross at the time of the earthquake, and then converted into an art hotel in 1996. In the evenings, a cheery chef from Bonn, called Karl-Heinz, wearing an apron and John Lennon-style spectacles, cooked schnitzels and roasts. His job – with a charitable organisation, he told us – was to train the hotel cooks in the art of German gastronomy. In a country of such ancient culinary arts, I silently questioned if this was really necessary, but Karl-Heinz was charming and the cooks seemed smitten with him. Outside in the garden, on benches shaded by trees, sat patients waiting to attend appointments at the neighbouring clinic, which was still operational and funded partly by the hotel. They would sit fanning themselves, while petting gentle stray dogs who had wandered freely into this leafy oasis from the hot streets.

Before dinner, prepared by Karl-Heinz and his team, we would join local men sitting happily drinking after work at the attached beer garden outside. Often, immediately upon seeing us, one of the men would stand, go to an apricot tree and reach skywards to pluck the choicest fruit, the one filled with most sunshine – and, without shared language, in place of words and welcome, he would put it down in front of us as a gift. Gratefully, I would split it open with my fingers, the smell heady, warm and aromatic, wondering if it was not an apple that was forbidden in the Bible, but a fiery-orange Armenian apricot. The temptation of them, how easily unbalanced they can make you with their pulpy ambrosia. I knew I would never again entertain a supermarket apricot at home, ruined by food-chain cold storage.

Inside the hotel hung the work of Ararat Sarkissian, a Yerevan-based artist born in Gyumri. His pictures are recreations of some of the hundreds of Armenian cross stones (khachkars) that were destroyed at an ancient Armenian cemetery by Azeri soldiers in Djulfa, in the Azerbaijani enclave of Nakhichevan, in 2005. Many have called the destruction a cultural genocide. 'From survival to destruction to a form of rebirth on paper',[15] as Sarkissian wrote in an accompanying book. We bought one of the artworks, already framed, and put it in the boot of the Lada, alongside a bag of apricots that we had been steadily adding to.

Gyumri, dating back to the eighth century and largely built of orange and black tuff, is a place that resounds with its own unique language. Though the modern settlement was largely destroyed in the earthquake, earlier history hangs on in the noodle-twist lanes of the old town, known as Kumayri, with its low-slung and teetering tsarist-era homes – all ironwork, cornices, art-nouveau doors and crumbling balconies that haven't seen fresh paint in decades. Here, where the smell is of dust, pickles, lavash and midsummer scented peaches, wool pelts dry in the sun, women sweep porches with hand-tied brooms and maroon cherries fall freely. Outside some homes, small daybeds languish in the shade, and all around, seeds are carried on the breeze and cats gaze out of windows. British folklorist and traveller Lucy Garnett (1849–1934), best known for her work in Turkey, wrote of Armenian houses across the Turkish border, in Erzurum, describing how, during the hot season, 'the family live briefly on the housetop, and the whole family frequently bring up their mattresses and cushions, and sleep "at the moon's inn" in company of their many domestic pets.'[16]

On Sunday morning, I traipsed through this old southern part of town until I reached the Russian church. Squat, built of black tuff, and with its tin roof glinting, it looked like a fairytale chapel. I had hoped to see a service, but the church was being refurbished. Painters were busy at work, reaching up from ladders, to touch up a giant golden Eye of Providence, enclosed in a triangle and surrounded by rays of light that shone on the ceiling. A few candles had been lit, but an attendant told me quietly, in Russian, that the church was closed to visitors. On seeing me, she ushered a dog outside, and then followed it out. I watched as she then sat on a three-legged stool while the dog, its eyes screwed up against the sun, tipped its head back to have the full length of its throat luxuriantly stroked.

I roamed on, until the backstreets led me into the city's park, which was cool, green and shady. Filled with the enjoyment of meandering through Gyumri's fruit-scented side streets, and glad to be out of the sun, I was drawn to an old-fashioned cash desk, painted with roses and falling leaves, its iron door shaded by a white lace curtain. The Ferris wheel in the park was not moving, but when I pointed at it, I was wordlessly sold a ticket anyway. I took the token and, in a hot dreamlike state, stepped into a gondola and sat down.

As I put my hands on the central pole to steady the swaying, three things happened: firstly, the fairground attendant began cranking a rusty lever which set the giant wheel in motion; secondly, I noticed that nobody else was on the ride, and possibly had not been for some time; and thirdly, as I shut my eyes, I felt my hands begin to sweat and shake. I smiled manically at my own stupidity and, as I opened my eyes ever so slightly to look down to the otherwise empty park, I saw a man filming me with his mobile phone. Was I the novelty, or the fairground ride? I glared down at him as the wheel rasped up and up towards the sun, which shone like a giant peach; then, with nothing around me except a foot platform and a couple of rusty bars, my eyelids did something they'd never done before, they began vibrating with fright. I clamped them shut again, my whole body rigid.

Soon, I realised that the babble of the city had completely fallen away, which meant I had reached the top. The only sounds were of my own breathing and the creaking of the rusty spokes. The ride paused. Waves of vertigo washed up and down my spine, flipping my stomach again and again. Hovering at the highest point, where each sick-inducing second felt like a minute, I remembered what day it was – and hoped, irrationally, that perhaps I would have the prayers of Gyumri's churches behind me.

I kept my quivering eyes firmly shut until the noise of the city slowly returned and I sensed I was back down. As the gondola came to a halt, I stepped off, wobbling, and thanked the attendant, who used his lever to shut down the ride again. At two hundred Armenian drams, or about fifty pence, this must be the ultimate in cheap thrills.

As soon as I was out of the park, head aching slightly from the combination of sun and stress, I shook out an Ararat Slim from its thin blue-and-white packet and lit it, hands trembling. I was eager for an Armenian brandy, though it was far too early, and the cafés were still busying themselves with morning coffees. Breathing heavily, I walked back through the Kumayri district, past the old beerhouse, which now has a quote from Gyumri's great satirist Poloz Mukuch (1881–1931) on the wall:

Neighbour: Brother Mukuch, when is a man full?
Poloz Mukuch: A rich man when he wants, a poor man when
he can.

On Shiraz Street, where the tumbledown buildings have portraits of pomegranates where windows once were, I sat on a bench and listened to Charles Aznavour's honeyed voice spilling out from a nearby café. Aznavour is heard everywhere in Armenia – in hotel lobbies, taxis and restaurants. Far more than Komitas. Christened Shahnour Aznavourian, he was born in Paris in 1924, his parents having escaped the Armenian genocide. 'I have that tragedy in my blood,'[17] he is quoted as saying. His song 'They Fell' is a reference to those who were forcibly marched into the desert. Regularly photographed through a blue cloud of cigar smoke, Azvanour died at the age of ninety-four, by which time he had a thousand songs to his name.

Today, Armenians still suffer the unbearable pain of 1915. The vivid memories of lived experience, passed down through the generations, are deeply internalised and keenly felt. The term 'genocide', typically attributed to the Polish-born Jewish lawyer Raphael Lemkin (1900–1959), stems from the atrocities committed against Armenians.[18]

Although Lemkin's mother and father were murdered in the gas chambers of Treblinka in 1943, many historians claim that the inspiration for the term came not from his own family catas-trophe but from much earlier, when he learned of the trial of the Armenian Soghomon Tehlirian, who had lost his entire family in the genocide. In March 1921, in Berlin's Charlottenburg dis-trict, Tehlirian had pulled out his Luger pistol and shot dead Mehmed Talaat, one of the Turkish pashas responsible for the Armenian massacres, with a single bullet. He was tried for murder, but was acquitted, and in later years worked as a postal clerk in America. When he died, he was buried in the Ararat Cemetery in Fresno, California. A popular revolutionary song in Armenia goes 'Let me tell you about the death of Talaat. Pour the wine, dear friend, pour the wine...'

Under the skin it all goes. Armenia's pain, and its beauty, etching itself into my heart and mind and marrow and soul. Its art, churches, food, mountains, ideas, music, humour, wine, flowers, hills. Its sheer survival.

~

At Gyumri's nineteenth-century Cathedral of the Holy Mother of God, also damaged in the earthquake, the Sunday service was busy. I crept in, heading up a narrow staircase to where the choir was singing. Below, the congregation crossed themselves in front of the altar. I stood mesmerised, listening and watching, tearful at the power of their devotion. Despite a diaspora in many coun-tries across the world, sadly many Armenian churches have been lost over time. In Moscow, the church on Armenia Lane was demolished in the 1930s; gone, too, is the little Armenian chapel in Penang, built in 1909.[19] Since that summer, I have sought out Armenian churches in Istanbul, Tbilisi, Rīga, London and Lviv, and there are many I would still like to see elsewhere, in Cairo, Isfahan and Paris.

Returning home, I unpacked dried apricots, apricots coated in chocolate and apricot-flavoured Ararat cognac, as well as my

treasured packets of Ararat Slims. The cross-stone artwork by
Ararat Sarkissian hangs in our bedroom, and I sometimes take it
down to look at it in detail, picking out the colours and textures.
But, more than anything that can be drunk, eaten or held in the
hand, I made a pact with myself not to ever let go of what I had
felt and learned in Armenia.

~

Evening in Edinburgh, and the wind whiffles in, flickering the
candle flames, making the kitchen wavy and saffron-hued, and
bringing with it pub voices and beer-soaked grunts. Soft Scots,
then Geordie, then stronger Glaswegian. Whisky words. The
clamour of children, the ruckus of thespians. Drunken pique
meets junkie howl. Then, the noise of plastic wheels rolling over
cobblestones: a suitcase. This is our collective soundtrack for
large parts of the year – especially the summer, when tourists
double the population – only leaving the city to us connoisseurs
of the cold in the frigid, wet, hard, long, festival-less months of
February and March, before they come fluttering back in again,
like migratory birds chasing the sun.

Darwin, oblivious to all, is snoring contentedly in the corner
of the kitchen, his smelly mohair blanket tucked underneath
him. I rub his velvety hound ears, still damp from trailing the
hills earlier, and give him a slice of salmon skin, oily and rust-
coloured, then I go back to drinking in the comforting scent of
the apricot biscuits baking in the oven – which, combined with
the evening hour, fills me with nostalgia. I think of the tenants,
owners and cooks who have stood right here in this kitchen
before me. Where did they go? What ghosts are here now?

I picture how others might once have lived here, in this kitchen, among the breadcrumbs, baskets of turnips, packets of
rice and pasta. How their words, dreams, hopes and promises,
their mealtimes, were once present within these walls. The

kitchen cannot exist without its past and, by inhabiting it now, I am experiencing a connection to those who came before me. They are part of the chemistry of the kitchen, its identity. And by acknowledging them, I am absorbed further into it.

By chance, as I began writing this book, a parcel arrived one Saturday morning. It was from our mortgage lender, and it contained historic ownership documents – a record of everyone who'd bought and sold our flat. The accompanying letter stated that, in our digital age, the paperwork no longer needed to be kept, so it had been posted out to us as the current owners. I gleaned a few clues, a few fickle threads, pulling out the musty papers of plans, agreements and legal letters. There were surprisingly few people who had been here, with several owners occupying the flat for decades. There was an army captain who'd moved back from his Berlin barracks, a woman who had left and moved to Seattle, another who went to Central Australia. Were they here by chance or by choice? Did they have a glow of home ownership, or did they feel entangled here?

Home is so thoroughly uncertain. So easily taken away. All it takes is the loss of a job, a divorce, an illness, a natural disaster, a war. A genocide. And in much the same way as the Armenians who were forced out of Ottoman Turkey lost their lives and their homes, Russia's bombardment of Ukraine has sent millions of Ukrainians fleeing theirs, just as countless Afghans, Syrians and Palestinians did before them, for so many years now. Families scattered in other towns and cities elsewhere, holding onto rusting keys, dreaming of return.

Apricot Cookies with Barberries

Outside of a few countries where apricots are exceptional straight off the tree (Armenia, Pakistan, Tajikistan and Afghanistan, for example), I prefer to buy good-quality dried ones to be soaked for hoşaf (see page 71) or baked into cookies for maximum sweetness. The barberries in these large buttery cookies – a nod to the Middle Eastern influences found in Armenian cooking – add a nice sour note.

MAKES 6 LARGE COOKIES

150g butter
80g honey
½ teaspoon orange
  blossom water
15 dried apricots, chopped
  into pea-sized pieces

20g barberries (or dried
  cranberries)
30g golden sultanas
100g ground almonds
150g plain flour
1 teaspoon baking powder

Melt the butter and honey in a saucepan and set aside to cool, then stir in the orange blossom water.

Next, soak the apricots, barberries and sultanas in boiling water for 10 minutes, then drain and pat dry.

In a large bowl, combine the ground almonds with the flour, baking powder and soaked fruit. Add the butter-honey mixture and mix to a soft dough.

Heat the oven to 180°C / 160°C fan / gas 4 and line a baking tray with baking parchment.

Divide the dough into six balls, then press flat into rounds about 12cm across. The dough will be very buttery, so use a spatula to transfer the rounds onto the baking tray, leaving a 2cm gap between them.

Bake, rotating the tray halfway through, for 15–20 minutes, until the cookies are golden at the edges and just set. Transfer to a wire rack to cool, then store in an airtight container.

CHAPTER TEN

Smashed

Not long ago, heartache gatecrashed the kitchen. Despite bountiful swaddling in my backpack, all three bowls, bartered for at a flea market in Uzbekistan, arrived broken. Rose medallion motifs shattered. Elegant rims, with gilding rubbed away over time, fractured. Red Cyrillic letters of factory marks scrambled and undecipherable. The pieces were beyond kintsugi, the art of 'golden joinery' that the Japanese are masters of; too small, even, for creating a 'one-of-a-kind mosaic', as websites suggested. Once so exquisite, the bowls ended up as little more than crude shards. I hung onto the fragments a while before guiltily tipping the lot away, cursing the airline, the baggage handlers and finally, myself.

These vintage bowls had almost made it into my luggage a dozen times before, but I had suppressed my cravings in antique shops and bazaars, worried not just about breaking them on the journey home, but also about disobeying the rules.

Before the death in 2016 of the authoritarian leader Islam Karimov, a man in power for almost thirty years, Uzbekistan was a place of bureaucratic paperwork, blatant corruption and busybody police. And often, it still is, especially for locals — though far less so for visitors, who nowadays are red-carpeted across borders, viewed as the latest lucrative spenders on the old Silk Road.

Karimov's Soviet-style economic policies made over-seas investors wary, and during those hard, paranoid years, Uzbekistan's development was almost suspended in time. Tourism was not officially encouraged, and foreigners were monitored closely. After registering with the migration police, I would carry with me, at all times, a slew of papers (chits from every hotel stay, plus photocopies of my visa, insurance papers, passport and onward flight tickets), ready for inspection by the police, who sometimes took visible satisfaction in wielding their powers. At land borders, and in airports, I was searched and questioned; laptop examined, medicines checked, all minor valuables declared. As for carrying back souvenirs that were not new – maybe an antique ikat robe, a vintage teapot or a Bukharan rug – the process was made difficult by ambiguous rules.

Collecting antiques is not something I do, but I craved those bowls. So cool and heavy in the hand, and pleasingly imperfect, dotted with tiny chips proving their history and usage. I desired them because I felt a connection to them, forceful as a magnetic pull. I had wanted them ever since I first saw them, in a secluded mountain valley in Central Asia, in the autumn of 2009.

~

Huddled outside a two-room wattle-and-daub house in the Pamir Mountains of Tajikistan were my new travel companions, two English men in their late twenties and their Tajik driver, Tatvik. Smoking cigarettes and talking about shutter speeds, they were filming the night sky, looking for Venus and hoping for shooting stars, while I was indoors organising my sleeping arrangements by candlelight. So isolated were we, and so cut off from skyglow – the glare created by homes, shops, streetlights and factories – that the light pollution was almost zero. To get here, I had hitched a ride with this trio of fellow travellers the previous day. I had met them, by chance, on the roadside in

Khorog, the small dusty capital of the region – a place enveloped by spires of mountains so steep and densely stacked that it is impossible to see beyond.

To reach Khorog, gateway to the High Pamirs, or bam-i-dunya ('roof of the world'), I had bought the last seat on a tiny Antonov An-28 aeroplane. After a screaming take-off from the Tajik capital, Dushanbe, we were in the air, with 7,000-metre-high mountains visible through every window. On clear days, the two-engine turboprop plane flies in between these peaks, rather than over them, meaning that at some points the wings were just a few metres away from sharp mountainsides. Nerves and excitement tingled in my stomach, and there was no talking in the aircraft as we all gazed in amazement at the clear views of vast turquoise lakes and the rolling brown hills below. A rumour still circulates that, in Soviet days, this was the only route for which Russia paid its pilots danger money and that, despite this, only one plane has ever crashed, not through pilot error but as a result of rocket fire from Afghanistan.

From Khorog, chain-smoking Tatvik, wearing his trade-mark leather cap, had taken to the wheel of an old UAZ-452 'Bukhanka' ('bread loaf') Russian jeep and had steered us along hairpin bends and past lakes to a tenuous-looking suspension bridge spanning the Bartang River, which was where the road ran out and hiking began. Once the four of us had crossed over, we climbed up and up, through tight groves of native silver birch trees, past a September drove of fat-tailed sheep, a whooping boy on a donkey and a flock of curly-horned mountain goats that scattered their peppercorn droppings as they went along. Finally, we arrived in a tiny hamlet ringed by lakes, further up the valley where one monumental mountain pushed and thrust into another. Swapping handfuls of Tajik somoni for tea and bread, we stayed at a couple of different houses. Den-like, and built from mud and clay, they had flat roofs where rounds of dung for fuel were drying out, along with apricot halves and animal skins.

In a Pamiri house, faith is woven into the fabric of the living areas. There are five sacred wooden pillars, reaching from the earthen floor to the ceiling. The first, my guidebook explained,[1] symbolises the Prophet Muhammed (and is where a baby's cradle would be placed); the second represents Ali, the prophet's son-in-law (a newly married couple will be seated at this pillar); the third symbolises Muhammed's daughter, Bibi Fatima (where the stove lives); and the fourth and fifth pillars are for brothers Hasan and Husayn, often marked by the horns of Marco Polo sheep. The valleys are too sparsely populated to warrant building mosques, so prayer happens indoors at home.

Comforts were the same in each low-ceilinged dwelling and, as we sat down, small adjustments were made by our elderly hosts — their sons working in Russia, their daughters and grandchildren tending to animals elsewhere — who shuffled in and out. The floor was quickly swept clean, cushions straightened, a bowl of biscuits put out, a candle lit. Warmness and softness. Rituals. A contrast to the stark wilderness outside. We travelers were so distant, so remote and removed from everything we knew; adrift from friends and family, news, responsibilities and urban concerns, little from our lives back home felt relevant, or even of interest.

Tatvik, unconvinced by star spotting, came inside, his gold teeth shining, and sat down to tell me about his life as a migrant worker in Russia, of the abuse he had suffered as a taxi driver but also of friends he had made in Moscow. We bumbled along in broken Russian and English, sharing a pot of green tea. Eventually he asked me if I would consider moving here, to one of the remotest mountain ranges on Earth, where it is -25°C in winter. 'Too cold for me, I think, Tatvik, beautiful as it is.' Through a gap in the door, I could see that a sheepdog had turned up. He was lying down, long as a lion, and pawing gently at the place where his ears once were – cut off as a precaution when he was a pup, so that wolves wouldn't have them.

On the padded sleeping platform by the dastarkhan (meal setting or tablecloth), where we had eaten our mutton dinner, I tucked my calves under my knees and pulled a thin floral-print duvet over my feet against the late afternoon chill. The sweat from the hike still clung to my clothes, and my lips were chapped from dehydration, high altitude and dust. Saffron-tinged light poured in through the traditional wooden skylight in the ceiling, which was made up of four concentric square layers that symbolised the four elements, with fire being the highest and therefore closest to the sun.[2] The bright rays shone straight onto a wooden shelf, where a single ox-blood bowl, a white rose medallion at its centre, glowed majestically.

The bowl instantly captivated me, drawing my eyes to it. How very curious, I thought, staring at it. I wondered if it was valued for its colours: the red indicative of fire and blood, the first things created by God; the white symbolising milk and light, the source of health and life.

But what really drew me to it, if I am honest, is how familiar it appeared. Slightly British, twee even, reminiscent of thatched-roof cottages and country fairs – but rather than finding a home in the Scottish Borders or the Cotswolds, here it was in the High Pamirs. At once irregular and extraneous, but then again not. Clearly treasured, the bowl suited the cosi-ness of the room, with its hearth and sheepskin rugs. And next to it were other precious things: a lute-like rubab with animal-gut strings; a spray of polyester roses; and a portrait of the Aga Khan, the current and forty-ninth hereditary Imam, who is revered as the noor ('light') of the Ismaili Muslims who live in these valleys.

Exhausted, we bedded down for the night, each taking a corner of the room, kept warm by the old-fangled stove.

~

After a breakfast of semolina and apricots, we trekked back down together and then I went on alone again. Stopping at the Saturday market in Khorog, where Afghan merchants cross the border bridge to trade once a week, I stayed overnight before setting off early the following morning, in a shared car, along the stomach-churning Pamir Highway to Dushanbe.

It was Ramadan, and our driver Zafar, gruff but quick to smile, drove for over fourteen hours without food or water, and not a single complaint was uttered – not at dangerous overtaking, car sickness, breakdowns or police checks, nor at the intense heat, dust and sheer drops. At one point, we were waved down by a shepherd, who offered us the chance to buy a freshly hunted marmot with Fanta-coloured fur and long, rat-like incisors; its fat, we were told, was good for easing aches and pains.

On the journey, I kept thinking about that eye-catching bowl, wondering where it had been made, if it was an heirloom, per-haps, or a wedding gift, or simply something charming picked up at a market. Then, at a roadside chaikhana (teahouse), our last rest stop, well into the evening hours, we ate rice soup, bread and honeyed melon – and drank tea, always tea, the timeless habit of it – as Zafar broke his fast. He only let his tiredness show as we neared the capital, all remaining energy visibly passing out of him. When we arrived in the city centre, he helped me with my backpack and polished a Pamiri apple on his shirt sleeve, until it shone like a mirror, then handed it to me as a parting gift.

After some downtime at Dushanbe's crumbling Hotel Vaksh – all dodgy plumbing (a hose, rather than a shower), cherry red-haired 'floor ladies' (who kept an eye on things) and dubious businessmen – I continued westwards. Bumping through Tajikistan's Fann Mountains, I somehow managed to suffer simultaneous bouts of car sickness and hunger.

Eventually, crossing the border into Uzbekistan, I travelled through Samarkand and on to holy Bukhara.

And it was there, at Akhbar House – one of the city's original guesthouses, built in the 1850s and formerly the home of a Jewish merchant – that I almost completely lost my composure when I caught sight of the dining room. The entire back wall was made up of small, elegant niches, and each one contained a single porcelain bowl, either white, blue or ox-blood. All had the same rose medallion motif in the centre – exactly the same design as the bowl I had admired in the tiny Pamiri house. Dozens of them. What *of* these bowls, I pondered as I ate my plov (the classic Uzbek rice dish) and tomato salad. Why are they so cherished? What do they say or represent? And how can everyday objects be so spectacular and emit such a powerful aura? An obsession started to stir.

~

What I have come to learn, over the years, is that these bowls are storytellers with seductive credentials, and that they tell more than one tale.

Firstly, they speak of Francis Gardner, who, in the eighteenth century, founded one of Russia's most successful porcelain factories. Gardner was probably born in Staffordshire, with ancestors in Aberdeen, but little is known about his background because paperwork offering clues to the family history was burned for fuel during the winter of 1925 at a country estate that had belonged to his relatives before it was seized by the Soviets for use as an orphanage.[3]

A seldom-seen memoir, occasionally referred to by ceramic historians and allegedly written by his grandsons in 1817, details how he was given special permissions and privileges to open his factory in the 1760s as a result of the earlier reforms of Peter the Great (1672–1725), who desired such things for Russia.

Gardner set off, papers in hand, to search for raw materials, finding resources of precious kaolin, the clay needed to make porcelain, in Chernihiv, Ukraine. His main challenge early on was securing workers, as foreigners were not allowed to employ serfs, but eventually he took on staff belonging to the family he had bought his estate from in Verbilki, north of Moscow.

Meissen porcelain from Saxony inspired the ceramists to create what came to be known as 'the Gardner rose', a design both British and Germanic-looking. When, in 1772, Catherine the Great (1729–1796) was gifted a porcelain dinner service from Berlin, she wanted something similar to be made within Russia, and it was Gardner's factory she commissioned to make porcelain tableware for the Winter Palace, a contract that surely proved the factory's success and cemented its reputation. Later, Nicholas I (1796–1855) put these original pieces into the Hermitage, in St Petersburg, where they were held until the Soviets sold them off, scattering them among collectors.[4]

After Gardner's death, in 1797, his family business began winning medals at trade exhibitions in Russia, and by the mid-1850s their porcelain was in demand throughout the Russian Empire. For the next fifty years, mass-produced bowls, teapots and cups aimed at the Central Asian market flooded the bazaars of cities such as Bukhara and Samarkand. This was bolstered by the sale of the factory, in 1890, to Matvei Sidorovich Kuznetsov, a shrewd businessman specialising in porcelain. He was also keen on producing designs with motifs popular in Silk Road cities and oasis towns, and soon affordable imitations of the Gardner-designed bowls, plates, teapots and pialas (handle-less teacups) were being produced. Seen as portable things of beauty, they were collected and treasured throughout Central Asia, and were often handed down as heirlooms. To protect the bowls and cups during their transport by horse and camel, intricately carved wooden and leather containers were fashioned, which were then put inside ornamental embroidered saddlebags. Carried in this way by nomads, the tableware travelled further and further afield, spreading throughout the region, into inns, teahouses, yurts, palaces and kitchens.

Harriet Sandys, a textile dealer who worked extensively in Pakistan and Afghanistan in the 1980s, explained in her memoir, *Beyond that Last Blue Mountain*, how the porcelain migrated with its owners, depending on the upheavals of war and conflict: 'When Uzbeks and Turkmen fled across the Amu Darya River to Afghanistan in the 1920s to escape a guerrilla uprising against Soviet repression, they brought their Gardner porcelain with them...'[5] As Sandys noted elsewhere, travellers on the hippy trail, passing through Afghanistan in the 1960s, might well have haggled for a kilim in Kabul over tea served in a Gardner piala a hundred years old.

Later, these valued bowls, given depth and meaning by the multiple hands that had held them, again moved en masse when the Soviets invaded Afghanistan in 1979. Millions of Afghan refugees crossed into Pakistan, selling their Gardner-ware in markets there. Sandys describes shopping in Quetta for antique saddlebags and cooling off in a chaikhana where tea was served in Gardner teapots and cups: 'The pieces were much cherished as status symbols, so much so that, if one was cracked or damaged, it was carefully and meticulously repaired with metal rivets.'[6]

Since my first sighting of Gardner-style crockery, I have seen it in every Central Asian country I have been to, everywhere from mountain homesteads to city emporiums. Bowls tend to be displayed as ornaments in teahouses and homes, but sometimes, out on the steppes or in other remote places, they are casually used, prey to wear and tear; form and function, bound up with tradition but part of normal life.

~

Now, in my fridge, there are two Gardner-esque bowls that did make it home safely. For twenty-four hours, each one has been sitting in the cold, on a shelf below a tightly bundled muslin bag of full-fat yoghurt seasoned with salt. Their job is to collect the whey as it slowly drains out of the yoghurt, leaving me with two bags of suzma, a yoghurt-cheese eaten in Central Asia, ready to be decanted into the bowls flavoured with chopped dill and crushed garlic.

I found these bowls, as well as a matching undersized teapot and piala, a year after the initial three bowls had arrived home broken, not so far from where I had first seen such things, in the ancient city of Khujand, in northern Tajikistan. I had negotiated a price, good-naturedly, in an unassuming antique shop and then had put them into my hand luggage, prepared for questions at Dushanbe airport (though there were none) – and, via many stops back to Edinburgh, I had carefully cradled them on the journey home, feeling this time that they were imbued with fortune and luck. Like the first set, I could tell they were not very old, and had probably come from an imitation factory. During the many years of production of Gardner-style crockery, the porcelain mark changed design several times, making it difficult for amateurs to age it precisely. But pleasingly, the bowls are very similar to the smashed ones: white, with pink rose-like medallions. And what matters to me is that they are here now.

The bowls are not treasured for their value, nor especially for their aesthetics. They are held dear because they are evocative, and because they forge a connection from Britain, where I was born and where Gardner came from, to Central Asia, a part of the world that has so influenced my life. And they are precious, too, because I saw such bowls during that first ever trip to the region – a journey which also happened to produce my first ever feature, sent to a newspaper editor from an internet café in Samarkand. Just as effectively as flavour, recipes and tastes, these bowls bring forth memories and feelings, drawing a link from my kitchen table back to Central Asia. Closing the distance between here, and there.

I worry sometimes about having removed these vintage bowls from their cultural context, and I wonder if it was crass of me to have done so; if, perhaps, in taking them from their homeland, something has been lost along the way. I think about whether they were really mine to take, even if they were for sale, and I consider how they might have been treated differently in other hands. Would they be used for porridge or soup or suzma, as I use mine? Or might they have been put on display? Am I the first to take them out of a family tree, or have they been passed around? What hints and signs might there be in the chips on their undersides?

But if such artefacts are cherished and made useful, as intended by their maker, rather than languishing on a shop shelf, or in a cellar, does that make their purchase more accept-able? These bowls, imbued with style and sense of place, pose so many questions. And how simply and remarkably they come alive in doing so.

I am glad that they are now, once again, at a table and in a kitchen. And I am aware that I have a responsibility to them. I hope that the more I use them over the years – eating from them and then washing them carefully by hand – the more they will become mine, but I also acknowledge that I will only ever understand a measure of their whole narrative.

~

Kitchens need a few well-worn, and well-used, things in their drawers and cupboards: objects suffused with nostalgia, a feeling not unlike homesickness, that have settled in and gained a hold. Tactile items with history in their grain or fibre, able to facilitate a route back to other people or other times; kept at hand over many years, and carrying the yesterdays of a place or a person that is loved. This might come down to your mother's mixing bowl or your grandmother's rolling pin, or perhaps a misshapen wooden spoon cherished for the memories it holds. Biographical, and therefore irreplaceable. To use such items is an act of remembrance.

Then there is the question of heirlooms. What if, like me, you do not have a personal cache of collectibles that has been passed down? What if everything has been thrown away, or lost? Might you, as I did, start accruing your own collection? Could you begin gathering meaningful things as an adult, with the wish that one day they would be passed on to someone who will care about them as you do, maybe even more so? I think so. I think you absolutely can.

These bowls, and the teapot and piala, are my treasured things, my true valuables. By bringing something of the chaikhana, the bazaar and the dastarkhan – places where the everlasting habit of pausing for tea plays out – to my Edinburgh kitchen, they help to ease my restlessness, reminding me that Central Asia will always be there. Now that they have become part of my own life story, I trust that, somehow, they'll be valued after I have gone.

~

Thinking about the smashed bowls and their replacements, these beloved kitchen companions, provides a momentary diversion from my primary anguish. But, no longer able to hold it at bay, I let it all come down. Tears fall fat and fast onto the table. Darwin is no longer here. Epilepsy has taken him.

After a string of dangerously long seizures, we tried an emergency drug treatment recommended by a canine neurologist only a month ago, but all it did was make him madly disorientated for a day and a half, frenziedly barking into the night. Before dawn, following two more seizures, there was a couple of hours of worn-out calm. I lay down with him on a rug in the sitting room, the curve of his back tightly tucked into my stomach. I stroked his paws, the softness behind his silky ears. I sang the songs that I had made up for him over the eight years we had been together, and I read him a Mary Oliver poem. The damage was there to see. He seemed already gone, utterly exhausted. As it got light outside, we lay still, gazing out of the window together, and I watched his eyes, soft and no longer scared, following the morning birds taking flight in the garden — free and alive, the day theirs.

With Darwin's epilepsy as drug-resistant as it was — and always had been, ever since the fits began when he was a puppy — we knew we had come to the end. There were no further treatments or pills or dosages to try, and the seizures, occasionally coming in clusters now, were taking everything out of him. It was no longer fair to carry on. The veterinary clinic was called, and we were told to bring him into the surgery before they opened for the day. We didn't know when we moved into our flat, the three of us, just before he was diagnosed, how much we would be in their consulting rooms over the years, or how practical it was to have them so nearby. James carried him slowly down the road; I followed, tears rolling off my cheeks, my whole body freezing cold, my heart racing. No choice, we knew. And Darwin, tranquil at last, seemed to know too.

It was a Saturday and the vet was not our usual one. She was young, and we had not met before, but her empathy and care couldn't have been greater. I trusted her immediately, and I kept thinking she looked like a hill walker, someone I would like, and would relate to; someone I could have a beer in the pub with. I clearly remember the brand of running shoes she wore, the length of her blonde hair, her skin, her nails, how she stood, almost every word she spoke. Details noted with journalistic eyes and ears because the moment was so critical. After a discussion, she then said the most humane and brave thing she could say, as I cried into Darwin's fur. 'If he was my dog, I would make the decision now...' We nodded, silently.

As he lay on the consulting table, I fed him the last two of the sardine biscuits I had recently baked for him, and then the needle went in. 'Oh, matey boy, matey boy, good boy...' said the vet in her gentle northern English accent, ever so quietly. Unusually, there was no noise, or even a flinch, from Darwin.

Weeping goodbye, I kept my hand on his chest until he took his last breath. The pain – a longing ache of sadness, mixed with disbelief and the sharpness of shock – hit my face, heart and stomach, and it stayed for days. Then weeks. Then months. It is still here as I write this; intensely so. And it will probably be here when you read this, too. On that day, James was covering the news desk from his home office and, as he filed urgent stories on Russia's latest atrocities against Ukraine, I stared into nothingness all afternoon. Sometimes we held hands.

Our lives are emptier now, the flat emptier still. And the kitchen is a different place, too. It was Darwin at my feet that so often made it. I know that now. But maybe more than ever, it is the kitchen – the steady, stable, unchanging kitchen – that I look to, because he is still here. And he always will be. His doughnut bed remains in the corner, and I say goodnight to him every evening before I go to sleep, wherever I am in the world. 'There is no love sincerer than the love of food,'[7] wrote George Bernard Shaw. Yes – except, perhaps, for the love of a dog.

Teahouse Brittle with Nuts and Cherries

One of my earliest memories of travelling in Uzbekistan was arriving at the Silk Road teahouse in Bukhara. Tired from the journey, I collapsed onto a chair and ordered a pot of green tea and a plate of sweets, which I recall were sugared almonds and sesame brittle. The crockery there was the popular navy-and-white 'cotton' design, but it is possible even today to stumble upon a traditional chaikhana where Gardner-esque teapots and pialas are still in use, though they are becoming increasingly rare. This brittle includes glacé cherries, which add some nice chewiness and colour, and are a nod to Central Asia's flavourful summertime cherries. Nutty brittle also makes for a great hill-walking snack – but wherever you choose to eat it, do be careful with your teeth as it is extremely sticky, chewy and hard, all at once.

MAKES 15–20 SQUARES

180g golden caster sugar
4 tablespoons honey
220g mixed sesame seeds, cashews and blanched hazelnuts (nuts roughly chopped)

30g butter
50g glacé cherries, chopped
1 teaspoon bicarbonate of soda

Before you start, make sure you have all your ingredients to hand, and your nuts and cherries chopped.

Line a baking tray with baking parchment.

Put the sugar and honey into a small pan over a medium-low heat and add 80ml of water. Do not stir, but keep an eye on it until the sugar has melted.

Turn the heat up to high and add the seeds and nuts – it is vital to keep stirring constantly now, while the sugar caramelises to a lovely dark golden colour. This can take up to 20 minutes, and it is important to let the mixture thicken and reduce down, otherwise the brittle won't set.

Remove from the heat and stir in the butter, then the cherries. Finally, stir in the bicarbonate of soda and mix thoroughly.

Carefully pour the mixture onto the lined baking tray. You want the mixture to be about 2cm deep: if necessary, make a border fence with the parchment by folding it up at the edges to stop it spreading. Leave to cool completely.

When entirely cool, turn out the brittle onto a chopping board and cut into neat squares. Serve, then keep whatever is left in an airtight container – it should be good for a couple of months.

CHAPTER ELEVEN

Clover Dumplings

Wrung out as rags, but safely back. Battered by strong winds, monsoon-like rain and the emotional intensity of our first hill walk without Darwin. Thirty miles by foot in the Highlands, not far from Loch Ness, over two days. *To heal* being the purpose of the excursion.

James and I had begun by climbing up into thick, low-hanging clouds, our foggy headspace matching the hampered outlook. Then, tugged onwards simply by the prospect of what lay beyond, we went striding across the sodden tops for several hours, until the weather eventually cleared to reveal theatrically sunlit hills that stretched on for miles and miles. The entire way, fair or not, we were accompanied by the primordial roar of stags in their autumn rut ricocheting around the valleys, their magnificent heads silhouetted above the sharp ridgelines where they stood on high. Them watching us, us watching them.

Walking is a lifeline, medication against bad thoughts. And the recipe for this cure is easy: lace up boots, establish a steady rhythm and cover some miles; remain open to the possibility of transformation; expel energy and keep on going – until, with each tendon doing its duty, and with new eyes, you start to feel a sense of being reborn.

Grief, though, grief is a tightrope. Each new day bringing with it a series of faltering attempts to gain toeholds of relief from its torment. The draining inevitability of falling off, again and again.

I stand up and open the window an inch, and Edinburgh's familiar malty-brewery breeze drifts in, along with faint wood-smoke — the scent of autumn coming. Apart from the low thrum of traffic, the streets are noiseless. A streetlamp comes on high above the flagstone courtyard and the candle flame sways, molten wax dripping down deeper into its buttery cleft. Giving in to a craving for hot bitter coffee, I fill the kettle and, once it has clicked off, I splash steaming water into the cafetiere and onto Italian ground coffee tipped straight from the packet. My tiredness is such that it takes effort to push the plunger down through the foggy glass cylinder smudged with fingerprints. Coffee will not interrupt sleep; it rarely does. Leaving the milk out for a second cup, I slump back down, not quite ready to go upstairs to bed, where James is already resting.

Feet and legs wise to the long miles clocked up, I trace a line through a thin film of dust on the dark oak of the kitchen table and try to fathom how I am feeling. Usually, I am happiest when traversing Scotland's uplands on foot, and the satisfaction that comes afterwards typically lingers on for days — but my heartsick pain is real and strong, and the silence of the room highlights, in neon, the lack of Darwin. Of him animating the kitchen, filling it. Scenting every detail, eager-eyed. Sometimes resigned, some-times impatient, always devoted. What I feel is a deep mournful-ness, paired with physical exhaustion. And this has resulted in a very specific and profound fatigue.

The candle flame pools golden onto the table, and I try to lean into the familiar feeling of gratitude and calmness that the kit-chen offers. This room that always waits for me, the place where each path begins and ends. This corner of the world, filled with a multitude of possibilities. And I find that its serenity does help, even now. Warmth is always present here, even during a storm.

~

Now, the coffee is cold, and the candle has burned down, its flame gone. Soon, I will go upstairs and rest. Soon, I must. Soon, I will be dead to the world for eight hours or more, putting a final full stop to our rambling adventure. I put the cafetiere in the sink and fill it with hot soapy water before closing the window, which has begun rattling with the wind. Switching off the light, I feel more tired than I have ever felt before. My skeleton knows that I am home now, and my bones sense that sleep is coming.

Putting the milk back in the fridge, a postcard catches my eye and I pull it from the fridge door. With a yurt and laughing children on the front, it stands out because it marks an anniversary. Two years ago, almost exactly: October 2020, a time spent picking up stories in Bishkek, capital of Kyrgyzstan, trying to improve my childlike Russian and then switching, briefly, to the role of news reporter when a violent crisis erupted. Slowly, I read my handwriting on the back of the card, describing to James the sun-soaked autumn parks and the pain of my early-morning lessons. It was written and mailed, I note, just before the trouble started.

Before I go upstairs, I decide that tomorrow, as a distraction from the grief, the kitchen and I will lower the drawbridge between Bishkek and here. We will return to Central Asia, together. My hope is that by doing so, by recalling a time of such potent stimulation, and by cooking what I ate there, I will ease my woes a little.

~

Freshly shot woodcock and pheasant, and baskets of blackberries and quince, are centre stage at the farmers' market close to my flat – proof that the season of game and full ripening has come, and a reminder that we are marching towards the clocks going

193

back. From the stallholders I have bought duck breasts, onions and carrots, ready for making a filling and moreish Central Asian plov. Perfect for autumn.

With the duck in the oven, I am now deaf to the world – with hands on duty, dicing onions, then peeling a handful of yellow carrots and chopping them into neat matchsticks until they pile up in a small golden haystack. Running a knife through a block of butter, I slide the fat from the blade into a heavy-bottomed casserole, adding a little rapeseed oil, and when it's all foaming nicely, I tip in the vegetables to caramelise. The rice goes in next, grains evened out with the back of a spoon, then a scattering of sour barberries and salt, and water to just cover the lot. First, a boil, then a simmer.

All that is needed now is for the clock to tick down, so I wait by the stove for as long as it takes me to drain a glass of wine. And then, with a pleasant freewheeling of the mind, I start to remember.

~

'You take delight not in a city's seven or seventy wonders, but in the answer it gives to a question of yours,'[1] wrote Italo Calvino in *Invisible Cities*. The answer, the guidance, I was hoping for in Bishkek, was for meaningful headway to be made with my Russian comprehension (Russian still being the language of the cities throughout Central Asia, though less so in villages).

A Kyrgyz friend had connected me with a teacher named Jarkyn, an acclaimed tutor of Russian at Bishkek's American University, who had begun her teaching career when Kyrgyzstan was part of the Soviet Union. During our introductory video-phone call, she apologised for her poor English – which was, in fact, excellent – and she added, with some pride, that she had privately tutored diplomats and employees of NASA. I liked her instantly and so, in September 2020, between the spring and autumn lockdowns in the UK, I called the Kyrgyz Embassy in London to check if it was reasonable and realistic to go. For months, the pandemic had separated me from Central Asia, the focus of my work and research, but I was still cautious about travelling. The official I spoke to assured me that it was ok to go, that the borders were open, and with that I booked a flight with no return date for flexibility. A tourist visa would give me sixty days – a good amount of time for language immersion.

My plan felt like a way of being present in the world again, after being apart from others for so long. A teacher, a timetable, a clean notebook; the satisfaction of absorption. I looked forward to slipping into a way of existing between different identities, places and languages. What I got, however, was something quite different.

~

My top-floor apartment, just off Pushkin Street, belonged to a solid three-storey block built for academics that was sandwiched between a stolovaya (canteen) and a school playground. The apartment had two rooms, each with a balcony (but both too crumbling to stand on), plus a cupboard-sized shower room. The bedroom overlooked a wide square dominated by the modernist concrete Philharmonic Hall, flanked by fountains and a statue of Manas, legendary hero of the Kyrgyz people, on horseback. The sitting room, above a tree-filled courtyard, got the afternoon light in autumn, and rays of sunshine would freely dance through the gauzy polyester curtains, fizzy and golden, washing onto the green velour three-piece suite. The kitchen, stocked with two saucepans, a frying pan and a set of shot glasses with a full carafe of vodka, was a dog-leg corner of this same room, with an island and two high faux-leather stools. And it was there that I would sit, reading and studying, while below in the courtyard a conspiratorial cluster of cats and their mewling kittens provided constant distraction. The shared stairway, perfumed with stale cigarette smoke, had walls painted a sallow mint-green colour – but only, in typical Soviet-era fashion, to hip height – and on every windowsill stood several wilting plants housed in old enamel cooking pots.

On my first day, unpacked and hungry, I edged down a badly lit unsealed road to a nearby Georgian restaurant that I had been to once before. The dining room, with blood-red and black Caucasian-style rugs on the floor, was busy with couples seated beneath large silk lampshades heavy with tassels. I ordered a glass of Georgian Saperavi wine and a Greek salad (ubiquitous in Central Asia) and, while waiting, devoured a plate of hefty khinkali dumplings, happily sucking the steaming-hot mushrooms and broth from each doughy pouch. I got used to listening and speaking a little Russian again, and, having ignored what I took to be glances of sympathy for my solo dining, walked back, nervous of potholes and cars driving too fast, too close, their headlights flashing.

Back on Pushkin Street, I punched in the four-digit code to the gate, pushed open the barrier and went crunching over the leaves in the courtyard. Not able to see even my feet in the dark, I had taken no more than twenty steps when a ferocious barking ripped through the night, followed by the sound of paws hitting the ground at speed. Then, with the woofing reaching a crescendo, it suddenly stopped. It stopped because the dog, which I could not see, had sunk its teeth into my leg, above my left ankle, before racing off again into the blackness. I had seen neither fur nor fang and had no idea of the dog's size or breed. Maybe it was a frustrated stray that had got trapped in the courtyard with the cats, I thought, as I sped, heartbeat racing, to my block, where I hastily pressed the fob onto the keypad. With the stairwell door shut behind me, I tentatively felt downwards: my trouser leg was torn, and I could feel wetness but could not tell if it was slobber or blood as the lights did not work. Gripping the wooden handrail, I inched up the concrete steps. Once I was safely upstairs in my apartment, I undressed. I could see tooth marks, but no blood. I shelved fears of rabies – unlikely with city dogs – and contacted the landlady. 'Oh, that's Jenny, she doesn't like strangers. I'm sorry, you just need to meet her.' I was given the number of her owner's apartment and said I would go over. Jenny, I thought. What a strange name for a canine assailant.

~

Quickly, I fell into a rhythm. Lying in bed at night, I would single out the city's night-time noises: drag-racing cars ripping up the main street, fireworks crackling somewhere to the west, students talking on benches below my bedroom window, the faint echo of a train whistling and, cartoon-like, a drunk falling over and swearing. I was soothed by picturing the scene out-side: the stained glass of the Philharmonic Hall, with its nomadic motifs – a horse, a goat, a ram – glowing like gems, the stout newspaper kiosk, the underpass where a fortune teller with gold teeth sometimes laid out her cards next to a pair of flask-wielding tea sellers who seemed to know everyone. The statue of Manas on horseback, shining bronze in the moonlight. The snowy Ala-Too Mountains, just there, just out of reach. All taken together, I thought it was undoubtedly the finest urban view in Central Asia. Every night, I would close the heavy maroon curtains, pic-turing it all, and listening carefully, completely still, until sleep wrapped me up.

In the mornings, I would pull the curtains back and watch as the wind shook golden leaves from the giant oak tree by my bedroom balcony, taking down acorns, too, loud as hailstones. With a mug of bitter black tea, I would make porridge with dried Kyrgyz apricots and mountain honey, while steeling myself for my lessons – which, taking place in the apartment, started before most offices opened. After lessons, shopping meant a trip to the sprawling and dusty Osh Bazaar, a mile away, to search for imported lemons from Tashkent, thin-skinned and heavy with juice, pomegranates, small knobbly cucumbers and yellow courgettes. Sometimes, I would go further, to Alameddin Bazaar, in the east of the city, where traders hung slabs of horse meat, big as car doors, above bruised-looking sheep's heads. And there, behind the butchers, I would buy tubs of sour cream, bottles of foamy kefir and nubbly tvorog (dry, sweet-ish cottage cheese) from Bishkek's chatty vendors, who bring the magic of the mountains to the city. The journey was always worthwhile, because Kyrgyzstan's rich pasturelands produce the purest milk imaginable.

One afternoon, carrying home a large bottle of homemade ryazhenka (similar to kefir, but with a sweet fudge-like flavour from milk that has been cooked at a low temperature), I met Jenny the dog. Armed with a packet of kibble, I knocked on my neighbour's door, as my landlady had advised, and out Jenny trotted, tail spinning. A small, fluffy black mongrel, in daylight she immediately, and deferentially, rolled onto her back for a belly rub.

Sometimes, a desire for imported wine sent me to the gourmet supermarket, 'Frunze', with its uniformed staff, air-conditioning and counters of ready-made lunches. Despite modern appearances, its name hints at Bishkek's past. From 1926 until 1991, Bishkek was called Frunze, after the moustachioed, and famously cruel, Bolshevik leader Mikhail Vasilyevich Frunze (1885–1925). Born in modern-day Kyrgyzstan, he doggedly lives on in a myriad of ways. Tucked behind Bishkek's Oak Park, its weeping willows glorious in autumn, there is Frunze the restaurant, with its trad-Russian menu offering herring, caviar and buckwheat; then there is Frunze Street and the Frunze Museum, built where his childhood cottage once stood. While many of

Central Asia's cities, in a surge of nation-building, have erased their Soviet pasts – renaming streets, razing buildings and removing monuments – Bishkek has, so far, been slower to join in. The old Lenin statue still stands in a prominent city-centre position, though it has been moved around. Not until the Soviet Union fell was the city's name changed to the more wholesome Bishkek, based on the name for a wooden paddle used to churn vitamin-rich mare's milk.

Bishkek is not always an easy city to live in. Fumes from old imported German cars, often with a million miles on the clock, belch out benzine, which mixes with smog from coal factories to create pollution so toxic that the city is almost unlivable in winter. There is crushing poverty, an active criminal under-world and political corruption, all of which corrodes dreams and ambitions. But the population is proud and protective of their city: a place of leafy sculpture parks, art galleries filled with embroidery and felt rugs, welcoming cafés and, in autumn, a sky that is almost always electric blue. And, it is somewhere that compels me. Each time I return, it unfurls a little more, teaching me new things.

~

'But you need to go out and meet people. Come with me to the family dacha at the weekend. There will be a birthday party, and my son will drive us.' How could I refuse? Jarkyn, my teacher, rounded off her generous invitation with a bite of a biscuit and a motherly nod. Then she returned to the whiteboard set up in the sitting room and, with two claps of her hands, we were back to learning. Hunched over a mint-green notebook, I tried to keep up through hot stings of frustration. Our lessons had gone on for a fortnight now, most mornings, and sometimes lasting for three hours. At times I thought my eyes, or entire head, would explode from the concentration. Jarkyn rarely registered my squirming. Surely I couldn't be that weak – it was merely a lesson, her glances seemed to say. But while Russian was not new to me, I could barely keep up.

From the outset, Jarkyn had said, without malice: 'You have to be broken down, to remove barriers. That is how you learn.' If we got stuck, she would pause, unwrap one of her favourite sweets – named Vecher (Russian for 'evening') – then would explain again why clock and watch are the same thing. In a country where it is normal to speak three or four languages, learning in Bishkek was a humbling experience. I felt exposed and on the back foot with everyone I encountered.

On leaving that day, Jarkyn presented me with two fried flatbreads, made after her morning's Quranic prayers, she told me. What unexpected kindness. Greasy and puffy as doughnuts, I devoured them both out in the courtyard, in the watery sun-shine, the pain of the day's lessons evaporating with every bite, while Jenny rolled in the leaves (ignoring me now) and the courtyard cats sunned themselves in a fluffy cluster.

The next Saturday, as promised, Jarkyn's son drove us out of Bishkek and into the countryside, towards a sharp-toothed cluster of snowbound peaks and faraway hills, where we could see horsemen, small as mice, out herding cattle with their dogs. Horses have utterly shaped the Kyrgyz way of life. The year was once planned around their grazing, with people and horses migrating together along historic routes to pasture. 'How are your legs?' one herder might ask another, the sentiment being that if your legs are good to ride, then all is well. If a favourite horse died, nomads would mourn it as they would a family member. And while true nomads and herders have all but disappeared today, if you go to a yurt in the mountains, you will still be offered kumis (mildly alco-holic mare's milk) with the first handshake.

We arrived at Jarkyn's family dacha, glad to be out of the city. Residents of the tiny hamlet, bisected by a burbling stream, were busy preparing for their friend's party (Raya, owner of the best garden, was turning fifty) and a harvest competition. In gardens blooming with roses, chickens roamed and vegetable patches thrived.

The village was almost completely female and ethnically Russian – although Jarkyn's sister-in-law, Gulya, whose garden we visited first, was Uyghur. We drank tea and sipped Kyrgyz 'cognac' on the terrace of Gulya's outdoor summer kitchen as she finished making duck plov in a wide kazan cooking pot for lunch. People came and went.

In this enclave of well-manicured gardens and clean air, with tangled hops tumbling over fences, it was clear that the women, bolstered by the power of strong female friendships, could count on one another, and they revelled in their shared oasis. Their dachas were extremely well kept and ordered; some even had wooden banyas (saunas). Most of the women had families and apartments in Bishkek, they explained, but being in the countryside was infinitely preferable. As the afternoon went on, we stopped by to meet different villagers, sitting on verandas, drinking tea and beer. I began to think of this gregarious gang as 'The All-Female Bishkek Dacha Collective'.

At the birthday party, the women spoke freely of the deaths of their beloved dogs, and their husbands, flicking their streaked hair and brushing down their leather leggings with hands tipped by glittery nails. Nothing was said about the parliamentary elections about to take place the next day. Everyone, I was told, was thoroughly sick of politics. The birthday speeches for Raya, given by each person sitting at the round table and broken up by cigarette breaks, were fully Russian in style, meaning that each guest gave an address not unlike an all-in-one personality assessment, love letter and end-of-year school report. Jarkyn whispered translated snippets to me: 'I love you. I will always love you. You are honest. You are hard-working… You are caring. You are a strong woman... You are a creative person, a wonderful cook,' and so on. The birthday supper was generous, artfully prepared by Raya herself. There was plate after plate of novi salat (a 'new-style' chopped salad of pear, beetroot, walnuts), roe on triangles of buttered bread, 'herring under a fur coat' (dressed herring) and smoky shashlik grilled in the garden. Then tea and vodka ('for fighting off viruses'). The conversation moved seamlessly from the women's hair colourants to their children's vegetarianism, family trees and multiculturalism ('My grandchild has seven nationalities!', 'Mine has nine!') and petty corruption, specifically police stopping drivers late at night for bribes.

I felt privileged to have been invited. At almost midnight, Jarkyn, her son and I thanked the dacha ladies for their enormous hospitality. And as we drove back to the city centre, the harvest moon low, wide and radiant, I felt a budding sense of belonging.

~

After the following Monday's lessson, Jarkyn and I went to Cafe Faiza, close to my apartment, for laghman noodles, pumpkin and lamb manti dumplings, a disc of golden non bread from the tandyr, which we tore up and shared, and green tea. Uyghur-run, and with the atmosphere of a canteen, Faiza has been popular with Bishkekers for twenty-plus years, and I too had become a regular, tending to order the same dishes and always sitting at the same table. We talked about our lessons, how I had learned the Russian word for pomegranate, 'granat' (which also means hand grenade). As we paid, splitting the bill, Jarkyn pulled out a large plastic jar from her handbag. 'My homemade sea buckthorn jam, it is good for you.'

I spent the afternoon sitting on the sofa in the luminous autumn sunlight, balcony doors open, writing a short script for

BBC radio. I had put out bread on the balcony, and my eyes flitted between the laptop screen and the blue tits that hovered and pecked, competing with the more boisterous myna birds. Bishkek felt particularly gentle that day, its streets golden with fallen leaves, its sky deep blue, with clouds fluffy as lambs. The story I was writing was a pleasant one, too, about a master restorer of traditional Kyrgyz costumes who I had met in the suburb of Archa-Beshik, with my young local friend Maya. My mood was positive, matching that of the city – or so I thought.

Suddenly, my mobile phone began lighting up with messages, the first from an experienced journalist friend: 'Are you ready to witness a revolution?' (Revolutions are not uncommon in Bishkek.) Then another: 'I'd stay inside if I were you.' The results of the parliamentary elections had just been announced and people were angry at the flagrant high-level corruption, I was told. I shut my laptop, slid on my running shoes and grabbed my bag.

~

Dashing down busy Chuy Avenue, in the direction of Ala-Too Square – the centre of uprisings in 2005 and 2010 – I joined dozens of men marching purposefully in the same direction. Many were wearing traditional white felt Ak-kalpak hats, and some were carrying red Kyrgyz flags strung onto long wooden poles. At the square, under another giant statue of Manas, a couple of thousand men and women shouted and cheered, some using loudhailers, accusing parties loyal to president Sooronbay Jeenbekov of vote-buying and intimidation. The fact that only four parties out of sixteen had passed the 7 per cent threshold for entry into parliament – all but one with ties to Jeenbekov – infuriated people. Joblessness was soaring, due to the pandemic 'fanning the flames', said one man. It struck me that the square, wide and devoid of obstructions or greenery, could have been purpose-built for revolutions. Close by, police and security forces were gathering, while buses poured into the city, filled with tough-looking men from the provinces, ready to join in, ready to fight. It was time for me to go home.

I carried on writing my script into the early evening, then stepped out to a nearby Turkish café with its cheery cooks and glass counter filled with Adana and Urfa kebabs. As my bowl of lentil soup arrived, I noticed that the café was oddly empty. There were none of the usual extended families, with screaming babies in highchairs being fussed over by grandmas. The only other occupied table was taken by two men, solid as icebergs; both were hunched over their meat, hard at work on the skewers, chomping without talking, all presence and stern bravado. Local dignitaries or criminals? It was difficult to tell. They were served by the staff, who were clearly nervous and skittish as young gazelles. Burning my tongue on my Turkish tea, I paid with the correct money, putting a wad of grubby notes into the faux-leather bill wallet and handing it to the waitress. As soon as I made to leave, the men left too, and the restaurant closed early.

Outside, on Kyiv Street, the air felt ripe for trouble. It was not yet eight-thirty, but the night was already engulfing and black. All the surrounding streets were dead and empty, and the atmosphere had shifted noticeably. A collective citywide tension was rising like an ominous vapour, so thick it was almost chewable. I marched fast on the uneven, slippery, leaf-strewn pavement and, turning a corner, found myself face to face with a drunk man, swaying and likely slugged by cheap vodka, with one hand on the wall to steady himself. Our eyes met briefly, then I instinctively began running, as sirens started up a block away.

Jamming the key into the lock, I double-bolted my front door behind me, heart thumping in my ears. The sounds of fighting were now deafening: whistling, shouting, screaming, unexplained booms, sirens, car horns and screeching tyres. Kneeling in the dark bedroom, I held the heavy velour curtain open a little, just enough to see groups of men running through the square. The terror in the pit of my stomach rose, tightening my chest like smoke. Suddenly, I felt extremely alone. I stood glued to the bedroom-balcony window, half obscured by the giant oak – which I was now even more grateful for, viewing it as a shock absorber between me and the city. Phone messages came in quickly: 'Stay indoors,' 'Keep the lights off and the door locked,' 'Move away from the window in case of gunshots.' Under an almost-full moon, the sky above Ala-Too Square and the nearby government headquarters flashed time and time again with explosions. Below the balcony, a gang of protesters stopped and sipped beer from cans, their faces aglow from the mobile phones they were typing into; then they were off again, metal bars in their hands, running into the darkness. Social media filled me in on what I could hear but could not see – that, down the road, police and security forces were breaking up crowds with water cannons, stun grenades and tear gas. What was this exactly? A putsch? A coup? A revolution?

Hungrily, I fed myself grim images, one after another, of men lying dead on the street, or kicking down doors of apartment blocks, like mine, then forcing their way in to gain cover and safety. It was as if the city, and all of us in it, had collectively entered a twilight zone. The world felt degraded and deranged. My apartment was solid, with strong locks and a steel front door, but I was effectively shipwrecked in it, with no safe way out. As the hours pressed on, I realised there had not been a single noise in the stairwell. No neighbours moving about or chatting or panicking. Most likely they had all hunkered down, having been in this situation before. I wondered if Jarkyn was with her family, and if my friend Maya was with hers. Alone, I felt real fear, blood-deep and hot.

The news, as it started to come in, was stunning. By the early hours, President Jeenbekov had fled the premises of the government headquarters and protesters had taken it over. Footage online showed in detail what I could make out in the distance: flames licking the top floor while white papers fell like snow, thrown from the windows. Audacious and emboldened, roaming protesters had seized other key government buildings, including the mayoral office right by my apartment. Now, it was chaos. Nobody was in charge.

For the whole night, I was poised like a gun dog by the window, as stun grenades and sonic booms rocked the sky. Then, at 5 a.m., just as I lay down to rest, the BBC news desk got in touch and asked if I would do a live report.

~

When morning finally dawned, I had never been happier to see it. I opened the balcony door and the net curtains billowed in and out, like the lungs of the city itself. The sky, grey and threatening rain, looked aged. But it was quiet. I went outside. On the streets, people looked pallid, jittery and weary. Discarded shells were scattered about and the bins on Kyiv Street, used as shields against the police, were still smoking. Many windows had been smashed. Unrest was spreading throughout the country, and reports claimed that last night in Bishkek several hundred had been injured, with at least one dead. What momentous events were to come?

As I was out surveying the nearby streets, messages came in from Jarkyn, telling me that all the shops were shut, and would I like some groceries? Then another message, from Maya: 'Meet me by the Manas statue, let's go and see.' I returned home, did my BBC report, and then went back outside to find Maya, who was wearing her trademark bucket hat.

'I was worried you'd be hungry,' she said, handing me a giant box of pastries. It was cold and cloudy, the mountains almost invisible, and I shivered from tiredness and the chill, but I was warmed entirely by such thoughtfulness. As we walked towards Ala-Too Square, the centre of the violence, she shared her frustrations. 'These politicians have been in power too long, many since independence in 1991. They do nothing for the people. They change parties and their opinions like they change their shoes.'

At the square, two men in black leather jackets scrambled onto a burnt-out car to get a better view of the throng of demonstrators, still thousands-strong, who huddled around the statue of Manas in the crisp air. A song by Mirbek Atabekov, 'This World', played loudly from a car stereo, its lyrics including the words 'Let's be purposeful, let's be respectful of the will of the people.' In a plastic gazebo, volunteers handed out bread and tea to protesters, suggesting they were settling in.

For the next couple of days, Maya and I were inseparable. We ate together and drank coffee, in cafés and at her apartment, and we talked about the remarkable photographs emerging from inside the stormed government headquarters. They showed the late-night intruders casually pausing their anarchic takeover, not to smoke cigarettes or to swig vodka, but instead gathering together for a civilised-looking cup of tea. Some of Maya's friends, mostly young students, had joined non-violent civil patrols as defence volunteers – known as druzhinniki ('friends' in Russian) – with the aim of protecting the city against looters and maintaining public order.

In Bishkek, people have learned not to bank on the police or the government, but to rely on one another. Late at night, these young, unarmed students bravely stood guard outside malls and cultural centres. 'We are protecting our Bishkek,' they would say. Their meeting hubs were restaurants, where other citizens dropped off food, bread and styrofoam trays of plov. Meanwhile, as the clean-up of central Bishkek started, Kyrgyzstan's newly appointed prime minister, Sadyr Japarov, who was serving a prison sentence for kidnapping until he was sprung out by his supporters during the troubles, announced elections would be forthcoming.[2]

Eventually, the straggle of Western reporters (including James) who had arrived to cover the unrest departed for other stories, and I too left Bishkek not long after, assuring Jarkyn that I would be back. Just before I left, Maya messaged me, saying she wanted us to try something together: 'Clover dumplings, can you imagine?' I could, and yet I couldn't. She had called ahead, and the cook had told her that while clover was not in season, they had a frozen batch of dumplings they would happily serve us.

We took a taxi to the café, out by the Madina fabric bazaar, sat at a table next to some worn-out-looking police officers and ordered the dumplings. The filling tasted like spinach, and they were slightly bland, but my taste buds were jazzed up by the very idea of them, as well as the sharp black vinegar we dipped them into. Peculiar, but moreish. The surprise of the clover dumplings became a metaphor for that time in Bishkek, which had given me improved language skills, a temporary home, a reporter's role – and most importantly, perhaps, unexpected friendships with Maya and Jarkyn.

~

In Edinburgh, the streetlights have come on suddenly like stars. Moonlight is filtering through the arch of stone steps that leads down to our front door, and the plov is almost ready – a rich quintupling of layers, all lightly spiced with cumin seeds and cayenne pepper. First, glossy onions, caramelised at the bottom of the casserole, then yellow buttery carrot matchsticks; on top of that, sour barberries and a thick blanket of rice, salted just right, then a scattering of seared duck seasoned with a lot of black pepper. It smells rewardingly like the one Jarkyn's sister-in-law cooked at her dacha, though I haven't cooked it in the same way. And as I sit down to eat it, remembering Darwin and thinking of my adventures in Bishkek, I know my appetite will not fail me, and it doesn't. Somehow, it outpaces the grief. I dig in and feel better, here in the kitchen. This enclosed space, so quiet and dark, the opposite of the noisy, confusing world outside.

After dinner, sitting in the too-narrow rocking chair below the window that squeezes my hips, I rock slowly, gradually emptying a tumbler of whisky and ice. And, thinking back, I feel a sense of guarded hopefulness and happiness from the memories of that particular visit to Bishkek, which felt like an exchange. I paid with a little time, money and curiosity, and it paid me back with insights, learning and friendship; the generosity of the city, how it had trusted me to tell its story.

Duck and Barberry Plov

This is a particularly appealing dish for when the leaves start to fall. It is based on the aromatic plov that I ate in an autumnal dacha just outside Bishkek, cooked outside and served before the harvest moon lit up the night. The method, not remotely authentic, is the easiest way to make something similar indoors, in a home kitchen.

SERVES 4

1 teaspoon cumin seeds
2 duck breasts, about 260g
  in total
fine sea salt and freshly
  ground black pepper

knob of butter
2 tablespoons rapeseed oil
2 onions, cut into thin
  half-moons
2 cloves garlic, thinly sliced

4 carrots, yellow or orange,
    cut into thick matchsticks
¼ teaspoon cayenne pepper
250g basmati rice

handful of barberries (or
    dried cranberries)
sea salt flakes

Place a small frying pan over a medium heat and toast the cumin seeds for a few minutes, until they start to lightly colour and release their aroma. Remove the seeds and, using a mortar and pestle, crush them lightly, just to break them down, then set aside.

Pre-heat the oven to 200°C/180°C fan/gas 6 and line a baking tray with foil.

Score the skin of the duck breasts at 2cm intervals, then season with salt and pepper. Place the duck skin-side down in a cold non-stick frying pan, then turn the heat on to medium-high. Cook for 5 minutes, without stirring or moving the pan – you want the fat to be well rendered, and the skin golden and crispy. Turn the duck over and seal the meat for a minute or so. Transfer the duck breasts to the baking tray, placing them skin-side up, then finish cooking in the oven until well done, about 15 minutes. Set the duck breasts aside, along with any juices, wrapped tightly in foil to keep them warm.

Meanwhile, tip any fat from the frying pan into a large casserole or heavy-bottomed saucepan, ideally one with a lid (or have foil ready to cover). Add the butter and oil to the casserole, followed by the onions, garlic, carrots, crushed cumin seeds and a large pinch of salt. Cook over a medium heat, stirring regularly until the vegetables are soft and caramelised. Grind a generous amount (about half a teaspoon) of black pepper over it all, then stir in the cayenne. Tip in the rice, using the back of a spoon to even it out, then sprinkle over the barberries and a quarter of a teaspoon of fine salt.

Slowly pour in just enough water to cover the rice and vegetables, then put the lid on (or cover with foil) and bring to a boil. Turn down to a simmer and cook for 10–15 minutes, until the rice is almost cooked and all the water has been absorbed. Remove from the heat and leave to steam for 5 more minutes.

Slice the duck breasts into bite-sized pieces and scatter over the rice, then put the lid (or foil) back on and let it all warm together for a couple of minutes. Plate it up immediately onto a large platter for everyone to share, scattering over some salt flakes and plenty of black pepper.

CHAPTER TWELVE

Night Cooking

Night cooking, when the kitchen offers a particular sort of shelter, carries a rare appeal. I don't do it often, but when I do, it is baking that feels most right. Main lights off, shoulders relaxed, hands doing the work. Combining slender half-moons of Bramley apple with midnight-hued blueberries and stirring through lemon juice (which quickly finds a cut on my thumb), I am making fruit strudel.

A crackly nocturne plays from the kitchen radio, and the spotlights beneath the wall cupboards shine onto the worktop, making the fruit glitter as it is gradually coated in sugar. I tip out a tot of Jamaican rum from the bottle into the cap, then another, pouring them into the mixing bowl. These are movements practised over time, done almost hypnotically.

Sometimes, cooking belongs to the night. But night-time is not just for sweet midnight feasts and eerie melodies. It is a time for prayers, lullabies, insomnia, flickering neon signs, strange hotels, dragging hours, fraught vigils and whirring movies of the mind. Overnight journeys, real or imagined. And storytelling. A time to summon up the past, to cross over into other lands.

So, with this strudel, I am casting a line back to Lviv, the Ukrainian city I visited most recently. Profoundly bookish and intellectually lively, it is a city of half-remembered stories that has changed hands and names many times over the centuries, coming under the control of Austria-Hungary, Russia, Poland,

Germany and the Soviet Union. As historian Karl Schlögel once wrote, it is a place of 'washed-out borders'.[1]

Lviv, Lvov, Lwów, Lemberg. City of lions.

Its history lives on in its great cafés, some of the finest in Europe; in the glass domes of elegant buildings, their floor tiles as striking as the finest Portuguese ones; in the faded ghost signs on the front of shops; and in ancient wooden beams engraved with the six-petal rosettes said to be a 'thunder mark',[2] a sign of the Slavic pagan god Perun. Little signs, if you know where to look, that help you to hear the city speak of its past.

Today, for Lviv, there is a new timeline. Life before Russia's brutal warmongering – the annexation of Crimea in 2014 and the full-scale invasion of wider Ukraine eight years later – and after. Lviv, where the flame of Ukrainian culture burns bright, is now, as I write, a place of armed civilians, air raids and continuous war preparations. Located far out west, only fifty miles from the Polish border, as the invasion began it became a natural hub for the displaced. Millions of internal refugees arrived at the train station, the westernmost point of the country's rail network, and emergency shelters, with cots and kettles, sprang up in office blocks and theatres. Sandbags were stacked against cathedral windows and, on the outskirts of the city, barricades were constructed, and road signs obscured, to throw off the enemy. Though far from the heaviest fighting, missiles hit critical infrastructure, including electricity supplies, and an area near the airport, killing and injuring civilians. 'We have to be vigilant because the enemy is getting more and more atrocious,' Lviv's mayor, Andriy Sadovyi, was reported as saying.[3]

After months of relentless attacks, Ukrainians carry on. What choice do they have? Thousands of immense, and immensely creative, efforts are made daily, by those fighting, by those carrying on with their lives inside the country, and by the diaspora outside Ukraine's borders. In Lviv, territorial defence volunteers go out on patrol, searching for Russian spies, while the Pravda ('truth') brewery converts beer bottles into molotov cocktails.[4]

~

In mid-November 2021, three months before Russia's invasion, after celebrating my birthday in Istanbul, I flew to Lviv and took a custard-coloured trolleybus from the city's small airport. Although I knew something of Kyiv and southern Ukraine – especially Odesa, a city I had spent time in while researching stories for my book *Black Sea* – I had never been to the west of the country.

Stepping off the trolleybus, I followed my map until I reached the soaring statue of Polish poet Adam Mickiewicz, marking the southern end of Viennese-looking Svobody (Liberty) Avenue, Lviv's central promenade. Opposite the statue, the George Hotel was unmissable. Puddles reflected its declining but still stately façade back at me, the strips of peachy-pink paint peeling off its frontage like bark from a tree. Detached, the hotel stood magnificently alone, the liquid light of new rain making it dazzle. I nurtured a fascination for this historic hotel, which I had begun to think of as a metaphor for the city.

Booking in for a week, the price of my room, paid in hryvnya, felt like a steal. From the lobby, I walked up a splendid marble staircase, flanked by wrought-iron balusters, first to a landing with an arched Art Nouveau-style stained-glass window depicting a woman draped in an orange robe, then further up to my floor where, with a heavy brass key, I opened the double doors to my room. Watery light poured in from the tall balcony windows, spilling onto the unvarnished oak parquet flooring – which gave off the sort of warm, slightly dusty smell that only old, unchanged things do. It was oddly reassuring, reminding me of my kitchen back home, with its faint damp-leaves-and-woodsmoke scent.

Furnished with a large, polished mahogany dining table in the centre of the room, onto which I unpacked a bag of mandarins carried with me from Istanbul, there was also a vintage dressing table and a pair of scallop-backed velvet chairs. Not a single sound came from the corridor, which was empty, just like the downstairs restaurant and the lobby that danced only with dust motes. But inside the bedroom, I sensed ghosts. The balcony was where, between concerts, the composer Franz Liszt once posed, waving to his fans. Honoré de Balzac had stayed at the George, too, drinking French wine and playing cards, en route to his lover, the Polish countess Princess Evelyn Hanska.[5] Opposite, the Roshen chocolate shop sign glowed red. Owned by former Ukrainian president Petro Poroshenko, nicknamed the 'Chocolate King', it was busy with shoppers filing in and out with bulging carrier bags. But compared to Istanbul's insatiable and consumer-heavy street life, Lviv seemed muted, silent, delicate and restrained. Sleet nibbled at the traffic below, which rattled over the wet cobblestones.

Tired from the early start, I sloped into the king-size bed, which was wooden and shaped like a giant sleigh, sucking the single Roshen chocolate wafer that had been left on the pillow. I slept soundly, then bathed in the high-ceilinged bathroom, unrenovated in decades but white and spotless. Afterwards, I plugged in the pink hair dryer which, after a couple of minutes, lit up a fiery orange and began to smoke furiously; unplugging it sparked an immediate, but quickly rectified, power cut.

By the afternoon, the wintry rain had stopped, and I strode out along Svobody Avenue. The city streets, with their steeples and bistros, felt wistful. There was none of the threat or stress of bigger cities: no growling traffic, no crowded pavements; just one smashed-up, wild-haired drunk hollering and crashing his way past Viennese-style and Neo-Baroque buildings, all with fine sculptural detail. Every bookshop window displayed the work of the great science fiction writer Stanisław Lem, author of *Solaris*, who was born here in 1921.

Then, looking even more glorious than its printed image on the twenty hryvnya banknote, the opera house appeared, its front façade decorated with carved comedy and tragedy masks and Lviv's coat of arms with its golden lion. Completed at the end of the nineteenth century, it was the first building in Lviv to have electric lighting, and its opening-night performance was the premiere of *Janek*, an operatic tale of highland life in the Carpathian Mountains.

Looking up at the opera house, hefty with its Corinthian columns and loggia arches, the idea that a subterranean river flowed beneath it seemed preposterous. But it was down there, quietly, privately, pushing on. Once, men would boat along the Poltva River in the open air, straight through the city centre, shooting ducks, but the Austro-Hungarian authorities, fed up with the waterway's pollution, infestations of mosquitoes and general stench, had its bed gradually driven underground in the nineteenth century.[6] By the time of the Second World War, over a hundred kilometres of the river's course had been covered, but there were early challenges. Shortly after the opening of the opera house, in October 1900, the ground beneath it began to sink, the asphalt waterproofing started failing and fissures began to appear in the walls. Not long afterwards, the building's architect, Zygmunt Gorgolewski, died of aortic paralysis.[7]

During the military parades of the Soviet era, heavy articulated vehicles were not allowed to approach the opera house for fear of cracking the foundations. Back then, when the avenue was named Lenin Boulevard, there stood a relatively modest, fourteen-metre-tall statue to the Bolshevik leader. Later, when the figure was toppled from its red granite plinth, it was rumoured that it had been built on fragments of Jewish tombstones. So many Lenin statues started 'falling' across

Ukraine as the Soviet Union crumbled, hundreds and hundreds of them, that the phenomenon was given a name, Leninopad, a quip translated as 'Leninfall'.[8]

Today, it is said that the Poltva can sometimes be heard flowing from the orchestra pit of the opera house and that eels, almost blind but keenly nosed, glide along in the river's murky undulations.

I walked back down Svobody Avenue, heading for Lychakiv cemetery, where gravesites were reserved for society's greatest, now a place of pilgrimage for the curious. After detouring briefly to Tyktora Street to see an old dairy shop that still bore pre-war inscriptions in Yiddish, Polish and German, I stopped at Nalyvaika Street, where a Jewish mikveh (ritual bathhouse) once stood.[9] Lviv's manhole covers tell another story, leading as they do down to the sewer systems where dozens of Jews hid during the Second World War, sheltering from the Nazis. Those who revealed their whereabouts for money, or blackmailed those in hiding, were known as shmaltsovniks. I went on further, until I came to a gateway to the sprawling necropolis.

Despite it being a Saturday morning, the graveyard, filled with carved angels and creeping vines, was deserted. I took off in no particular direction, crunching along its well-kept pathways, which were heavy with the smell of rain on fallen leaves. Opened in 1786, Lychakiv spans 42 hectares and has, within its walls, tens of thousands of graves, 2,000 burial vaults, 500 sculptures and reliefs and several family chapels (including the Polish family of the doomed opera-house architect, Gorgolewski).[10] It is a cemetery of mixed cultures, reflecting the city's past, with gravestones marking the burial sites of Polish poets and Austrian governors, Armenian archbishops and Ukrainian singers. In the newest section, the polished black granite gravestones of Ukrainians who died defending Crimea in 2014 were surrounded by a sea of colour, made up of hundreds of lanterns, memorial candles, fresh bouquets of white lilies and potted chrysanthemums. From the top of a nearby slope, mass Soviet-era housing stretched out into the distance, wrapped in a light November mist.

Back towards the entrance, crows flapped their greasy-looking wings right above the grave of Ivan Franko (1856–1916), one of Ukraine's best-known writers, who was born not far from Lviv, near Drohobych. His grave is topped with a monumental cubist-style statue of a muscular, shirtless man lifting a pickaxe; he is stoic-faced, perhaps symbolising Franko's encouragement of Ukrainian solidarity, or his courage for writing in Ukrainian at a time when the intelligentsia wrote in Polish and German. Ivan Franko dined at the George Hotel's restaurant, and anniversary celebrations of his work have been held there too.

But it was another writer, born in the same region as Ivan Franko, that I thought of as I trudged back through Lviv's muted streets. Born into a family of Polish Jewish shopkeepers in 1892, Bruno Schulz spent almost his entire life in Drohobych, leaving in 1910 to study architecture in Lwów, but only staying for a year due to ill health. Sickly and unmarried, he wrote loosely biographical, intensely vivid short stories and sketched fanciful drawings, merging truth with myth in an attempt to transform his constrained world into a rich and symphonic place. Often compared to Franz Kafka, Schulz's work has been widely admired by other writers, including Philip Roth, Isaac Bashevis Singer and Cynthia Ozick.

His 1934 masterpiece, *Sklepy cynamonowe* (*The Cinnamon Shops*) was a triumph of the imagination, one where Schulz created a magically fluid world, in contrast to his own circumstances: 'I used to call them cinnamon shops because of the dark panelling of their walls. These truly noble shops, open late at night, have always been the objects of my ardent interest. Dimly lit, their dark and solemn interiors were redolent of the smell of paint, varnish, and incense; of the aroma of distant countries and rare commodities. You could find in them Bengal lights, magic boxes, the stamps of long-forgotten countries, Chinese decals, indigo, calaphony from Malabar, the eggs of exotic insects, parrots, toucans, live salamanders and basilisks, mandrake roots, mechanical toys from Nuremberg, homunculi in jars, microscopes, binoculars, and, most especially, strange and rare books, old folio volumes full of astonishing engravings and amazing stories.'[11]

In 1941, the Nazis brought to an end hundreds of years of Jewish life in Drohobych, and on 19 November 1942 an SS officer shot Bruno Schulz with a pistol. It remains unclear today where Schulz is buried; with no grave to visit, one of the finest writers of the twentieth century remains in the realms of imagination, even in death.

But there is something. As I was finishing this book, the Ukrainian poet Ilya Kaminsky uploaded a photograph to Twitter, on 2 December 2022, with these words: 'In the midst of war in Ukraine a monument to writer Bruno Schultz [sic] has just been erected this week.' The photograph shows the memorial, in Drohobych, in the snow. A framed mural propped behind a bench, depicting a man, hand on chest, hat on head, looking over rooftops, it appears to have been inspired by *Spotkanie* (*The Meeting*), one of the few oil paintings by Schulz.

~

That evening, the George Hotel's restaurant, despite its welcoming white tablecloths, remained largely unoccupied. Some guests, I was told, were at the attached 24-hour casino for slots and blackjack. In the tranquil room, I ordered a bowl of borsch and a plate of trout, and thought of the hotel's many incarnations over the years. In the 1790s, the site was occupied by an inn born from a restaurant called Under Three Hooks, which had been considered the best in all Galicia (a historical region that included Lviv and Kraków). Later, in 1811, it became Hotel de la Rus, in a new building, and the owners, the George Hoffman family, would put on firework displays for their guests, as well as concerts and carnivals in the gardens. In June 1905, en route to Vienna, the Shah of Iran, Mozaffar ad-Din Shah Qajar, block-booked rooms at the George for his entourage. Local news-paper journalists, covering his stay with interest, reported that the shah had been eager to try everything the restaurant had to offer, often ordering five times more than his fellow diners. The final bill for his stay was equivalent to the cost of a ten-room apartment, yet he managed to negotiate a discount before leaving on his private train.[12]

I rested well that night, in the coolness of the giant bed, wrapped in quietude. Before the current war, Lviv's population was on a par with that of Kraków, yet it drew only a fraction of the tourists, helping it to maintain a hushed atmosphere. And stillness seemed central to its psychology now, too, with the silence of the city in early winter surely adding to the sense of nostalgia.

~

At breakfast the following morning, a man in a grey Adidas tracksuit took a seat at the piano and, with long graceful fingers, began playing Chopin. As I listened and worked my way through a plate of fresh blini with raspberry jam, a group of stocky men in leather jackets took it in turns to file up to the corner bar – from where, after whispering to the waiter, they'd return to their table with a carafe of vodka to toast their breakfast meeting. The other diners, mostly from Poland and Belarus, seemed to take no notice of either the pianist or the thick-necked men.

My plan for a solitary Sunday in Lviv had been determined by the art historian Vita Susak, when she told me about her home city over the phone before I set off: 'In the beginning of the 1990s, Lviv was very grey, very dark, and we had only two or three restaurants. Now, the city has grown an enormous stomach. You can see so many cafés. Go to Svit Kavy, this is the place for the best coffee and strudel, and whatever you do, don't miss the Armenian Cathedral. The church is active, and the interior murals are extraordinary.'

With the church bells ringing, I walked first to Kotliarska Street, stopping opposite number eight, where I had a clear view of Café Sztuka. By its entrance were several striking hand-painted 'ghost signs' in Yiddish and Polish – for 'books' and 'chocolates' – letters and words that stitch together loss, time and shared memories. I crossed the road and went inside the former store, now a café filled with old lace curtains, grand wooden dressers, cross-back bistro chairs, floral frescos and ceramic-tile stoves. On the walls were vintage photographs, posters and newspapers. The coffee was fine, the other tables empty, but really it was all about the building – itself a travel guide to the past, a soliloquy to what once was. Idealised but still deeply atmospheric, and bolstered by the fact that in 1906, the great Yiddish satirist Sholem Aleichem briefly lived across the street, at number one. '[It] offers a picture of order, breadth, and beauty! A sight to feast the eye…'[13] he wrote of Lviv. Aleichem had arrived at a time of pogroms in Kyiv, but while he was living on Kotliarska Street, he spent time at the Jewish Intellectual Club, attended performances by Jewish travelling theatres, and met with Ivan Franko at the Café Monopol, opposite the George Hotel. Little of that world exists today. But the vestiges of those times that persist have the power to suddenly stop you on a street corner.

And what of the Scottish Café on Shevchenka Avenue? A plaque gave some clues. During the interwar years, it was a meeting place for the Lwów School of Mathematics, where, over cups of coffee, difficult research problems were discussed – notably, functional analysis and topology. When a solution was found, a hand would be raised, and with the words, '*Waiter, the book, please!*' it would be noted down, in what came to be known as the Scottish Book.[14] Prizes, in the form of wine, brandy and once even a live goose, were offered for particularly impressive explanations. At first, the mathematicians pencilled their equations directly onto the marble tabletops, but the markings irked the waiters – and the analysis was, of course, wiped away at the end of each night. Then, one day, the wife of the great Polish mathematician Stefan Banach arrived with a large notebook, and there was no going back.

I ambled on through Rynok Square, where once there was a swift trade in dark, rich sweet wines from Greece, Cyprus, Spain and Italy, which gave rise to some of the largest drinks cellars in Europe. Martin Gruneweg, a merchant from the Baltic port city Gdańsk, noted in 1606 that, 'At any one time you can see over one thousand wine barrels stacked up in Rynok Square.'[15]

Suddenly, there was a change in the light, and snow started falling. Children went running past the old cream-and-pink-painted town houses, their mouths open to catch snowflakes on their tongues. The whiteness of fresh snow shone against the blackened seventeenth-century Catholic burial chapel of Hungarian merchant Georgi Boyim, its walls so densely covered with sandstone sculptures that it resembled a blurry, three-dimensional Hieronymus Bosch painting. And, right by it, Svit Kavy.

Stepping inside, I found men in suits having meetings, students studying, women dressed in fur coats, writers scribbling in notebooks, people meeting up, chatting and sharing news. Nobody ordered takeaway, because they came for the experience: to sit and be enfolded by other worlds, other lives and loves – yours to slip into, momentarily, for the price of a coffee.

Not too many choices on the simple menu, either, therefore no need to weigh up appetites versus desires. Svit Kavy reflected my longings back at me. For the world to slow down a bit, for there to be quiet places still. For there to be magic in the ordinary and pleasure in the senses, available to everyone.

I sat at a table in the corner, so that I could see the whole room, under wooden beams and next to a wall of antique coffee grinders, clasping my hands around a hot cup of coffee made by baristas who exuded a subtle fizz of pride. My slice of strudel, manageable at about the size of a deck of cards, was matchless. Best in class. The crispy dough was so paper-thin as to be almost translucent, and the icing sugar, lightly dusted on, was as white as the snow that was still falling outside.

How smells and flavours pull at the imagination, delivering us to other places. I would give my all to go back to Svit Kavy, the room overheated and cosy as a Carpathian wood cabin. I still have the scent of that sharp-sweet strudel in my nostrils. The smell, the taste, the 'feelings' of a city — so often the essence of a place is passed down the generations through mealtimes and memories — are also for the outsider, the one looking in, as valuable as its history, architecture and civic life. They offer a way to identify with the city, to connect with it.

Reluctantly leaving the sanctuary of Svit Kavy, a hundred or so paces took me to the Armenian Cathedral, the first stones of which were laid in the fourteenth century. Worshippers filed inside, dressed in scarlet shawls and dark-coloured winter coats; some crooked and elderly, some still learning to walk. I followed the congregation into the dim light. Sublime singing praised God, and the service was conducted in both Ukrainian and Armenian. Above, Jan Henryk de Rosen's arresting murals glowed with gold leaf. Folkloric images, crosses and lambs represented the ancient traditions of Armenia; and the murals, depicting the last supper and the crucifixion, were as radiant and luminous as Vita Susak had promised. Commissioned by the Armenian archbishop of Lwów, de Rosen finished the work in 1929, while another Polish artist Józef Mehoffer painted the ceilings. Over his lifetime, de Rosen designed so many murals and mosaics that he once described them as 'like the pebbles on the shore of the sea',[16] impossible to count – though it is hard to imagine that any could be more awe-inspiring than these.

Heading back to the George Hotel, I stopped at an open square, the site of Lviv's Perpetuation Memorial. This marks the place where the Great City Synagogue, Beth Hamidrash, and the late sixteenth-century Golden Rose Synagogue once stood, before all were destroyed by the Nazis in the 1940s. Now called the Space of Synagogues, at its centre is an outdoor installation of thirty-nine stone tablets, some with quotes from the memoirs and diaries of rabbis and thinkers chiselled into them.

The quotes, in Hebrew, Ukrainian and English, tell something of life before, during and after the Holocaust. I was particularly struck by the words of Debora Vogel. Born in 1900, in a Galician town called Bursztyn (now in western Ukraine), she was a friend, correspondent and muse to Bruno Schulz, and their letters formed a basis for his short-story collection *The Cinnamon Shops*. Her exquisite prose poems were written in Polish and Yiddish, and her work has recently experienced a modest revival in literary circles. Along with her family, Debora Vogel was murdered by the Nazis in 1942, during the liquidation of the Lviv ghetto. On her memorial tablet today is this extract from her poem 'Grey Streets':

The streets are like the sea
they reflect the colour of longing
and the difficulty of waiting

As I took the trolleybus back to the airport, I made a wish to return, not knowing, of course, what terror was coming; how soon we would all speak the language of war once again.

~

In Edinburgh, at the stove, slowly the butter begins foaming in a small frying pan. I tip in breadcrumbs, with a sprinkling of cinnamon, and stir gently as they turn golden. Rich and sweet-smelling, the buttery crumbs will go into my strudel filling to bolster it; to support the fruit, giving it extra bite, extra texture. The pastry sheets are papery thin, and I take off my rings so as not to snag them. They are not quite see-through, though, and that is the test: Austrian pâtissiers say you must be able to read a love letter through the strudel sheaves. Leaning on the flavours of apples and cinnamon, this strudel is ideal for the start of the cold season.

Why bother, you might ask, when you can buy a perfectly good strudel? Because baking is a series of alchemic collisions, which, hopefully, add up to a deliciously harmonious thing to eat. And those steps, and that belief, and the effort poured in? It is about as gratifyingly far from the sterile world of consumerism as it is possible to get. In short, it is a mindful practice, and a defence when faith has failed, and the deepest gloom descends.

Midnight. News from Ukraine comes on the radio. Stories echoing those that James has been reporting on, those that he tells me about, sometimes in horrifying detail, in the evenings when we sit together in the kitchen. Since February, there has been so much to take in, the news so fast-moving, so repugnant and terrifying. The Mariupol theatre blast. Putin vowing to 'purify' Russia of 'traitors'. Children born in bomb shelters. The same Russian generals who destroyed Syrian cities now being deployed again. The humiliation of the Russian Army, and the absurdity of paid pundits and troll factories. The ongoing threat of nuclear war. Britain's dirty money and the London 'laundromat'. The Russia-watchers we know, who are all scrambling to make sense of Putin's 'strategy'.

We discuss, too, Russia's media blackout and how rapidly any pretence of autonomy and freedom has disappeared. And how Russia's future, which will affect us all, is now so wildly and dangerously uncertain. And we talk of journalists and friends who have fled Moscow for Almaty, Tbilisi, Istanbul and Yerevan. Westerners, mainly, who had made their careers — and let down their guards, to some degree — in Russia, after the Soviet Union fell. Some admit that they had perhaps been naive, that they were foolish to ever believe that Russia would take a different path from the 1990s onwards. But many clung to a belief that good would prevail, 'despite all the chaos and evidence of corruption and human rights abuses', as one friend wrote to me. The word 'duped' cropped up in correspondence more than once.

News agencies in Ukraine posted photos online of Lviv's Rynok Square, where the Student Council hung framed diplomas for young people who had put down their books, taken up arms and died in the fighting to defend Ukraine. Students who now would never receive their certificates. 'They wrote the history of the country's struggle but they could not finish their story,'[17] the statement read. Dozens and dozens of reports, pages and pages of news copy. Lives ruined and families destroyed. Future generations who will never forgive what Russia has done. The world, especially Europe, for ever changed.

Gripped by war for so many months now, how long can Ukraine endure? I think of the camaraderie of those fighting and risking their lives, not just for their freedoms but for ours as well, and I wonder what stronger ties there could be in life. Tighter than family, bonded by shared experience and bravery.

But for now, they are busy piecing their weapons together, again and again.

Wine makers, close to the Black Sea coast, and not far from the front line, say they are still working tirelessly, eager to ensure that Ukraine has plenty to drink when it celebrates its victory. Everyone believes them. One night, I dreamt of sending a love letter to Odesa, strapped to a kite that was carried on the wind across the Black Sea. And I think of the marvellous George Hotel, which quite rightly values its soul over modernisation, and how it is, once again, witness to another war. Standing firm, as if on its own private island in the city.

~

Brushing the pastry sheets with melted butter, I coat the next and the next, layering and tucking in the filling, rolling and straightening, like making a soft, cushioned bed.

How fragile peace is. How perishable home is. All of it so easily lost. Home is many things; it is fixed for some, movable for others. An instinct, or four walls. Either way, it is surely foolish to ever take it for granted.

This kitchen is home, but I know how easily the things inside it that make it 'home' can disappear. Not only the terrible loss of Darwin, but all of it. Bread, fruit and milk spoil. Plants die. Glassware breaks. Paper – that holds words, essays, recipes – is so easily torn or burned, lost or thrown away. But for now, I have to believe that the kitchen is a protector. Somewhere to feel safe. I acknowledge how fortunate I am, for it was only chance and luck that put me here. I hang on to the reassurance of it, as best I can, pressing into the kitchen's familiar soundness.

As the night pushes on, finally the strudel is ready. Its papery edges are golden and blueberry-stained, and a little apple juice is foaming nicely around the crinkly edges. Memory tells me that there was no rum in the version I ate in Lviv, at Svit Kavy – but no matter, precious fragments of the city are now here in my mind, and inside the kitchen.

Through the solitary window, eye to Edinburgh, leaves blow about in the strengthening breeze. Sitting down with James, I pour out tea and we eat the strudel at the table – just us, a candle, a vase of sunflowers and a single lemon in a fruit bowl, one side of it gone to greenish dust. Satisfying and redemptive, the strudel demands seconds, despite the hour. Then, blowing out the candle, we stand up, turn off the light, and begin walking up the stairs.

Apple, Blueberry and Rum Strudel

A satisfying strudel for the long-haul months of winter. Of course, you could buy something similar in the shops, but home-made strudel is undoubtedly better, and this is fairly effortless to prepare and relatively economical (if you already have the rum knocking about).

MAKES 1 LARGE STRUDEL

2 large acidic apples (around 400g), such as Bramley, peeled, cored and sliced into thin half-moons
200g blueberries
80g caster sugar
grated zest and juice of 1 lemon
1–2 tablespoons rum

6 large sheets filo pastry
120g butter
40g white breadcrumbs
pinch of ground cinnamon
2 tablespoons flaked almonds
1 tablespoon icing sugar
cream or vanilla ice cream, to serve (optional)

Put the apples and blueberries in a large bowl and toss with the caster sugar, lemon zest and juice – and rum, if you fancy it (though don't let the rum have too much input). Set aside to let the flavours meld for 15 minutes.

Bring the filo out of the fridge and let it come to room temperature, then unwrap it and cover with a damp tea towel to stop it drying out.

Next, make the buttered breadcrumbs. Heat a frying pan over a gentle heat and add 10g of the butter. When it has melted, add the breadcrumbs and cinnamon and brown until golden. Set aside.

Pre-heat the oven to 180°C/160°C fan/gas 4 and line a large baking tray with baking parchment.

To assemble the strudel, melt the remaining butter in a small saucepan. Place a sheet of filo pastry onto the damp tea towel and brush it with butter. Lay another sheet of pastry on top and paint again with butter. Repeat this process until you have used all the sheets of filo, saving a little butter to brush over the top of the strudel later.

Stir the breadcrumbs into the fruit filling and mix well. Heap the filling along one of the long sides of the pastry, about 2cm in from the edge, then tuck the ends of the pastry in and roll up to enclose the filling as carefully and tightly as you can manage. Transfer the strudel seam-side down onto the baking tray.

Brush the strudel with the remaining butter and sprinkle the almonds over the top. Place in the oven and bake for 40 minutes, then turn up the temperature to 200°C/180°C fan/gas 6 for 10 more minutes or so, until fully golden all over. Leave to cool on the baking tray.

Once the strudel is cool, dust with icing sugar. Cut into slices and serve with cream or vanilla ice cream, both good accompaniments, but it is equally delicious by itself.

NOTES

A SUBTERRANEAN HOMECOMING

1   De Marco, Camillo, 'Review: *Europa*', www.cineuropa.org/en/new
    sdetail/407631/

2   Ruskin, John, *The Ethics of the Dust* (New York: John Wiley & Son,
    1866), p. 145

3   'Chloroform a knockout discovery', www.scotsman.com/arts-and-
    culture/chloroform-a-knockout-discovery-1673859

4   'Stevenson House: History', www.stevenson-house.com/history/

5   Zinik, Zinovy, 'Happy traveller', www.the-tls.co.uk/articles/happy-
    traveller/

6   McNeill, Florence Marian, *The Scots Kitchen* (London: Mayflower,
    1974), p. 78

7   Smith, Joe, 'The history of the Edinburgh colonies and how they got
    their name', www.edinburghlive.co.uk/news/edinburgh-news/hist
    ory-edinburgh-colonies-how-name-18059666

8   Stevenson, Robert Louis, *Edinburgh: Picturesque Notes* (London:
    Seeley & Company, 1896), p. 2

1   WINTER MELONS

1   Torolsan, Berrin, 'The Sweet Taste of Summer', *Cornucopia*, Issue
    39, 2008, p. 115

2   Ibid., p. 116

3   Ibid., p. 114

4   Carruthers, Douglas, *Beyond the Caspian* (Edinburgh: Oliver and
    Boyd, 1949), p. 6

5   Eden, Caroline, 'The Magic of Uzbek winter melons', *Financial
    Times*, 29 November 2019

6   Babur, *Memoirs of Zehir-Ed-Din Muhammed Baber: Emperor of Hindustan* (London: Longman, Rees, Orme, Brown, and Green; Edinburgh: Cadell and Co., 1826), p. 33

7   Ibid., p. 60

8   Paris, Harry S. et al., 'Medieval Emergence of Sweet Melons, Cucumis Melo (Cucurbitaceae)', *Annals of Botany*, vol. 110, no. 1, 2012, pp. 23–33

9   *The Travels of Ibn Battuta, A.D. 1325–1354, Volume 3* (Cambridge: Cambridge University Press, 1971), p. 547

10 O'Donohue, John, *Benedictus: A Book of Blessings* (London: Random House, 2007), p. 64

11 Burnes, Alexander, *Travels into Bokhara* (London: Eland Publishing, 2012), p. 192

12 Burnaby, Frederick, *A Ride to Khiva: Travels and Adventures in Central Asia* (Cambridge: Cambridge University Press, 2011), p. 278

13 'Gilbert White's House & Garden: Hotbeds', www.gilbertwhitesho use.org.uk/hotbeds/

14 'Recipes from Scotland, 1680s to 1940s: Jams and Preserves, Melons', digital.nls.uk/recipes/themes/preserves/melon.html

15 Switzer, Stephen, *The Practical Kitchen Gardiner* (London: Tho. Woodward, 1727), p. 94

16 Lloyd, Christopher, *Gardener Cook* (London: Frances Lincoln, 1997), p. 27

17 Twain, Mark, *Pudd'nhead Wilson* (London: Chatto & Windus, 1894), p. 141

2 RUSSIAN RAILWAY PIES

1   Collingham, Lizzie, *The Biscuit* (London: Random House, 2020)

2   Ferlinghetti, Lawrence, 'Russian Winter Journal, February–March 1967', www.yalereview.org/article/russian-winter-journal-febru ary-march-1967

3   Ibid.

4   Nabokov, Vladimir, *Nabokov's Congeries* (New York: Viking Press, 1968), p. 128

5   Ibid., p. 480

6   Martyris, Nina, ' "Lolita" And Lollipops', www.thenabokovian.org/ sites/default/files/2018-01/NABOKV-L-0026833___body.htmlm

7 Ferlinghetti, 'Russian Winter Journal'
8 Ibid.
9 Smith, Alison K., *Cabbage and Caviar* (London: Reaktion Books, 2021), p. 97
10 Norman, Henry, *All the Russias* (New York: Scribner's Sons, 1902), p. 110
11 Blanch, Lesley, *From Wilder Shores* (London: John Murray, 1989), p. 25
12 Collingham, *The Biscuit*, p. 124
13 Ibid., p. 180
14 Bryson, Bill, *Notes from a Small Island* (London: Transworld, 1995), p. 282
15 Dostoyevsky, Fyodor, *Buried Alive: Or, Ten Years Penal Servitude in Siberia* (London: Longmans, Green and Co., 1881), p. 31
16 Thomson, Catriona, 'Scotland's Larder', www.foodanddrink.scotsman.com/producers/artisan/scotlands-larder-kirstie-campbell-of-seabuckthorn-scotland/
17 Manley, Deborah (ed.), *The Trans-Siberian Railway: A Traveller's Anthology* (Oxford: Signal Books, 2009, ebook)
18 Akinsha, Konstantin, 'Culture in the crossfire', www.theartnewspaper.com/2022/03/25/ukraine-culture-in-peril
19 Goldstein, Darra, *Beyond the North Wind* (New York: Ten Speed Press, 2020), p. 111

3 SNOW FALLS ON SULTANAHMET

1 Stone, Norman, 'Othmar's Dream', *Cornucopia*, Issue 35, 2006, p. 62
2 Toralsan, Berrin, 'Sweet Endings', *Cornucopia*, Issue 62, 2021, p. 136
3 'B² Bill Brown's Bridges: Bosphorus Bridge 1973', www.b2.co.uk/world-bridges/bosphorus-bridge/
4 'The Art of Idling', *Cornucopia*, Issue 52, 2015, p. 160
5 Freely, John, *Strolling Through Istanbul* (London: I.B. Tauris, 2010), p. 294
6 Kelly, Laurence, *Istanbul: A Traveller's Reader* (London: Robinson, 2015), p. 174
7 Stone, Norman, 'Crimea', *Cornucopia*, Issue 36, 2006, p. 36

8   Sebag Montefiore, Simon, 'A Turkish Pepys', *Financial Times*, 9 October 2010

9   Torolsan, 'Sweet Endings', p. 135

10 'Queen of Hearts', *Cornucopia*, Issue 52, 2015, p. 106

11 Rosenberg, Michelle, *The 50 Greatest Explorers in History* (Barnsley: Pen and Sword History, 2022), p. 28

12 'Hekimbaşı Salih Efendi Yalisi', www.cornucopia.net/guide/listi ngs/sights/hekimbasi-yali/

13 Sarsilmaz, Meltem, 'Boza', www.dailysabah.com/life/2020/01/12/ boza-a-wintry-treat-journeying-from-ancient-mesopotamia-to-the-caucasus-the-balkans-and-beyond

14 Charitonidou, Martha, 'The tradition of salep orchids' harvesting in NW Greece and its effects on orchid conservation', https://globalorchidtrade.wixsite.com/home/post/2020/04/15/ the-tradition-of-salep-orchids-harvesting-in-nw-greece-and-its-effe cts-on-orchid-conserva

15 Eden, Caroline, 'The magic and mystery of Turkey's chestnuts', *Financial Times*, 26 November 2021

16 'The Absolute Guide to Istanbul', *Cornucopia*, Issue 40, 2008, p. 50

4 BETTER A DINNER OF HERBS

1   Kaye-Smith, Sheila, *Kitchen Fugue* (New York: Harper & Brothers, 1945), p. 191

2   Grissmann, Carla, *Dinner of Herbs: Village Life in 1960s Turkey* (London: Eland Publishing, 2016), p. 113

3   Ibid., p. 109

4   Ibid., p. 38

5   Ibid., p. 116

6   Ibid., p. 88

7   Bedford, Sybille, *Jigsaw* (London: Eland Publishing, 2005, ebook)

8   Torolsan, Berrin, 'Meatball Wizard', *Cornucopia*, Issue 22, 2000, p. 106

9   Rustaveli, Shota (trans. Venera Urushadze), *The Knight in the Panther's Skin* (Tbilisi: Sabchota Sakartvelo Publishers, 1979)

10 Grissmann, *Dinner of Herbs*, p. 116

11 Ibid., p. 88

12 Preface to *Elene Akhvlediani Grand Masters of Georgian Art* (Tbilisi: Baia Gallery, 2016)

13 Grissmann, *Dinner of Herbs*, p. 47

14 Eyre, Hermione, 'Interview: Carla Grissmann', *Steppe – A Central Asian Panorama*, issue 8, 2010, p. 28

5 BALTIC SYMPHONIES

1 'Riga Central Market: History', www.rct.lv/en/about-us/history
2 Information boards at the Museum of the History of Riga and Navigation, www.rigamuz.lv
3 'Leģendas: Vilhelma Ķuzes saldumu karaliste' (Kuze's Kingdom of Sweets), www.db.lv/zinas/legendas-vilhelma-kuzes-saldumu-karali ste-149916
4 'Saldā Latvija' (Sweet Latvia), www.laikmetazimes.lv/2013/03/04/ latvijas-zimolu-legendas-saldumu-razotaji/
5 'Riga's Nativity of Christ Cathedral', www.liveriga.com/ en/3877-riga-s-nativity-of-christ-cathedral

6 JOURNEY FOOD

1 Birkett, Rosie, *The Joyful Home Cook* (London: HarperCollins, 2019), p. 40
2 McNeill, Florence Marian, *The Scots Kitchen* (London: Mayflower, 1974), p. 318
3 Stafford, Ed, *Expeditions Unpacked* (London: White Lion Publishing, 2019), p. 88
4 Ibid., p. 54
5 Ibid., p. 104
6 Blanch, Lesley, *From Wilder Shores* (London: John Murray, 1989), p. 63
7 Blanch, Lesley, *Round the World in Eighty Dishes* (London: Grub Street, 2012), p. 10
8 Blanch, *From Wilder Shores*, p. 62
9 Bedford, Sybille, *A Visit to Don Otavio* (London: Eland Publishing, 2002), p. 19
10 Hansen, Valerie, *The Silk Road* (Oxford: Oxford University Press, 2012), p. 93
11 Stein, Marc Aurel, *Innermost Asia Detailed Report of Explorations in Central Asia, Kan-Su and Eastern Īrān* (National Institute of Informatics – Digital Silk Road Project, Digital Archive of Toyo Bunko Rare Books doi:10.20676/00000187), dsr.nii.ac.jp/ toyobunko/T-VIII-5-A-a-3/index.html.en

12 Food product (Chinese), www.britishmuseum.org/collection/obj ect/A_1928-1022-130

13 'Obituary, Lady Jekyll', *The Times*, 29 January 1937

14 Jekyll, Agnes, *Kitchen Essays* (London: Persephone Books, 2009), p. 177

7 CARRIED AWAY BY A CLOUDBERRY

1   Martin, Seamus, 'Casualty of an ignoble nobility', www.irishtimes.com/news/casualty-of-an-ignoble-nobility-1.298043

2   'Mr. Henry Seebohm', *The Spectator*, archive.spectator.co.uk/article/7th-december-1895/29/mr-henry-seebohm

3   'Beinn nan Oighreag, hill of the cloudberrries', www.scotsman.com/news/beinn-nan-oighreag-hill-cloudberries-2465497

4   Amundsen, Roald, *My Life as an Explorer* (Cambridge: Cambridge University Press, 2014), p. 70

5   Ferguson, Donna, 'The secret of how Amundsen beat Scott in race to south pole? A diet of raw penguin', www.theguardian.com/environment/2021/may/16/the-secret-of-how-amundsen-beat-scott-in-race-to-south-pole-a-diet-of-raw-penguin

6   Williams, Isobel, 'Shackleton's Scurvy – Or Its Absence', www.isobelpwilliams.com/2018/10/05/shackletons-scurvy-or-its-absence/

7   'Adolf Lindstrøm', www.basecampexplorer.com/spitsbergen/arctic-dictionary/adolf-lindstrom/

8   Nielsen-Bobbit, Jaughna, 'A Guide to Cloudberries', www.scandinaviastandard.com/a-guide-to-cloudberries-all-about-the-norths-most-sought-after-fruit/

9   Brown, Hamish, *Climbing the Corbetts* (Dingwall: Sandstone Press, 2012), p. xii

10 Muir, John, 'Through Florida Swamps and Forests', www.vault.sierraclub.org/john_muir_exhibit/writings/a_thousand_mile_walk_to_the_gulf/chapter_5.aspx

8 SOUP AND A SPARROW

1   'Polish painting returned to Warsaw after 67 years on missing list', www.theguardian.com/world/2011/jul/27/polish-painting-returned-to-warsaw

2   'POLIN Museum of the History of Polish Jews: About the Museum', www.polin.pl/en

3   Minshull, Duncan, *While Wandering: A Walking Companion* (London: Random House, 2014), p. 177

4   Taylor, Matthew, 'White Europe: 60,000 nationalists march on Poland's independence day', www.theguardian.com/world/2017/ nov/12/white-europe-60000-nationalists-march-on-polands-indep endence-day

5   'Dancing Auschwitz: I Will Survive', www.janekormanart.com/ the-new-dance

6   McKittrick, Casey, *Hitchcock's Appetites*, www.bloomsburycollecti ons.com/book/hitchcocks-appetites-the-corpulent-plots-of-des ire-and-dread/ch5-childhood-and-the-challenge-of-fat-masculinity

7   'A Clockwork Orange and Nadsat', www.anthonyburgess.org/a-clockwork-orange/a-clockwork-orange-and-nadsat/

8   Freedland, Jonathan, ' "Thou shalt not be indifferent": from Auschwitz's gate of hell, a last, desperate warning', www.theguard ian.com/world/2020/jan/27/thou-shalt-not-be-indifferent-from-auschwitzs-gate-of-hell-a-last-desperate-warning

9 CHEAP THRILLS

1   Butlin, Roy, *The Little Book of Scottish Rain* (Edinburgh: Birlinn, 2018), p. 37

2   'David Hume's Letters: The Philosopher as cook', www.chirnsid ecommongood.org/david-humes-letters/

3   McNeill, Florence Marian, *The Scots Kitchen* (London: Mayflower, 1974), p. 82

4   Carruthers, Amelia (ed.), *Writers on... Food: A Book of Quotes, Poems and Literary Reflections* (Writers On..., 2016, ebook)

5   Wilde, Oscar, *The Picture of Dorian Gray* (London: Random House, 2007), p. 71

6   Belk, Russell W., 'Possessions and the Extended Self', *Journal of Consumer Research* 15, no. 2, 1988

7   Mandelstam, Osip, *Journey to Armenia* (London: Notting Hill Editions, 2011), p. 89

8   Grossman, Vasily, *An Armenian Sketchbook* (London: MacLehose Press, 2013, ebook)

9   'Renowned Architect of the 20th century: Founder of the New Armenian Architecture', www.alexandertamanian.com

10 Harutyunyan, Tigran, *Yerevan: Architectural Guide* (Berlin: DOM Publishers, 2018), p. 27

11 Walker, Christopher J. (ed.), *Visions of Ararat* (London: I.B. Tauris, 2005), p. 32

12 'Armenian PM Says Almost 3,800 Soldiers Killed In War With Azerbaijan', www.rferl.org/a/armenian-deaths-karab akh-war/31425644.html

13 Church, Michael, 'Komitas', www.classical-music.com/composers/komitas

14 Harutyunyan, *Yerevan: Architectural Guide*, p. 269

15 Sarkissian, Ararat, *Cross Stones* (Yerevan: self-published, 2006)

16 Garnett, Lucy Mary Jane, *The Women of Turkey and Their Folk-lore*, Volumes 1–2, (London: David Nutt, 1890), p. 202

17 Vincent, Sally, 'Aznavour: Me, I'll take the laughter and the tears', www.theguardian.com/lifeandstyle/2000/mar/25/weekend.sally vincent

18 Ignatieff, Michael, 'The Unsung Hero Who Coined the Term "Genocide"', www.newrepublic.com/article/114424/raphael-lem kin-unsung-hero-who-coined-genocide

19 Demoyan, Hayk, *Armenian Churches and Monasteries* (Yerevan: self-published, 2019)

10 SMASHED

1 Middleton, Robert and Thomas, Huw, *Tajikistan and the High Pamirs* (Hong Kong: Odyssey Guides, 2008)

2 Ibid., p. 644

3 Ross, Marvin C., *Russian Porcelains* (Oklahoma: University of Oklahoma Press, 1968), p. 3

4 Ibid., p. 50

5 Sandys, Harriet, *Beyond that Last Blue Mountain* (Cowes: Medina Publishing, 2018), p. 84

6 Ibid.

7 Shaw, George Bernard, *Man and Superman* (The Floating Press, 2012), p. 64

11 CLOVER DUMPLINGS

1 Calvino, Italo, *Invisible Cities* (London: Vintage, 1997), p. 38

2 Leonard, Peter, 'Kyrgyzstan: Japarov seizes all levers of power', www.eurasianet.org/kyrgyzstan-japarov-seizes-all-levers-of-power

12 NIGHT COOKING

1 Mitterbauer, Helga and Smith, Carrie, *Crossing Central Europe: Continuities and Transformations, 1900 and 2000* (Toronto: University of Toronto Press, 2017), p. 141

2 Kovalska, Areta, 'A Protection Symbol for the Home', www.forgottengalicia.com/a-protection-symbol-for-the-home-the-six-petal-rosette-on-the-crossbeams-of-galicia

3 Arraf, Jane, 'A Russian Strike Hits Lviv', www.nytimes.com/2022/04/18/world/lviv-russia-strike-ukraine.html

4 Fielder, Jez, 'Ukrainian brewery fuels community Molotov cocktail drive', www.euronews.com/culture/2022/02/27/ukrainian-brewery-in-lviv-appeals-on-social-media-for-molotov-cocktail-donations

5 'About the Hotel', www.georgehotel.com.ua/about.html

6 Lemko, Ilko, *The Legends of Old Lviv* (Lviv: Apriori, 2018), p. 50

7 'Prosp. Svobody, 28 – Lviv Opera House', www.https://lia.lvivcenter.org/en/objects/opera-house/

8 Premiyak, Liza, 'Looking for Lenin', www.calvertjournal.com/features/show/5790/lenin-soviet-monument-ukraine

9 'Jewish Lviv: 100 addresses', www.lia.lvivcenter.org/en/storymaps/100-addresses-mobile/

10 'Lychakiv cemetery', www.lia.lvivcenter.org/en/objects/lychakiv-cemetery/

11 Schulz, Bruno (trans. Celina Wieniewska), *The Fictions of Bruno Schulz: The Street of Crocodiles & Sanatorium Under the Sign of the Hourglass* (London: Picador, 2011), p. 61

12 Lemko, *The Legends of Old Lviv*, p. 57

13 Simkin, Mark (trans. Miriam Feyga Bunimovich), 'Sholem Aleichem's Creative Encounters in Lviv', www.ukrainianjewishencounter.org/en/sholem-aleichems-creative-encounters-lviv-commemoration-100th-anniversary-departure-eternity/

14 'The Lviv Scottish Book', www.math.lviv.ua/szkocka/

15 Lemko, *The Legends of Old Lviv*, p. 130

16 'Jan Henryk de Rosen', www.alchetron.com/Jan-Henryk-de-Rosen

17 'Diplomas that will never be issued', www.zahid.espreso.tv/diplomi-yakikh-nikoli-ne-vidadut-u-lvovi-zgaduyut-studentiv-zagiblikh-unaslidok-rosiyskoi-agresii

INDEX

INDEX

ACKNOWLEDGEMENTS

I'd like to sincerely thank all at Bloomsbury, especially Rowan Yapp, Faye Robinson, Ros Ellis and Emily North for seamless organisation and affable guidance through the whole process. To Alison Cowan, who so patiently and cheerfully ploughed through the copy, a million thanks. I am also grateful to my brilliant agent Jessica Woollard for encouraging me with the idea from the very start.

The following extended many different forms of kindness, support and friendship during the creation of this book, both online and in real life, that helped me get by and therefore, to write: Jarkyn Almazbekovna, Howard Amos, Nadia Beard, Paul Brummell, Jess Cooper, Lyse Doucet, Boris Dralyuk, Megan Eaves-Egenes, Anna Frame, Julia Gorodetskaya, Jill Gorringe, Nagihan Haliloğlu, Zukhra Iakupbaeva, Maya Ibraeva, Sophie Ibbotson, Kate Ide, Yörük Işık, Signe Johansen, Joshua Kucera, Oksana Maksymchuk, Alexandra Matts, Devon Magliozzi, Nicola Miller, Meagan Neal, Monisha Rajesh, Dan Richards, Vilija Rudyte, Yasmine Seale, Coşkun Sener, Helen Stokes, Amelia Stewart, Judith and Duncan Sugden, Matthew Teller, Alex Robertson Textor, Jean Wiley and my generous in-laws.

To Diana Henry, our correspondence means so much to me, thank you for your words and humour over the years we've been in touch. Thank you, also, to my friend Emily Couch for inspiring me to write about myth-status meals (things we ate once that we know we'll likely never have again). For me, it was chłodnik with pear in Poland for Emily it was a Bukharan plov in Uzbekistan. And special thanks, too, to Darra Goldstein and Rosie Birkett for allowing me to adapt their recipes which I love so much – pirozhki and pasties, respectively.

As ever, *Cornucopia* magazine has been a rich source of ideas and insights. Thank you to my editor John Scott who is a friend and a huge inspiration, and someone who has, over the years, so generously opened doors to so many other worlds and other lives.

Thank you to booksellers everywhere! As a former bookseller, I appreciate all you do, really and truly. I'd like to thank my local bookshops in Edinburgh in particular who've shown me such support since I moved here. Polly and Jonathan and the entire team at Golden Hare Books, Euan and the brilliant booksellers at Portobello Bookshop, the charming staff at Topping and Co. and Waterstones Princes Street (whose café I write in most weeks), and all the staff at Blackwells. When I first moved to Edinburgh your welcoming spaces meant so much to me (and they still do).

And to those bookshops in the USA who have stocked my books and supported my work over the years, especially Kitchen Arts & Letters, Harvard Book Store, Omnivore Books, Book Larder and Now Serving. I hope to see you soon.

My heartfelt thanks to James, my husband, and to my dad, Dave: you are both always there for me. And, lastly, to Noriko Kumagai, to whom this book is dedicated, not only are you a constant source of happiness, you also taught me the true meaning of friendship.

~

The author and publisher would like to thank the following for permission to reproduce quotations. Excerpts from *Dinner of Herbs: Village Life in 1960s Turkey* by Carla Grissmann are reprinted by permission of Eland Publishing. Quotations from *My Life as an Explorer* by Roald Amundsen reproduced with permission of The Licensor through PLSclear. And W.W. Norton & Company for permission to quote from *Russian Winter Journal, February–March 1967* by Lawrence Ferlinghetti. Excerpts from Lesley Blanch by permission of Peters Fraser and Dunlop. And thanks to Medina Publishing for kind permission to reprint *Beyond that Last Blue Mountain* by Harriet Sandys. All excerpts from *Cornucopia* magazine are reprinted with generous permission from its editor, John Scott.